Wisconsin

Atlas & Gazetteer™

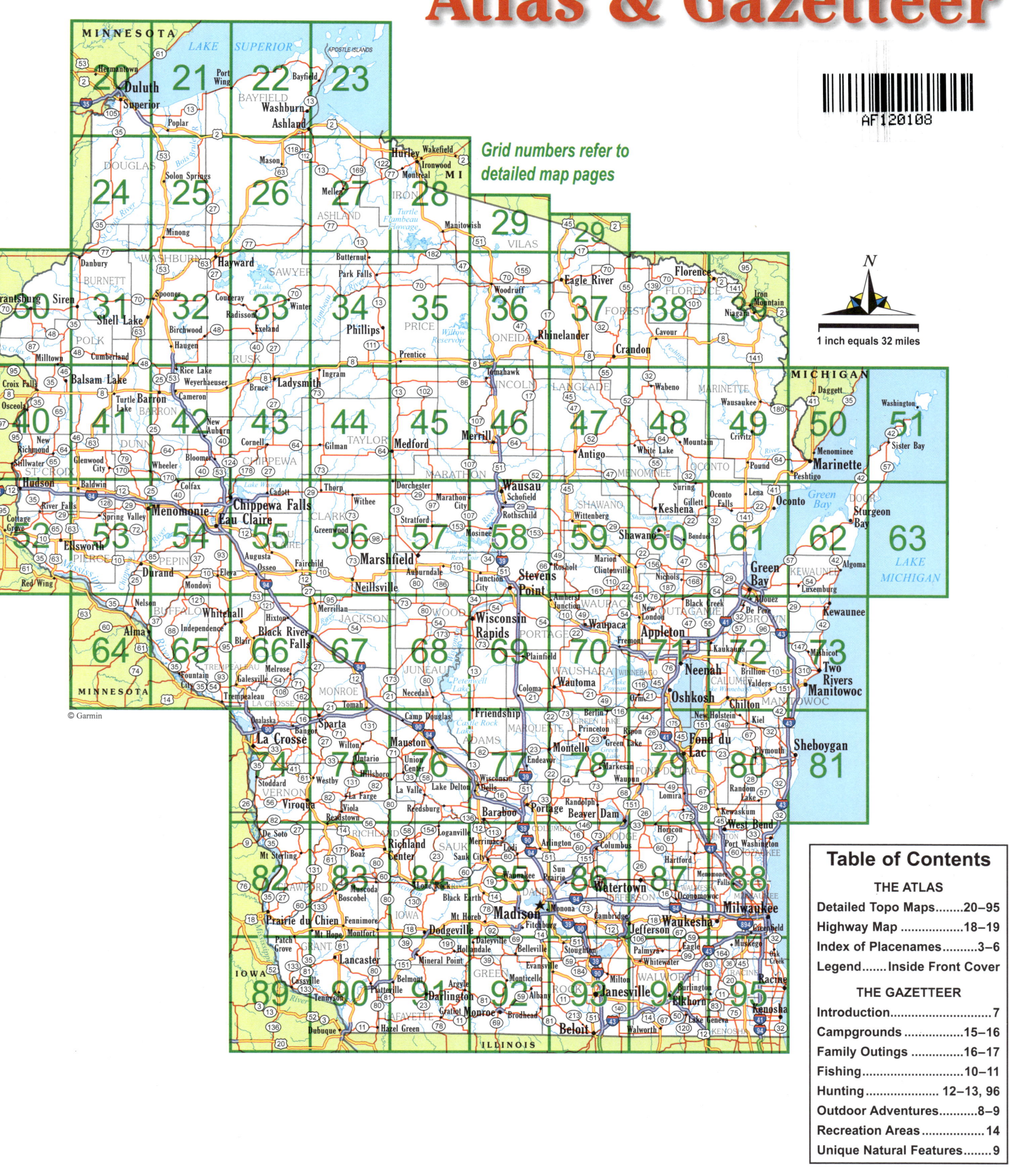

Grid numbers refer to detailed map pages

1 inch equals 32 miles

AF120108

SIXTEENTH EDITION.
Copyright © 2024 Garmin Ltd. or its Affiliates. All rights reserved.
2 DeLorme Dr. Suite 200, Yarmouth, Maine 04096
www.garmin.com/DeLormeAtlas
Printed in Canada.

Important Notices

Garmin has made reasonable efforts to provide you with accurate maps and related information, but we cannot exclude the possibility of errors or omissions in sources or of changes in actual conditions. GARMIN MAKES NO WARRANTIES OF ANY KIND, EITHER EXPRESS OR IMPLIED, INCLUDING THE WARRANTIES OF MERCHANTABILITY AND FITNESS FOR A PARTICULAR PURPOSE. GARMIN SHALL NOT BE LIABLE TO ANY PERSON UNDER ANY LEGAL OR EQUITABLE THEORY FOR DAMAGES ARISING OUT OF THE USE OF THIS PUBLICATION, INCLUDING, WITHOUT LIMITATION, FOR DIRECT, CONSEQUENTIAL OR INCIDENTAL DAMAGES.

Nothing in this publication implies the right to use private property. There may be private inholdings within the boundaries of public reservations. You should respect all landowner restrictions.

Some listings may be seasonal or may have admission fees. Please be sure to confirm this information when making plans.

Safety Information

To avoid accidents, always pay attention to actual road, traffic and weather conditions and do not attempt to read these maps while you are operating a vehicle. Please consult local authorities for the most current information on road and other travel-related conditions.

Do not use this publication for marine or aeronautical navigation, as it does not depict navigation aids, depths, obstacles, landing approaches and other information necessary to performing these functions safely.

Index of Placenames

Linton 94 E3
Little Black 45 E5
Little Chicago 45 F8
Little Chute 71 C8
Little Eau Claire 58 C3
Little Hope 70 B2
Little Kohler 80 F3
Little Norway 85 E5
Little Point 79 A7
Little Prairie 94 B3
Little Rapids 72 B2
Little Rose 57 C6
Little Sturgeon 62 B2
Little Suamico 61 D7
Little Waupon 58 E4
Livingston 90 A4
Loddes Mill 85 C5
Lodi 85 B7
Loganville 84 A3
Lohrville 70 F2
Lombard 56 A1
Lomira 79 E7
London 86 E3
Lone Rock 76 A2
Lone Rock 84 D2
Long Lake 38 C2
Longwood 56 B3
Lookout 65 A7
Loomis 49 D7
Loreta 84 B2
Loretta 34 B1
Louis Corners 80 A3
Louisburg 90 E3
Loveland Corners 32 F3
Lowell 86 B4
Lowville 85 A8
Loyal 56 D3
Loyd 84 A1
Lublin 44 F2
Luck 30 F4
Luco 79 B7
Ludington 55 B6
Lugerville 34 C3
Lund 53 F6
Lunds 60 D2
Luxemburg 62 F1
Lykens 40 B4
Lymantown 34 B4
Lyndhurst 59 B8
Lyndon Dale 78 E3
Lyndon Station 76 C4
Lynn 56 E4
Lynxville 82 C3
Lyons 94 D4

M

Mackeys Spur 45 B5
Mackville 71 B7
Madge 32 D2
Madison 85 E8
Madsen 72 E4
Magnolia 93 C5
Maiden Rock 53 F5
Malone 80 B1
Malvern 37 E5
Manawa 70 A4
Manchester 78 D3
Manitowish 28 E3
Manitowish Waters 28 E4
Manitowoc 73 E5
Manitowoc Rapids 73 E5
Mann 57 E6
Maple 21 F6
Maple Bluff 85 D8
Maple Grove 74 C2
Maple Heights 79 A8
Maple Hill 43 F8
Mapleton 87 D7
Maplewood 62 C3
Marathon 57 A8
Marathon City 57 A8
Marblehead 79 D8
Marcellon 78 E1
Marcy 88 D2
Marengo 27 B5
Maribel 72 C4
Marinette 50 E2
Marion 59 D8
Markesan 78 D3
Markton 48 E2
Marlands 36 A1
Marquette 78 C2
Marshall 86 D2
Marshfield 57 D6
Marshland 65 E7
Martell 53 B5

Martinsville 85 D6
Martintown 92 E1
Marxville 85 D6
Marytown 80 A1
Mason 26 B3
Mather 68 D1
Mattoon 47 F7
Mauston 76 B3
Maxville 53 F8
May Corner 49 F8
Mayfield 88 B1
Mayville 79 F6
Mazomanie 85 D5
McAllister 50 C1
McCartney 90 C1
McCord 35 F8
McFarland 86 F1
McKays Spur 36 E1
McKinley 31 F6
McNaughton 36 D3
Meadow Valley 68 D1
Mecan 78 B1
Medary 74 B2
Medford 45 E5
Medina 71 C6
Medina Junction 71 C6
Meehan 69 A6
Meeker 88 C1
Meekers Grove 90 D4
Meeme 80 A4
Meggers 72 F2
Mellen 27 C6
Melnik 73 C5
Melrose 66 E3
Melrose Park 71 F6
Melvina 75 B5
Menasha 71 D7
Menchalville 72 D4
Mellen —
Menomonee Falls 88 D2
Menomonie 53 B8
Menomonie Junction 53 A8
Mequon 88 C3
Mercer 28 E3
Meridean 54 D1
Merrill 46 D2
Merrillan 67 A5
Merrimac 85 A6
Merton 87 D8
Meteor 33 D5
Metz 70 D4
Middle Inlet 49 C7
Middle Ridge 74 B4
Middleton 85 E7
Middleton Junction 85 E7
Midway 94 B4
Mifflin 90 A4
Mikana 32 F3
Milan 57 A6
Milford 86 E4
Mill Center 61 E5
Mill Creek Community 58 F2
Milladore 57 E8
Millard 94 C1
Millhome 80 A3
Millston 67 D6
Milltown 30 F4
Millville 82 E4
Milton 93 B7
Milton Junction 93 B7
Milwaukee 88 E3
Mindoro 66 F3
Mineral Point 92 C3
Mineral Point 91 A6
Minersville 27 B5
Minnesota Junction 79 F5
Minocqua 36 B1
Minong 25 F5
Misha Mokwa 53 F8
Mishicot 73 C5
Modena 65 A5
Moeville 52 D4
Mondovi 54 F2
Monico 37 F6
Monitor Corners 87 D7
Monches 87 D8
Monona 85 E8
Monroe 92 D2
Monroe Center 68 E4
Montana 65 B6
Montello 77 C8
Montello Corners 77 C7
Monterey 87 D7
Montfort 83 F8
Montgomeryville 83 B5
Monticello 92 C2
Montreal 28 B1
Montrose 92 A2
Moon 58 C1
Moon Valley 85 A6
Moose Junction 24 D3
Moquah 22 F3
Morgan 61 C5
Morrison 72 C3
Morrisonville 85 C8
Morse 27 D6
Morton Corner 52 C4
Moscow 91 B8

Mosel 81 B5
Mosinee 58 C2
Mosling 60 B4
Mount Calvary 80 B1
Mount Hope 83 F5
Mount Hope Corners 54 D3
Mount Horeb 85 F5
Mount Ida 83 F5
Mount Sterling 82 B4
Mount Tabor 75 D8
Mount Vernon 85 F6
Mount View 58 A1
Mount Zion 83 C6
Mountain 48 D3
Mukwonago 94 A4
Murat 44 D4
Murphy Corner 71 B8
Murry 33 F6
Muscoda 83 D8
Muskeg 21 F8
Muskego 95 A6
Myra 88 A2

N

Nabob 88 A1
Namekagon 26 D3
Namur 62 D1
Nasbro 79 E7
Nashotah 87 E8
Nashville 37 F7
Nasonville 57 E5
Naugart 46 F1
Navarino 60 E3
Necedah 68 F3
Neda 87 A7
Neenah 71 D7
Neillsville 56 F3
Nekoosa 68 B4
Nekoosa Junction 68 B4
Nelma 37 A8
Nelson 64 A4
Nelsonville 59 F5
Nenno 87 A8
Neopit 59 A8
Neosho 87 B7
Neptune 84 A1
Nerike 53 F6
Neshkoro 78 A1
Neuern 62 F1
Neva 47 D6
Neva Corners 47 D6
Nevels Corners 83 A7
Nevins 56 F4
New Amsterdam 66 F1
New Auburn 42 D3
New Berlin 88 F2
New Diggings 91 E5
New Fane 80 E1
New Franken 61 F8
New Glarus 92 B2
New Holstein 80 A2
New Hope 59 F5
New Lisbon 76 B2
New London 71 B5
New Miner 68 D3
New Munster 95 E5
New Paris 80 C3
New Post 33 B6
New Richmond 40 E4
New Rome 68 D4
Newald 38 D1
Newark 93 E5
Newbold 36 D3
Newburg 88 A2
Newburg Corners 74 C4
Newry 75 C5
Newton 73 F5
Newton 74 E3
Newtonburg 73 F5
Newville 93 B7
Niagara 39 D7
Nichols 60 F3
Nichols Shore Acres 71 E6
Nobleton 32 E2
Nora 86 E2
Norma 55 A5
Norman 73 B6
Norrie 59 B5
Norske 59 E5
North Andover 89 B8
North Bay 95 B8
North Bend 66 E3
North Branch 66 A3
North Bristol 86 C1
North Cape 95 B6
North Clayton 83 A6
North Creek 65 C8
North Fond du Lac 79 B7

North Freedom 76 F4
North Grimms 72 D3
North Hudson 52 A2
North La Crosse 74 B2
North Lake 87 D8
North Leeds 85 B8
North Lowell 87 A5
North Menomonie 53 B8
North Prairie 87 F8
North Readfield 71 C5
North Red Wing 52 E3
North Shore 93 A8
North Star 58 E4
North York 27 B5
Northeim 73 F5
Northfield 66 A3
Northland 59 E5
Northline 52 A2
Northport 51 C7
Northwoods Beach 32 B4
Norton 42 F1
Norwalk 75 B6
Norway Grove 85 C8
Norway Ridge 68 E1
Nutterville 46 F3
Nye 40 C3

O

Oak Center 79 D6
Oak Creek 95 A8
Oak Grove 87 A5
Oak Hall 85 F8
Oak Hill 87 F6
Oak Knoll 94 A4
Oak Orchard 61 C7
Oak Park 86 E2
Oakdale 75 A8
Oakfield 79 D6
Oakland 31 B5
Oakland 86 F3
Oakley 92 E3
Oakridge 53 E5
Oakwood 71 F6
Oakwood 95 A7
Oconomowoc 87 D7
Oconomowoc Lake 87 E7
Oconto 61 B8
Oconto Falls 61 B6
Odanah 23 F6
Ogema 45 A5
Ogdensburg 70 A3
Oil City 75 C7
Ojibwa 33 C7
Okauchee 87 D7
Okee 85 B6
Old Albertville 54 A3
Old Ashippun 87 C7
Old Badger Mills 54 B4
Old Camp McCoy 67 F6
Old Lebanon 87 C6
Oliver 20 E2
Olivet 53 C6
Omro 71 E7
Onalaska 74 A2
Oneida 61 F5
Ono 53 E6
Ontario 75 C7
Oostburg 80 D4
Orange Mill 76 A1
Orchard Grove 80 F2
Oregon 92 A4
Orfordville 93 D5
Orihula 70 D4
Orion 83 C8
Ormsby 47 D5
Orva 28 B1
Osceola 40 C2
Oshkosh 71 E7
Osman 72 F4
Osseo 55 E6
Ostrander 70 B4
Otis 46 C2
Otsego 86 A2
Ottawa 87 F7
Ottman Corners 52 D4
Oulu 21 F7
Ourtown 80 D4
Owen 56 A3
Oxbo 34 B2
Oxford 77 C7

P

Packard 50 B1
Packwaukee 77 C7
Paddock Lake 95 E6
Padus 48 A2
Palmyra 94 A2
Paoli 92 A3
Pardeeville 78 E1
Parfreyville 70 B2
Paris 95 D6
Park Falls 34 B4
Park Ridge 58 F3
Parkland 20 E4
Parnell 80 D2
Parrish 46 B4
Patch Grove 82 F4
Patzau 24 A2
Paukotuk 71 F7
Pearson 47 B7
Pecks Corners 77 E5
Peebles 79 B8
Peeksville 27 F7
Pelican Lake 47 A6
Pelishek Corners 72 B4
Pell Lake 94 E4
Pella 59 C8
Pembine 39 E7
Pence 28 B1
Peninsula Center 51 F5
Pennington 34 F4
Pensaukee 61 C7
Pepin 64 A3
Peplin 58 C2
Perkinstown 44 D2
Peru 59 E5
Peshtigo 50 F1
Petersburg 83 C5
Pewaukee 88 E1
Peyton 20 E4
Pheasant Branch 85 E7
Phelps 29 B6
Phillips 34 D4
Phipps 25 F8
Phlox 47 F7
Piacenza 71 D5
Pickerel 47 B8
Pickett 79 A5
Pierceville 86 D2
Pigeon Falls 66 A2
Pike Lake 87 B8
Pike River 26 B2
Pilsen 73 A5
Pine Bluff 85 E8
Pine Creek 65 E7
Pine Grove 54 B3
Pine Grove 72 A4
Pine River 46 E2
Pine River 70 D2
Pinehurst 54 B4
Pipe 79 A8
Pipersville 87 D6
Pittsfield 61 E5
Pittsville 68 A2
Plain 84 B3
Plainfield 69 D7
Plainville 77 C5
Platteville 90 C4
Pleasant Corners 53 F6
Pleasant Prairie 95 E7
Pleasant Ridge 84 E3
Pleasant Valley 74 C2
Pleasantville 66 A1
Plover 69 A7
Plugtown 83 C5
Plum City 53 E6
Plymouth 80 C3
Point Comfort 79 A7
Pokegama 20 E3
Poland 72 A4
Polar 47 E7
Polifka Corners 72 D4
Polley 44 E1
Polonia 58 E4
Poniatowski 57 A7
Popcorn Corners 27 E6
Poplar 21 F5
Popple River 38 C1
Porcupine 53 E7
Port Andrew 83 C7
Port Arthur 43 B6
Port Edwards 68 B4
Port Washington 88 A4
Port Wing 21 D8
Portage 77 E7
Porterfield 49 E8
Porters 93 E7
Portland 75 C5
Portland 86 C3
Poskin 41 B8
Post Lake 47 A6
Postville 92 B1
Potosi 90 C2
Potosi Station 90 D2
Potter 72 E2

Potts Corners 75 D6
Pound 49 E6
Powell 28 F4
Powers Lake 94 E4
Poy Sippi 70 E3
Poynette 85 A8
Praag 65 B6
Prairie Corners 90 E3
Prairie du Chien 82 E2
Prairie du Sac 85 B5
Prairie Farm 41 D8
Pratt Junction 47 A6
Pray 67 B7
Preble 61 F7
Prentice 35 F5
Prescott 52 C2
Presque Isle 29 D5
Preston 83 F7
Price 55 E7
Primrose 92 A2
Princeton 78 B2
Prospect 88 F1
Pucketville 52 F4
Pulaski 61 D5
Pulcifer 60 B4
Purdy 74 F3
Pureair 23 D5

Q

Quarry 72 E3
Queenstown 45 B5
Quinney 71 F8

R

Racine 95 C8
Radisson 33 D6
Radspur 26 E1
Randall 30 D1
Randolph 78 E3
Random Lake 80 E3
Range 41 B6
Rangeline 57 C7
Rankin 62 E3
Rantz 36 C1
Raymond 95 B7
Raymore 67 F6
Readfield 71 C5
Readstown 83 A5
Red Banks 61 E8
Red Banks 70 C4
Red Cedar 54 D1
Red Cliff 23 C5
Red Mound 74 F2
Red River 60 C1
Red Rock 91 D7
Redgranite 70 F2
Reeds Corners 78 C4
Reedsburg 76 F3
Reedsville 72 D3
Reeseville 86 B4
Reeve 41 D7
Regina 59 B7
Reifs Mills 72 D4
Reighmoor 71 E5
Renet Lake 95 F6
Requa 55 E6
Reseburg 56 A1
Reserve 32 B4
Retreat 82 A3
Rewey 90 B4
Rhine 80 B3
Rhinelander 36 E4
Rib Falls 57 A8
Rib Lake 45 C6
Rib Mountain 58 A2
Rice Lake 42 A2
Richardson 41 C6
Richfield 88 C1
Richford 69 F8
Richland Center 83 B8
Richmond 94 C1
Richwood 87 C5
Ricker Bay 71 E7
Ridgeland 42 D1
Ridgetop 39 B5
Ridgeway 84 F3
Riley 85 E6
Ring 79 A6
Ringle 58 B4

Rio 86 A1
Rio Creek 62 E2
Riplinger 56 C4
Ripon 78 B4
Rising Sun 82 A4
River Falls 52 B3
River Hills 88 D3
Rivermoor 71 E5
Riverside 24 F2
Riverside 91 D7
Riverview 20 F2
Roberts 52 A3
Rochester 95 C5
Rock Elm 53 D6
Rock Falls 54 D2
Rock Springs 76 F4
Rockbridge 83 A8
Rockdale 86 F3
Rockfield 88 C2
Rockland 74 A4
Rockmont 20 F4
Rockton 75 D7
Rockville 90 C2
Rockville 80 A3
Rockwood 73 D5
Rocky Corners 58 D2
Rocky Run 58 F2
Rodell 55 D6
Rogersville 79 C6
Rolling Ground 83 B5
Rolling Prairie 79 F5
Romance 74 E2
Rome 87 F6
Roosevelt 37 E5
Rose Lawn 60 E4
Rosecrans 72 C4
Rosedale 66 E4
Rosendale 79 B5
Rosendale Center 79 B5
Rosewood 95 C5
Rosholt 59 E5
Rosiere 62 D2
Ross 75 E5
Ross Crossing 92 B3
Rostok 62 F3
Rothschild 58 B2
Rouse 27 C8
Rowleys Bay 51 D6
Roxbury 85 C6
Royalton 70 A4
Rozellville 57 C7
Rube 72 F4
Rubicon 87 B7
Ruby 43 D8
Rubys Corner 50 D1
Rudolph 58 F1
Rugby Junction 88 B1
Rural 70 B2
Rush Lake 78 A4
Rusk 54 B1
Rutland 92 A4
Rutledge 90 E2
Ryans Corner 62 F2

S

Sabin 83 A7
Saint Anna 80 A2
Saint Anthony 87 A8
Saint Catherines Bay 71 E8
Saint Cloud 80 B1
Saint Croix Falls 40 B3
Saint Francis 88 F4
Saint Germain 36 B3
Saint John 72 D1
Saint Joseph 74 C3
Saint Kilian 79 E8
Saint Lawrence 87 A8
Saint Martins 95 A6
Saint Marys 75 B6
Saint Michaels 80 F1
Saint Nazianz 72 F3
Saint Peter 79 B8
Saint Rose 90 D4
Salem 53 E9
Salem 95 E6
Salem Oaks 95 E6
Salmo 23 D5
Sampson 61 C5
Sanborn 26 B4
Sand Bay 22 B4
Sand Creek 42 E2
Sand Lake 40 B3
Sand Prairie 83 C6
Sandrock 28 C2
Sandstone Bluff 78 B3
Sandusky 84 A2
Sandy Bay 73 B6
Sandy Hook 90 E2

Sarona 32 D1
Sauk City 85 C5
Saukville 88 A3
Saunders 20 B3
Sauntry 25 C5
Saxeville 70 D2
Saxon 27 A8
Saylesburg 87 B7
Saylesville 87 F8
Sayner 36 A3
Scandinavia 70 A2
Schmidt Corner 59 E6
Schnappsville 57 A7
Schneyville 92 E2
Schofield 58 B2
School Hill 80 A4
Schultz 92 C2
Scotts Junction 75 A6
Sechlerville 66 B3
Sedgwick 27 A7
Seeley 26 E1
Seminary Springs 86 D1
Seneca 82 C4
Sextonville 84 B1
Seymour 60 F4
Seymour 54 C4
Seymour Corners 91 D5
Shady Dell 83 F5
Shamrock 67 D5
Shanagolden 27 F6
Shantytown 58 D4
Sharon 94 F1
Shawano 60 C2
Shawtown 54 C3
Sheboygan 81 C5
Sheboygan Falls 80 C4
Shelby 74 C2
Sheldon 43 C8
Shell Lake 31 D8
Shennington 68 F1
Shepley 59 B6
Sheppard 67 C5
Sheridan 70 B1
Sherman Center 80 E3
Sherman Corners 37 F7
Sherry 57 E8
Sherry Junction 47 D7
Sherwood 67 A8
Sherwood 72 D1
Shiocton 71 A6
Shirley 72 B3
Shoemaker Point 62 D1
Shopiere 93 E7
Shorewood 88 E4
Shorewood Hills 85 E8
Shortville 56 F3
Shoto 73 D5
Shullsburg 91 E5
Sidney 56 F2
Silica 79 B8
Silver Creek 80 E2
Silver Lake 95 E5
Sinsinawa 90 E3
Sioux 22 D4
Siren 31 C5
Sister Bay 51 D5
Six Corners 93 C8
Slab City 60 D3
Slabtown 87 F6
Slades Corners 94 E4
Slateford 91 B6
Slinger 87 B8
Slovan 62 F2
Snell 47 F5
Snells 71 D7
Sniderville 72 B1
Snows Corner 52 D4
Sobieski 61 D6
Sobieski Corners 61 D6
Soldiers Grove 83 A5
Solon Springs 25 C5
Somers 95 D7
Somerset 40 E3
Sono Junction 52 A2
Soperton 48 A2
South Beaver Dam 86 A4
South Byron 79 D7
South Chase 61 D6
South Itasca 20 E4
South Kenosha 95 E8
South Milwaukee 95 A8
South Randolph 78 F3
South Range 20 F4
South Superior 20 E3
South Wayne 91 E8
Sparta 75 A5
Spaulding 67 B8
Speck Oaks 67 C7
Spencer 57 C5
Spirit 45 A6
Spirit Falls 45 A7
Split Rock 59 D7
Spokeville 56 D4
Spooner 32 C1
Sprague 83 D2
Spread Eagle 39 B6
Spring Bank Park 67 F6

Spring Brook 32 A2
Spring Green 84 D3
Spring Grove 78 B3
Spring Prairie 94 C4
Spring Valley 53 B6
Springfield 94 D4
Springfield Corners 77 A7
Springfield Corners 85 C7
Springstead 35 A6
Spring Valley 80 A4
Springville 74 E4
Spruce 61 A5
Spur 46 C2
Stanberry 32 A3
Stangelville 73 A5
Stanley 55 A8
Stanton 40 D4
Star Lake 29 F7
Star Praire 40 D4
Starks 37 E5
State Line 95 F8
Stearns 92 D2
Stebbinsville 93 B6
Steinthal 72 F3
Stetsonville 45 F5
Steuben 83 D5
Stevens Hill 62 B4
Stevens Point 58 F3
Stevenstown 66 F2
Stiles 61 B6
Stiles Junction 61 B6
Stitzer 90 A2
Stockbridge 71 E8
Stockholm 64 A2
Stockton 58 F3
Stoddard 74 D2
Stone 93 A5
Stone Lake 32 C3
Stonebank 87 D8
Story 92 A3
Stoughton 93 A5
Stratford 57 C7
Strawbridge 90 E4
Strickland 42 A3
Strongs Prairie 68 E3
Strum 54 F4
Sturgeon Bay 62 B4
Sturtevant 95 C8
Suamico 61 E6
Sugar Bush 61 F8
Sugar Grove 83 A6
Sugar Island 87 C6
Sullivan 87 F6
Summit Center 87 E7
Summit Corners 87 E7
Summit Lake 47 B5
Sumner 42 B2
Sun Prairie 86 D1
Sunnyside 20 F3
Sunnyside 86 F1
Sunrise Bay 71 D7
Sunset 46 F3
Superior 20 E3
Superior Village 20 E3
Suring 60 A4
Sussex 88 D1
Sutcliffe Corners 75 C8
Sutherland 26 B2
Sweetheart City 49 C7
Swiss Historical Village
92 B2
Sylvan 83 A6
Sylvan Mounds 86 F3
Sylvania 95 C7
Symco 59 F8

Thorp 56 A1
Three Lakes 37 C6
Tibbets 94 C2
Tichigan 95 B5
Tiffany 93 E8
Tigerton 59 D6
Tilden 42 F4
Tilleda 59 C8
Timberland 31 E7
Tioga 56 D1
Tipler 38 B2
Tisch Mills 73 B6
Tobin 95 E8
Token Creek 86 C1
Tomah 67 F7
Tomahawk 46 A1
Tonet 62 E1
Tony 43 A8
Topside 22 F1
Torun 58 E3
Towerville 82 A4
Townsend 48 C2
Tracy Corners 60 C3
Trade Lake 30 D3
Trade River 30 E3
Trego 32 B1
Tremble 61 E6
Trempealeau 65 F8
Trenton 52 E3
Trevino 64 A3
Trevor 95 E6
Trimbelle 52 D3
Tripoli 35 F7
Trippville 75 C8
Troy 94 B3
Troy Center 94 B3
Truesdell 95 E7
Truman 91 C5
Tuckaway 88 F3
Tuleta Hills 78 B3
Tunnel 76 B1
Tunnel City 67 F7
Tunnelville 75 E6
Turtle Lake 41 B7
Tuscobia 32 F2
Tustin 70 D4
Twelve Corners 71 A7
Twin Bluffs 84 C1
Twin Grove 92 E3
Twin Lakes 95 E5
Twin Town 41 B7
Two Creeks 73 C6
Two Rivers 73 D6
Tyler Forks 27 C7
Tyran 38 A4

U

Ubet 40 B4
Ulao 88 B3
Underhill 60 B4
Union 90 B3
Union 93 B5
Union Center 76 D1
Union Church 95 B6
Union Grove 95 C6
Unity 57 B5
University of Wisconsin
Experiment Station 22 F4
Upper French Creek 66 D1
Upson 27 C8
Urne 54 F1
Utica 86 F2
Utley 78 C4
Utters Corners 94 C1

T

Tabor 95 B8
Tadpole Corners 32 B1
Taegesville 46 F1
Tamarack 65 D8
Tarrant 54 E1
Taus 72 D4
Tavera 83 B6
Taycheedah 79 B8
Taylor 66 B3
Tell 65 B5
Tennyson 90 C2
Tess Corners 95 A6
Theresa 79 F7
Theresa Station 79 F7
Thiensville 88 C3
Thiry Daems 62 E1
Thompson 87 C8
Thompsonville 95 B7
Thornapple 43 B6
Thornton 60 C1

V

Valders 72 E4
Valley 75 D7
Valley Junction 67 E8
Valmy 62 B4
Valton 76 E1
Van Buskirk 28 B2
Van Dyne 79 A7
Vaudreuil 67 C5
Veedum 68 A2
Veefkind 56 D4
Vernon 95 A5
Vernon Station 95 A5
Verona 85 F7

Vesper 68 A3
Victory 74 F2
Victory Center 88 C2
Victory Heights 93 E6
Vienna 94 C4
Vignes 62 D4
Viking 53 B5
Vilas 86 E1
Village Hall 88 D3
Vinnie Ha Ha 93 A8
Viola 75 F6
Viroqua 74 E4

W

Wabeno 48 A2
Wagner 50 C1
Waino 21 E7
Waldo 80 D3
Waldwick 91 B7
Wales 87 F8
Walhain 62 F1
Walsh 50 D1
Walworth 94 E2
Wanderoos 40 C4
Wards Corners 84 A2
Warrens 67 E7
Warrentown 53 E5
Wascott 25 E5
Washburn 22 E4
Washington 51 B7
Washington Island 51 B7
Waterbury 67 B7
Waterford 95 B5
Waterford North 95 B5
Waterloo 86 D3
Watertown 87 C5
Waterville 87 E7
Waubeka 80 F3
Waucousta 80 D1
Waukau 71 F5
Waukesha 88 F1
Waumandee 65 C6
Waunakee 85 C7
Waupaca 70 B2
Waupun 79 D5
Wausau 58 A2
Wausau Junction 58 A2
Wausaukee 49 B7
Wautoma 70 E1
Wauwatosa 88 E3
Wauzeka 82 E4
Waverly 53 D6
Waxdale 95 C8
Way 20 F4
Wayne 79 F8
Wayside 72 C3
Webb Lake 31 A7
Webster 31 B5
Weedens 80 D4
Wein 57 B7
Weirgor 33 D5
Wells 72 E2
Wentworth 21 F5
Wequiock 61 F8
Werley 83 F5
West Allis 88 F3
West Almond 69 C7
West Bancroft 69 C7
West Baraboo 77 F5
West Bend 88 A1
West Bloomfield 70 D3
West De Pere 72 A2
West Denmark 30 F4
West Granville 88 D2
West Kraft 46 A1
West La Crosse 74 B1
West Lima 75 E6
West Milwaukee 88 F3
West Prairie 65 E7
West Prairie 74 F3
West Rosendale 79 B5
West Salem 74 A3
West Sweden 30 F4
Westboro 45 B5
Westby 75 D5
Westfield 77 A7
Weston 53 C7
Weston 58 B3
Westport 83 C6
Weyauwega 70 B3
Weyerhaeuser 42 B4
Wheatland 95 D5
Wheeler 41 F8
Whispering Pines 71 C8
Whitcomb 59 C6
White City 75 E8
White Creek 76 B4
White Lake 48 E1

White Oak 91 E5
White River 27 A5
Whitefish Bay 88 D3
Whitehall 66 B1
Whitelaw 72 D4
Whitewater 94 B1
Whiting 58 F3
Whittlesey 45 D5
Wickware 42 B1
Wilcox 61 A8
Wild Rose 83 B7
Wild Rose 70 D1
Wildwood 53 B5
Willard 56 D2
Williams Bay 94 E3
Willow Creek 88 C1
Willow Springs 88 D1
Wills 25 A7
Wilmoore Heights 78 A4
Wilmot 95 E5
Wilson 55 B7
Wilson 53 A6
Wilton 75 B7
Winchester 28 D4
Winchester 71 D6
Wind Lake 95 B5
Wind Point
Windsor 85 C8
Winnebago 71 E7
Winneboujou 25 A7
Winneconne 71 E5
Winter 33 C7
Wiota 91 D8
Wisconsin Dells 77 D5
Wisconsin Junction 37 E8
Wisconsin Rapids 69 B5
Withee 56 A3
Wittenberg 59 C6
Witwen 84 B4
Wolf Creek 30 F2
Wonewoc 76 D1
Wood 76 E1
Woodboro 36 E3
Wooddale 32 E4
Woodford 91 D8
Woodhull 79 C6
Woodland 87 A7
Woodland Corner 24 E2
Woodlawn 47 A8
Woodman 83 E5
Woodruff 36 B2
Woodstock 75 F8
Woodville 53 A5
Woodworth 95 E7
Worcester 35 E5
Wrightstown 72 B1
Wuertsburg 57 A6
Wyalusing 82 F2
Wyeville 67 F8
Wyocena 78 F1
Wyoming 84 D2

XY

Yarnell 32 D4
Yellow Lake 31 B5
Yellowstone 91 B7
York 66 A2
York Center 86 C2
Yorkville 95 C6
Young America 80 F1
Yuba 75 E8

Z

Zachow 60 D4
Zander 73 B5
Zenda 94 E3
Zion 71 F6
Zittau 71 D5
Zoar 47 F8

Introduction

With more than 15,000 lakes and many miles of shoreline along Lake Michigan, Lake Superior, and the Mississippi River, Wisconsin offers endless possibilities for water sports. Along the Great Lakes, sandy beaches, lighthouses, quaint villages and coastal islands present scenic backdrops for fishermen and sailors. Interior lakes, rivers and streams provide options for swimming, water skiing, canoeing and whitewater rafting. Beautiful forestlands, hills, and meadows attract visitors to the outdoors for hiking, biking, horseback riding, skiing and snowshoeing. Sunny beaches, colorful fall foliage, sparkling winter snows and a variety of museums and cultural events leave visitors with year-round recreation opportunities.

As a starting point, the Gazetteer features a selection of activities for all ages and activity levels. For a more comprehensive list of destinations and activities contact the following state and federal agencies.

RECREATION

The Wisconsin Department of Tourism provides information on a wide range of activities including performing arts, spectator sports, outdoor recreation and excursions. The State Department of Tourism also provides information on cultural attractions such as museums, galleries, ancient Indian ruins and history of early European explorers. Wisconsin offers numerous trails for hikers and bikers, as well as miles of rivers and streams for paddlers of all skill levels. Wisconsin has more than 40 waterfalls that attract painters and photographers each year. To make your travel planning easier, Wisconsin is divided into three tourism regions each with its own selection of attractions. In addition to information on events and activities, the Wisconsin Department of Tourism office also supplies maps, brochures, and information about accommodations.

Wisconsin Department of Tourism
www.travelwisconsin.com
(800) 432 8747

The state of Wisconsin has over 100 state parks, forests, wildlife areas and recreation areas providing places for camping and outdoor activities. These parks offer nearly 2000 miles of trails so outdoor enthusiasts can hike, bike, horseback ride, cross-country ski or snowshoe. The state lands include thousands of miles of waterfront for swimming, boating, water skiing and fishing. Tour a 1000-year-old archeological site, visit the home of architect Frank Lloyd Wright, or investigate any of the other museums and historic sites highlighting the state's rich history. The State Department of Natural Resources can assist visitors with information on planning, reservations, regulations, fees and activities on both state and county lands.

Wisconsin Department of Natural Resources
www.dnr.wisconsin.gov
(888) 936-7463

Wisconsin contains millions of acres of federal lands designed to encourage outdoor recreation. A wide range of outdoor activities occur year-round in the 1.5 million acre Chequamegon-Nicolet National Forest. Operated by the National Park Service, the Ice Age National Scenic Trail allows access to landscapes formed by massive ice sheets that dominated North America 15,000 years ago. Dozens of other scenic sites and recreational areas offer visitor activities surrounding features of historic and geologic interest. Wildlife refuges preserve valuable ecosystems and allow limited opportunities for wildlife viewing, photography and educational programs. For additional information on recreation activities on federal lands contact the following agencies.

National Park Service
www.nps.gov/state/wi

Chequamegon-Nicolet National Forest
www.fs.usda.gov/cnnf
(715) 362-1300

National Wildlife Refuges
www.fws.gov/refuges
(800) 344-WILD

US Army Corps of Engineers
www.corpslakes.us

TRAVEL

The Wisconsin Department of Transportation (WisDOT) works to promote traffic safety and assist travelers. WisDOT operates more than 30 rest areas along major highways, with restrooms, picnic areas and travel information. To make travel planning easier, WisDOT provides highway maps and information on public transportation, as well as travel by bicycle, train and ferry.

WisDOT also maintains roads of scenic or historic interest as scenic byways or rustic roads. Scenic byways highlight state routes of both scenic and historic interest. Rustic roads, however, are lightly traveled rural roads that attract hikers, bikers and motorists. Road conditions vary, as surfaces sometimes consist of dirt or gravel. To avoid confusion with state highways, rustic roads are marked with distinctive yellow and brown signs.

To improve safety, motorists can access up-to-date information on road conditions, weather delays and travel restrictions. Road Weather Information System (RWIS) displays real time weather information from automated sensors at nearly 60 sites throughout the state.

Wisconsin Department of Transportation
www.wisconsindot.gov

If you plan to travel outside the US, you can receive information and assistance from US Customs and Border Protection. This agency will provide information about travel requirements, documents, travel alerts and wait times at border crossings. For information about passports, contact the US Department of State.

US Customs and Border Protection
www.cbp.gov
(877) 227-5511

Passport Information
www.travel.state.gov
(877) 487-2278

STATE FACTS

Admitted to the Union:
  May 29, 1848; 30th state; name is a French corruption of an Indian word whose meaning is disputed
Capitol: Madison
Size: 65,498 square miles
Population: 5,892,539 (2022 estimate)
Nickname: Badger State
Motto: Forward
Bird: Robin
Flower: Wood Violet
Tree: Sugar Maple
Mineral: Galena
Animal: Badger
Fish: Musky (Muskellunge)
Fossil: Trilobite
Insect: Honeybee
Song: "On Wisconsin"
Major Ports: Milwaukee, Duluth-Superior, Green Bay, La Crosse, Prairie du Chien
Lowest point: Lake Michigan, 579 feet
Highest points:
  Timms Hill .... 1,952 feet
  Pearson Hill .... 1,951 feet
  Rib Mountain .... 1,940 feet
  Sugarbush Hill .... 1,938 feet
  East Hill .... 1,875 feet

Major Lakes:
  Lake Winnebago .... 137,708 acres
  Lake Pepin .... 27,813 acres
  Petenwell Lake .... 23,040 acres
  Lake Chippewa .... 15,300 acres
  Lake Poygan .... 14,102 acres
  Castle Rock Lake .... 13,955 acres
  Turtle–
    Flambeau Flowage ..... 13,545 acres
  Lake Koshkonong .... 10,460 acres
  Lake Mendota .... 9,842 acres
  Lake Wisconsin .... 9,000 acres
Largest Cities (with population):
  Milwaukee 563,305
  Madison 272,903
  Green Bay 106,095
  Kenosha 98,484
  Racine 76,462
Major Rivers:
  Wisconsin River .... 430 miles
  Oconto River .... 209 miles
  Fox River .... 200 miles
  Chippewa River .... 183 miles
  Black River .... 160 miles
Major Industries: Dairy Products (milk, butter, cheese), Farming (corn), Machinery, Paper Manufacturing, Beer, Tourism

FISHING AND HUNTING

With its vast forestlands and thousands of miles of waterways Wisconsin offers unlimited opportunities for hunting and fishing. The Gazetteer features a selection of fishing and hunting locations on state and federal lands.

It is important to be familiar with local rules, regulations and restrictions before hunting or fishing in any area. The following agency provides information on hunting and fishing regulations in the state of Wisconsin.

Wisconsin Department of Natural Resources
www.dnr.wisconsin.gov
(888) 936-7463

CAMPGROUNDS

Campgrounds with a variety of different facilities are located on state, federal and private lands. The public campground symbol, as shown in the Legend (see inside front cover), identifies campgrounds located within national forests and parks. For information on fees, services and reservations at public campgrounds contact one of the state or federal agencies listed above. The Gazetteer also lists information on private campgrounds that are members of the Wisconsin Association of Campground Owners (WACO). To locate private campgrounds in this Atlas, look on the appropriate map for the campground symbol and corresponding four-digit number. Public campgrounds located on state and federal lands can be identified by the symbol indicated in the Legend.

Wisconsin Association of Campground Owners,
www.wisconsincampgrounds.com
(608) 582-2327

Outdoor Adventures

HIKING

ANVIL TRAIL SYSTEM – Chequamegon–Nicolet National Forest – 37 B7 System of trails used for hiking and cross-country skiing. Twelve miles of marked trails over gently rolling to hilly terrain. Trailhead at parking lot across from Anvil Lake Campground. Side trail to Franklin Lake open for summer hiking.

BLACK LAKE TRAIL – Loretta – 33 A8 Trailhead at parking lot on FR 1666. Loop trail around Black Lake. Excellent views of lake.

BRULE–ST CROIX LAKE TRAIL – Brule – 25 A7 Marked snowmobile trail used for hiking through Brule River State Forest. Route crosses varied terrain in Brule River Valley. Trailhead at parking area on SR 27. No camping along trail. Numerous access sites.

EMMA CARLIN TRAIL SYSTEM – Palmyra – 94 A2 Trailhead at parking lot off CR Z in Kettle Moraine State Forest—Southern Unit. Loop trail winding through meadows and rolling oak and pine forests. Only loop trail in forest open to winter hiking and snowshoeing.

ESCANABA TRAIL – Boulder Junction – 29 F6 Marked trail over hilly, wooded terrain winding around five lakes. Trailhead at parking area on Nebish Lake Road. Three loops allow shorter routes. Open to cross-country skiing. Shelter along route.

EUROPE BAY HOTZ LOOP – Newport State Park – 51 D7 Trailhead at picnic area. Trail extends north along Lake Michigan from Newport Bay to Europe Bay. Route passes through maple and beech forest, meadow, bogs and along sand beach. Views of Death's Door Passage, Plum Island, Detroit Island and Pilot Island Lighthouse.

FLAMBEAU HILLS TRAILS – Chequamegon–Nicolet National Forest – 35 A5 Eleven separate trails, from 1 to 23 miles in length. Trails cross streams and South Fork of Flambeau River and give access to many lakes. Three parking areas and two rustic campgrounds. Open to hunting, cross country skiing and horseback riding. Trail bike riding in designated areas. Trailhead at parking area on east side of Blockhouse Lake on FR 153.

GREAT RIVER STATE TRAIL – Onalaska – 74 A1 State trail in unglaciated portion of west central Wisconsin from Onalaska to Trempealeau National Wildlife Refuge. Passes through Mississippi River Valley. Surrounded by steep bluffs. Trailhead at parking lot on South Second Street. Open to hiking, biking and snowmobiling.

ICE AGE NATIONAL SCENIC TRAIL – Polar – 47 E7 Trail corridor extends nearly 1,200 miles through Wisconsin from Lake Michigan to Saint Croix River. 600 miles of completed trail passes through hardwood forests and lowland bogs featuring evidence of glacial activity, including drumlins, eskers and kettles. Completed trail segments connected by road. Access at several parking and rest areas. Designated state trail.

INDIAN MOUND TRAIL – High Cliff State Park – 71 D8 Trailhead at family campground in park. Marked trail through several prehistoric Native American effigy mounds. Mounds vary from 25 to 285 feet in length and were probably used as ceremonial or burial mounds.

JONES SPRING AREA TRAIL – Chequamegon–Nicolet National Forest – 48 C2 2,000-acre area set aside for non-motorized use. Seven miles of marked trails for hiking and cross-country skiing. Access to numerous lakes. Walk-in campgrounds at Fanny Lake. Numerous access points.

LAUTERMAN NATIONAL RECREATION TRAIL – Chequamegon–Nicolet National Forest – 38 B2 Trail system used for hiking and cross-country skiing. Route follows ridge along Pine River and circles Lost Lake. Trail over rolling terrain connects to northern hiking loop around Perch Lake. Trailhead at Lost Lake Campground. Several parking and access points.

MICHIGAN RAPIDS HIKING TRAIL – Chequamegon–Nicolet National Forest – 38 F3 Easy, marked hiking trail along Peshtigo River. Scenic features include rapids, river islands and rock formations. Trailhead at Burnt Bridge.

MOUNT VALHALLA TRAIL – Washburn – 22 D3 Marked loop located in Mount Valhalla Recreation Area once used as training area by US Olympic Ski Team in Chequamegon–Nicolet National Forest *(see Recreation Areas)*. Trailhead at chalet. Scenic ridge and hill offering views of Lake Superior. Trail also passes Sunbowl—large valley with little tree growth. Birch Grove Campground along trail.

NORTH COUNTRY TRAIL – Mellen – 27 C6 Trail corridor extends about 4,800 miles from Vermont to North Dakota. Over 60 miles of trail pass through Chequamegon–Nicolet National Forest featuring rocky outcrops, scenic overlooks, lakes and streams. Several access points along trail allow for shorter trips. Designated state trail.

PERROT RIDGE TRAIL – Perrot State Park – 65 F8 Trailhead at South Contact Station. Ancient Native American burial mounds at trailhead route over Reeds Peak and Perrot Ridge (elevations from 400 to 500 feet). Views of Mississippi River Valley.

POPPLE RIDGE TRAIL – Langlade – 48 D1 Located in Chequamegon–Nicolet National Forest *(see Recreation Areas)*. Trailhead at parking area off Forest Road 2122. Marked trail proceeds east following old truck trails through variety of timber types. Several access points. Primitive camping permitted along trail.

ROCK LAKE TRAIL – Namekagon – 26 E2 National Recreational Trail. Trailhead at parking lot on CR M. Marked trail system for hiking and cross-country skiing. Alternate shorter loop trails.

ST PETERS DOME TRAIL – Sanborn – 26 C4 Scenic route leads to St. Peter's Dome, offering panoramic views. Passes 70-foot-high Morgan Falls. Trailhead at parking area on FR 199. Primitive camping area.

TOWER TRAIL – Idlewild – 62 B3 Route follows old paved roadway along highest bluff in park. 75-foot observation tower offers panoramic views of Green Bay, Door County and Michigan. Trail descends slowly to edge of bluff where it drops sharply to Sturgeon Bay shoreline. Route continues along shore through archway of cedar trees, turning west at North Campground for return to trailhead. Trailhead at parking lot at Powatoni Ski Hill.

ZILLMER TRAIL – Kettle Moraine State Forest—Northern Unit – 80 E1 Marked loop trail over hilly terrain offers scenic views of area. Open to cross-country skiing. Alternate shorter loops. Trailhead at parking area on CR SS.

BIKING

DEVILS LAKE LOOP – Baraboo – 77 F5 Route begins on designated bicycle path off Walnut Street and follows along south range of Baraboo Hills to Devils Lake at Devil's Lake State Park. Terrain ranges from easy to difficult as route progresses from valley to bluffs. From bicycle path, route heads west to South Shore Road where road narrows, then east on South Lake Road to SR 113. Heads south to left turn on CR DL to junction with SR 78, traveling in northeasterly direction. Loop finishes with left turns on Durwards Glen Road and McLeish Road, crossing Columbia Sauk County line back toward Devil's Lake State Park on Tower Road.

LAKE MONONA LOOP – Madison – 85 E8 Loop consists of varied bikeways. Begins with bicycle path off Spaight Street, follows John Nolen Drive and circles Lake Monona passing through Law and B. B. Clarke Parks and Olbrich Gardens. Continues from path on Waunona Way to Midmoor and Winnequah Roads to Atwood Avenue. Then follows Lakeland Avenue and Rutledge Street to Spaight Street to complete loop.

MADELINE ISLAND – La Pointe – 23 D5 Route begins at La Pointe Ferry Dock heading east on CR H to south shore of island. Continues on Hagen and Haines Roads to Big Bay State Park for swimming and camping. Doubles back to Black Shanty Road heading north intersecting with CR H again. Views of North Channel and Bayfield. Alternate routes throughout island.

MENOMINEE RIVER CENTURY LOOP – Marinette – 50 E1 Route follows Menominee River and begins on SR 180, travels north to McAllister and CR JJ, heading east over Menominee River and Wisconsin–Michigan state line to SR 577. Heads south to 18th Avenue, then West Drive to 25th Street to Hattie Street over bridge. Loop finishes with Riverside Avenue to Van Cleve Avenue and SR 64, then west back to SR 180.

OAK LEAF TRAIL – Milwaukee – 88 F4 Multiple loops connect parks and neighborhoods within Milwaukee County. Varied tour includes connecting trails, park paths, park and parkway drives and municipal streets.

OMAHA BIKEWAY – Sprague – 68 D2 Route begins at Necedah National Wildlife Refuge and travels west on 9th Street passing Sprague–Mather Flowage turning south on 5th Avenue to 16th Street and 6th Avenue. Route continues on Grand Dike Road to Headquarters Road. Follows SR 21 Necedah and SR 80 north. At intersection with SR 21 follows CR G until reaching 19th Street east and 17th Avenue north. Route passes Petenwell Flowage to 16th Avenue and travels west on 12th Street. Heads north on CR G and intersects, then turns north on CR G and intersects, then north on 12th Avenue and 9th Street to complete loop.

OSHKOSH LOOP – Oshkosh – 71 F6 Route begins at Rainbow Park on Fox River. Travels south to Punhoqua Street to Graham Avenue to Eagle Street south, to Oshkosh Avenue. Turns south on Westfield Street, east on Taft Avenue and south on Campbell Road, passing Steiger Park Trail and paralleling Fox River. Continues south to Idaho Street, then east to Sixth Avenue and north on South Main Street, crossing Fox River. Turns southeast on Ceape Avenue and south on Broad Street to Bay Shore Drive. Heads north on Lake Street with views of Lake Winnebago. Turns northwest to Rosalia Street, Washington Avenue, west to Hazel Street, then north to Menominee Park for swimming and picnicking. Continues north around Lake Winnebago to Hazel Street and Menominee Drive, then turns west on East Murdock Street. Heads south on Main Street until Nevada Avenue, heading west. Turns south on Jackson Street, west on Congress Avenue, passing Paine Art Center and Arboretum and then crosses Fox River, returning to Rainbow Park.

POINT BEACH RIDE – Two Rivers – 73 D6 Route begins at Neshotah Park and passes through Point Beach State Forest on Rustic Road O, heading northeast to Rustic Road V. Sights include Rawley Point Light. Views of Lake Michigan and sandy swimming beaches. Route heads north to Nuclear Road and Point Beach Nuclear Plant turns west on Tapawingo Road, south on Tannery Road and west on Benzinger Road. Then south to meet Rustic Road V, through Mishicot to East Shore Road, south on Manitou Drive and east on Crystal Spring Road. At intersection of SR 147 heads north to Maplewood Road and south on Tannery Road. Continues southeast on Riverview Road to forest entrance. (Alternative 15-mile loop heading southwest at Lakeshore Road and Rustic Road V intersection.)

RACINE COUNTY BIKE TRAIL – Racine – 95 C8 Route begins at South Street and Douglas Avenue in Racine, connecting with portion of MRK Trail to Seven Mile Road. Travels west to Waukesha Road, south and west again on Five Mile Road passing through Raymond Center. Heads south on 108th Street, west on CR K and north on Britton Road. Continues west on Burmeister Road to Wind Lake Road to Loomis Road, around Wind Lake (alternative off-road bicycle path here). From Loomis Road heads south to Pioneer Road, north on Settler Avenue and west on Homestead Road to Town Line Road. Heads north to North Lake Drive and south on Marsh Road. Then Ranke Road to Buena Park Road and towns of Waterford and Rochester. From Rochester, follows CR FF (Academy Road and Heritage Avenue) to Honey Lake Road through Burlington. Route continues to Milwaukee Avenue heading south to Pine Street and northeast on Jefferson Street to Main Street. From Main Street northeast to Browns Lake Drive to Ketterhagen Road. Turn north on CR J (English Settlement Avenue) and east on Church Road. Heads south on South Britton Road, east on Spring Street and south again on 59th Drive turning east on SR 11. Route continues south on 59th Drive, crossing I-94 to 105th Street to Braun Road. Route may end at Elmwood Park or continue short distance to North Shore Trail.

SUNSET TRAIL – Peninsula State Park – 51 E5 Route follows bicycle trail north from park around peninsula on Shanty Bay and connects with return route over scenic back roads to Fish Creek park office. Heads south at path end, to Hemlock Road and Middle Road, intersecting with bicycle trail and completing loop. Smooth, graveled trail surface.

WASHINGTON ISLAND – Detroit Harbor – 51 C7 Route begins at Washington Island Ferry Line dock and CR W (Lobdell Point Road), to Detroit Harbor Road, heading north on Range Line Road to Lakeview Road. Turns east to Eastside Road, then north to Mountain Road. Passes Mountain Park Lookout and intersects Jackson Harbor Road to Jackson Harbor. In Jackson Harbor, take Karfi Ferry to Rock Island State Park. Return route follows Jackson Harbor Road to CR W (Main Road) with views of Washington Harbor and Schoolhouse Beach. CR W (Main Road) continues to Detroit Harbor. Alternate route around South Shore Drive and Sand Dunes Public Beach.

PADDLING

BARABOO RIVER – Baraboo – 77 F5 Put-in at bridge on Highway 113. Upper portion winds through farmland then passes through narrows. Several access points at bridges. Route joins Wisconsin River with take-out two miles downstream at Dekorra.

BEAR RIVER – Lac du Flambeau – 35 A8 Put-in below dam at outlet of Flambeau Lake. Upper portion meanders through marsh. Numerous access and campsites along route. Take-out at Murray's Landing on Flambeau Flowage. Route suitable for novices. Class I.

BLACK RIVER – Black River – 67 B5 Put-in at Halls Creek canoe landing in Black River State Forest. Slow-moving river, suitable for beginners and popular with fishermen. Slow to medium current, to confluence with Mississippi River. Dam portage at Black River Falls. Rolling terrain. Camping at Hawk Island. Take-out at Irving.

BOIS BRULE RIVER – Brule River State Forest – 25 B6 Put-in at Stone's Bridge canoe landing on CR S. Scenic route through Brule River State Forest. Stretch above US 2 bridge, with rapids suitable for novices. Lower portion for experienced canoeists only. Two portages around Class III–IV Lenroot and May Ledges rapids. Take-out at canoe landing at river mouth on Brule River Road. Bois Brule and Copper Range Campgrounds located on forest land. Class I–IV.

CHIPPEWA RIVER – Eau Claire – 54 C3 Put-in at boat launch off Menominee Street. Easy stretch past sandstone cliffs, wooded shores and sandy beaches. Numerous access sites along route. Take-out at SR 35 bridge above confluence with Mississippi River.

CLAM RIVER – Webster – 31 C5 Put-in at Highway 35 bridge. Easy route suitable for beginners. Fallen trees occasionally block river. Flatwater paddling on Clam Flowage. Take-out at Highway F bridge.

FLAMBEAU RIVER – Flambeau River State Forest – 34 C3 Put-in at landing on Nine Mile Creek. Popular whitewater route. Upper portion of trip includes Class I rapids and some fast water. Lower portion includes numerous Class II rapids and several Class III rapids where portages may be necessary in high water. Dam portages. Water slows at Lake Flambeau. Wilderness scenery. Rustic campgrounds along river. Numerous access sites. Take-out at Flambeau Lodge. Class I–III.

FOX RIVER – Portage – 77 E7 Put-in off SR 33 Street. Route begins on Portage Canal connecting Wisconsin and Fox Rivers. Easy paddle along historic trade route. Dam portage. Flatwater paddling on Buffalo Lake. Take-out in Montello.

KICKAPOO RIVER – Ontario – 75 C7 Put-in at canoe landing at intersection of SR 33 and SR 131. Slow-flowing river meanders through farmland and past limestone and sandstone bluffs. Subject to flooding. Numerous access sites at bridges. SR 131 parallels river. Camping at Wildcat Mountain State Park. Take-out at La Farge.

MANITOWISH WATERS – Northern Highland– American Legion State Forest – 29 F5 Put-in at boat landing on Island Lake. Nearly a dozen small lakes joined by streams. Numerous access sites and campsites along lakes, rivers and streams.

MISSISSIPPI RIVER – Wyalusing – 82 F2 Put-in at boat landing. Signed canoe route through sloughs and backwaters. Wildlife and bird-watching.

NAMEKAGON RIVER – Trego – 32 B1 Put-in at Trego Park. Route within boundaries of St. Croix National Scenic Riverway. Portage at Trego Dam. Joins St. Croix River. Class I rapids above Big Island. Numerous access sites and campgrounds along route. Take-out at Riverside Landing. Class I.

PESHTIGO RIVER – Cavour – 38 E2 Put-in at Big Joe campground in Chequamegon–Nicolet National Forest. Portion above CCC Bridge suitable for beginners. Middle portion of section includes short, rocky rapids, possibly hazardous for novices. Portages may be necessary due to fallen trees blocking river. Class I–II rapids nine

miles above Burnt Bridge. Final leg of trip requires portages at Michigan Rapids and the Dells. Take-out at CR L. Class I–II.

RED CEDAR RIVER – New Auburn – 42 E2 Put-in at village park on CR V. Route suitable for beginners. Moderate, steady current. Numerous access sites. Take-out at park on Tainter Lake.

ST CROIX RIVER – Riverside – 24 F2 Put-in at Riverside Landing on SR 35. Rustic scenery along St. Croix National Scenic Riverway. Rapids range from Class I in summer and autumn to Class II–III during spring flooding. Numerous access and campsites along route. Take-out at canoe landing at SR 70 bridge. Class I–III.

TURTLE–FLAMBEAU FLOWAGE – Mercer – 28 E2 Put-in at Lake of the Falls County Park on CR FF. 18,900-acre flowage includes nine lakes with over 150 miles of shoreline and many undeveloped islands. Numerous state campsites. Wind can cause heavy waves on large, shallow lakes.

WAUPACA CHAIN O' LAKES – Waupaca – 70 B2 Put-in at public landing on Taylor Lake. 22 spring-fed, interconnected lakes, ranging in size from 2.5 acres to over 115 acres. Depths vary to almost 100 feet. Smooth paddling—no wake speed limit on all but largest lakes (Rainbow, Round, Columbian and Long Lakes).

WISCONSIN RIVER – Sauk City – 85 C5 Put-in at US 12 bridge. Fast-moving, sometimes shallow river. Shifting sandbars. Water level can fluctuate several feet. Primitive camping on public islands. Take-out at Tower Hill State Park.

WOLF RIVER – White Lake – 48 E2 Put-in off Sunny Waters Ln. Rugged route, for expert canoeists only, through Menominee Indian Reservation. Numerous Class II rapids. Some Class III–IV rapids. Portage around falls. Take-out in Keshena. Class II–IV rapids.

YAHARA RIVER – Waunakee – 85 D8 Put-in at boat ramp. Mainly flatwater route through Lake Mendota, Lake Monona, Mud Lake, Lake Waubesa and Lake Kegonsa. High winds may

make canoeing hazardous on Lake Mendota. Lock connects Lakes Mendota and Monona. Take-out at Lake Kegonsa State Park.

YELLOW RIVER – Spooner – 31 C8 Put-in at Green Valley Rd. Route suitable for novices with easy rapids and riffles. Flatwater canoeing on Rice, Yellow and Little Yellow Lakes. Take-out at bridge below Little Yellow Lake on CR U.

Unique Natural Features

BRADYS BLUFF PRAIRIE – Perrot State Park – 65 F8 Dry prairie situated on steep Mississippi River bluff rising 460 feet above river. Over 100 plant species including big and little bluestem, side-oats grama, northern dropseed, prairie clovers and rough blazing star. Hiking trail.

CATHEDRAL OF PINES – Chequamegon–Nicolet National Forest – 48 C2 One of few remaining stands of virgin pine in Wisconsin. 20-acre parcel in Chequamegon–Nicolet National Forest. Pine trees ranging from 200 to 400 years old. Great blue heron rookery.

CAVE OF THE MOUNDS – Blue Mounds – 85 F5 Guided tours through limestone caverns. Stalactites, stalagmites, crystallized rock formations and underground pools. Lighted, paved walkways.

CAVE POINT COUNTY PARK – Valmy – 63 A5 20-foot-high limestone bluff along rocky Lake Michigan shoreline. Assortment of shallow caves hollowed out by wave action. Largest cave 40 feet deep.

CHIWAUKEE PRAIRIE – Kenosha – 95 F8 Large prairie featuring plant species native to both wet and high prairie habitats. Series of sandy beach ridges (small ridges superimposed on large ones) paralleling Lake Michigan. Varied, colorful wildflowers.

CREX SAND PRAIRIE – Grantsburg – 30 B3 Remnant of sand prairie once covering extensive portions of northwestern Wisconsin. Eastern half of area is wildlife refuge.

CRYSTAL CAVE – Spring Valley – 53 B6 Guided tours through three-level cave. Upper two levels result of dissolution of limestone rock. Larger, lower level formed by underground river. Stalactites and stalagmites. Displays on caves, cave life, exploration and conservation.

DELLS OF THE EAU CLAIRE – Hogarty – 46 F4 1.5-mile gorge along Eau Claire River with 20- to 30-foot-high walls. River drops nearly 65 feet through gorge. Potholes up to five feet in diameter. Unique and varied plant life.

DEVIL'S LAKE STATE PARK – Baraboo – 85 A5 Rock formations include Turk's Head, Elephant Rock, Balanced Rock and Devil's Doorway. Glacial features include erratic boulders, kettle, potholes and extinct glacial lake bed. Baraboo Bluffs, sheer 400-foot-high cliffs, on west side of park. Cold air flow from bluffs provides habitat for unusual, northern plant species. Areas of dry prairie and red oak and maple forest on top of bluffs.

DEWEY HEIGHTS PRAIRIE – Nelson Dewey State Park – 89 C7 Large, dry lime prairie on 800-foot-high Mississippi River bluff. Exposed cliffs and ledges. Prairie dominated by big and little bluestems, side-oats and hairy grama; June, Indian and porcupine grass.

DRIFTLESS AREA – Wildcat Mountain State Park – 75 D7 Southwestern portion of Wisconsin that escaped glaciation can be seen from observation point. Low plateau deeply cut by stream valleys. Rough topography contrasts with ice-formed landscape of other parts of state.

EAGLE CAVE – Blue River – 83 C7 Guided tours through Wisconsin's largest onyx cave. Rock formations.

GRANDDAD BLUFF – La Crosse – 74 B2 600-foot-high bluff overlooking La Crosse and Mississippi Rivers.

GREENBUSH KETTLE – Kettle Moraine State Forest – 80 C2 Outstanding example of kettle. Scenic overlook and interpretive display near parking lot.

HASKELL NOYES WOODS – Kettle Moraine State Forest – 80 E1 Old growth transition forest with rich ground flora and significant glacial features. Upland hardwood forest dominated by sugar maple and red oak.

KICKAPOO INDIAN CAVERNS – Wauzeka – 82 E4 Guided tours through largest caverns in Wisconsin. Underground lake and 40-foot-high Cathedral Room. Lighted, cement walkways. Native American Museum features artifacts and handcrafts.

KOHLER PARK DUNES – Kohler–Andrae State Park – 81 D5 Park contains active and stabilized dunes. Several thickly vegetated interdunal ponds. Common plants that stabilize dunes include sand reed, Canada wild rye, marram grass, common and trailing juniper, sand cherry and willow species.

MILL BLUFF STATE PARK – Camp Douglas – 76 A1 Unique, flat-topped, cliff-sided rock formations rising abruptly from surrounding plain. Larger mesas, smaller, more abrupt buttes and slender pinnacles range in height from 80 feet to over 120 feet. All once stood as islands in glacial lake.

MT PISGAH HEMLOCK-HARDWOODS – Wildcat Mountain State Park – 75 D7 Relict stands of hemlock, yellow birch and white pine. Rare plant species found on cliff faces. Hiking trail.

NATURAL BRIDGE – Natural Bridge State Park – 84 B4 Wind-carved sandstone arch. Bridge opening is 25 feet wide and 15 feet high; top standing 35 feet above ground level. Rockshelter at base of bridge is 60 feet in width, with maximum depth of 30 feet.

NEWPORT CONIFER HARDWOODS – Newport State Park – 51 D6 Northern hardwood forest composed of white birch, sugar maple, beech and ash. 3-to-8-foot-high wall of dolomite blocks crossing site, former shoreline of glacial lake.

OLD MAN OF THE DALLES – Interstate State Park – 40 B3 Rock feature resembling human profile, found in sheer walls of deep gorge along St. Croix River. Gorge named The Dalles carved by glacial meltwater, with walls rising 150 feet above river. Frost and weathering formed other rock features including Devil's Chair, Lion's Head and Turk's Head.

PARFREYS GLEN – Merrimac – 85 A6 Deep gorge cut through sandstone conglomerate. Shaded cliffs harbor northern flora including white pine, yellow birch, mountain maple and rare cliff plants. Unique aquatic ecosystem.

PARNELL ESKER – Kettle Moraine State Forest – 80 D2 Classic example of glacial esker. Accessed by hiking trail.

PIER NATURAL BRIDGE PARK – Rockbridge – 83 A8 Long finger of rock, 60 feet long and 80 feet wide. Ends abruptly where ledge toppled and stands on end below cliff.

POPE LAKE – Hartman Creek State Park – 70 B1 Only undeveloped water body in heavily developed chain of lakes. Clear, deep lake with clay bottom. Rich in aquatic plants. Bordering wetlands of tamarack and winterberry.

POTHOLES – Interstate State Park – 40 B3 Potholes ranging in size from small, shallow depressions to giants 25 feet in diameter and up to 80 feet deep.

RIDGES SANCTUARY – Baileys Harbor – 51 F6 1,001-acre area of wooded bogs, sandy ridges, marshy areas and Lake Michigan beach. 28 species of rare orchids native to Wisconsin. 13 plant species on state's endangered and threatened list. Hiking trails and boardwalk system.

ROCHE-A-CRI – Roche-A-Cri State Park – 69 F5 Prominent butte rising 300 feet above surrounding plain. Composed of Cambrian sandstone, butte once island in glacial lake. Indian petroglyphs found in several locations.

ROCKY ARBOR STATE PARK – Wisconsin Dells – 77 D5 Sandstone gorge originally cut by Wisconsin River now flowing 1.5 miles east of park. Rock walls, ledges and formations.

SPRUCE LAKE BOG – Kettle Moraine State Forest – 80 D1 Undisturbed, shallow bog surrounding kettle lake. Many carnivorous plants including pitcher plants, sundews and bladderworts. Tamarack and black spruce forest surrounds bog. Boardwalk.

ST PETERS DOME – Chequamegon–Nicolet National Forest – 26 C4 Pink granite summit, approximately 1,600 feet above sea level. Views of Lake Superior.

TIMMS HILL – 6 miles East of Ogema – 45 A6 Highest point in Wisconsin, 1,951.5 feet above sea level. Observation tower.

WHITE KAME – Kettle Moraine State Forest – 80 D1 One of many kames located in Kettle Moraine State Forest—Northern Unit. Easily spotted because of white color.

WHITEFISH DUNES – Whitefish Dunes State Park – 63 A5 Among largest sand dunes in Wisconsin. Tallest, Old Baldy, rises 93 feet above lake level. Site contains all stages of succession from open beach through northern forest of maple, beech and hemlock. Rich and diverse plantlife. State natural area.

WISCONSIN DELLS – Wisconsin Dells – 77 D5 Seven-mile stretch along Wisconsin River where sandstone cliffs rise more than 100 feet above water. Dam separates Upper and Lower Dells. Rock formations include Stand Rock, Demon's Anvil and Visor Ledge.

WYALUSING STATE PARK – Wyalusing – 82 F3 Park is site of many geological features including caves, waterfalls and rock formations. 500-foot-high bluffs cut by Wisconsin and Mississippi Rivers. Pure stands of black walnut trees in mature forest.

Streams

NUMBER, BODY OF WATER	PAGE & GRID	BROOK TROUT	BROWN TROUT	LAKE TROUT	RAINBOW TROUT	LARGEMOUTH BASS	SMALLMOUTH BASS	MUSKELLUNGE	PIKE	WALLEYE
1000 Alder Creek	33 C5	•								
1003 Alder Creek	27 B8	•								
1006 Allen Creek	67 B5	•	•							
1009 Aniwa Creek	47 F5	•								
1012 Apple Creek	27 C8	•								
1015 Armstrong Stream	38 E3	•	•							
1018 Augustine Creek	27 D8	•								
1027 Bark River	22 C2	•	•		•					
1030 Barr Creek	27 B7	•								
1033 Beaver Brook	32 C1	•	•							
1036 Beaver Creek	55 C6	•	•							
1051 Big Rib River	45 D6	•	•							
1060 Black Earth Creek	85 D6	•	•		•					
1066 Bois Brule River	25 B7	•	•		•					
1075 Bradley Creek	59 E5	•								
1078 Brule Creek	37 A8	•	•							
1081 Brule River	38 A1	•	•							
1084 Buffalo River	55 E7	•	•							
1090 Caldron Falls Flowage	49 B5						•	•	•	•
1093 Camp C Creek	35 B5	•								
1096 Camp Eight Creek	38 E1	•								
1099 Campbell Creek	77 B5		•							
1102 Carpenter Creek	34 E3		•							
1105 Casey Creek	21 F7	•	•		•					
1114 Cedar Springs Creek	70 E3	•								
1117 Chaffee Creek	69 F8		•		•					
1120 Clam River, South Fork	31 E7	•	•							
1123 Clearwater Creek	47 C5	•								
1126 Cody Creek	38 C3	•								
1132 Cranberry River, East Fork	22 D2	•	•		•					
1138 Creek 19-16	55 F6	•								
1141 Dalton Creek	48 D1									
1144 Deer Creek	32 E4	•	•							
1153 Dent Creek	59 C6	•								
1156 Devils Creek	43 A5	•	•							
1162 Drew Creek	47 E8	•								
1165 Duncan Creek	42 E4	•								
1174 Eddy Creek	33 C5	•								
1177 Eighteen Mile Creek	26 C2	•	•							
1180 Elvoy Creek	37 A8	•	•							
1183 Embarrass River, Middle Branch	59 B6	•								
1186 Embarrass River, North Branch	59 B6	•	•							
1189 Emmons Creek	70 C1		•							
1192 Empire Creek	24 A2	•								
1195 Engle Creek	42 A1	•								
1198 Evergreen Creek	47 D8	•	•							
1201 Evergreen River	47 D8	•	•							
1207 Flag River	22 D1	•	•		•					
1210 Flume Creek	59 E5	•	•							
1213 Flume Creek	59 E5	•	•							
1216 Forbes Creek	48 C4	•								
1219 Fourmile Creek	22 E3	•	•		•					
1225 Frieberg Creek	27 A8	•								
1228 Garland Creek and Springs	29 E7	•								
1231 Godfrey Creek	32 B3	•								
1237 Green Meadow Creek	46 A3	•								
1243 Harvey Creek	38 F4	•								
1246 Hay Creek	48 C4	•								
1249 Hendricks Creek	38 C3	•								
1252 High Falls Reservoir	49 C5						•	•	•	•
1258 Hills Pond Creek	48 D2	•								
1261 Hines Creek	48 D3	•								
1264 Holmes Creek	49 A7	•								
1267 Indian Creek	48 B2	•								
1270 Iron River, East Fork	21 E8	•	•		•					
1276 Jackson Creek	59 D6	•								
1279 Javorsky Creek	27 C7	•								
1282 Jennie Creek	36 F3	•								
1285 Jones Creek	37 C8	•	•							
1288 Kentuck Creek	37 A7	•								
1294 Kinnickinnic River	52 B2	•	•							
1297 Krause Creek	27 C6	•								
1408 Lamon-Tangue Creek	38 D4	•	•							
1411 Langley Creek	35 C8	•								
1462 Lawler Creek	32 F4	•								

Streams, *continued*

NUMBER, BODY OF WATER	PAGE & GRID	BROOK TROUT	BROWN TROUT	LAKE TROUT	RAINBOW TROUT	LARGEMOUTH BASS	SMALLMOUTH BASS	MUSKELLUNGE	PIKE	WALLEYE
1414 Leer Creek	59 E6	•	•							
1417 Lepage Creek	39 B5	•								
1420 Little Balsam Creek	24 A2	•	•							
1426 Little Pine Creek	46 B2	•								
1429 Little Pine Creek, East Branch	69 F8	•	•							
1432 Little Plover River	69 A7	•								
1435 Little Popple River	38 D1	•								
1438 Little Sioux River	22 D4	•			•					
1444 Little Waupee Creek	48 E3	•								
1468 Lunch Creek	69 F8	•	•							
1471 Lund Creek	38 D4	•								
1474 MacIntire Creek	38 D4	•								
1477 Main Creek, Middle Fork	34 F1	•								
1480 Main Creek, South Fork	44 A1	•								
1483 Maple Creek	33 D5	•								
1489 McCann Creek	42 D4	•								
1492 McCauley Creek	48 D3	•								
1495 McDonald Creek	37 B8	•								
1498 McKenzie Creek	31 E5		•							
1504 Mecan River	69 F8	•	•				•			
1507 Middle Inlet	49 C6	•	•							
1510 Mill Creek	67 E7	•								
1516 Minong Flowage	24 E4									•
1522 Mishonagon Creek	36 A1	•								
1525 Mosquito Brook	25 F8	•	•							
1528 Mt Vernon Creek	92 A2	•	•				•			
1531 Murphy Creek	49 E6	•	•							
1543 Neenah Creek	77 B6		•							
1549 New Wood River	45 C8	•								
1561 Oconto River, First South Branch	48 E3	•	•							
1564 Oconto River, North Branch	48 C3	•	•				•			
1567 Oconto River, Second South Branch	48 D2	•	•							
1570 Oconto River, South Branch	48 E2	•	•				•			
1576 Onion River	22 D4	•	•				•			
1582 Parker Creek	52 A4	•	•							
1591 Pemebonwon River, North Branch	39 E7	•								
1594 Pemebonwon River, South Branch	39 E5	•								
1600 Peterson Creek	70 A2	•								
1606 Pigeon Creek	32 E4	•								
1612 Pike River, Little South Branch	49 A6	•								
1615 Pike River, North Branch	39 F6	•	•							
1618 Pine Creek	39 C5	•								
1621 Pine River	70 D2	•	•							
1624 Plover River	59 A5	•	•				•			
1627 Poncho Creek	58 F4	•								
1630 Prairie River	46 A4	•	•							
1633 Prairie River, North Branch	46 B2	•	•							
1639 Price Creek	34 D2	•								
1645 Radley Creek	70 C2		•							
1648 Railroad Creek	59 B5	•								
1657 Richie Creek	45 A7	•								
1660 Riley Creek	38 C2	•								
1663 Riley Creek	38 A3	•								
1666 Roche-A-Cri Creek	69 D6	•	•				•			
1672 Rock Creek	38 F3	•								
1669 Rock Creek	38 D3	•								
1681 Rowan Creek	85 A7	•	•				•			
1684 Rullands Coulee Creek	74 C4	•								
1687 Sand Creek	42 D3	•								
1690 Sand Creek	31 E7	•								
1702 Sidney Creek	38 E4	•								
1705 Silver Creek	46 B4	•								
1708 Sioux River	22 E4	•	•				•			
1711 Siphon Creek and Springs	29 E7	•								
1714 Snow Falls Creek	48 C3	•								
1717 Soper Creek	67 E5	•								
1720 Soules Creek	70 E1	•	•							
1723 Spencer Creek	48 A2	•								
1726 Spikehorn Creek	39 D7	•								
1729 Spirit River Flowage	46 A1						•	•	•	•
1732 Spring Brook	27 C5	•					•			
1735 Squaw Creek	45 A7	•								
1738 Squaw Creek	49 A8	•								
1750 Sucker Creek	32 E3	•								
1753 Sullivan Creek	39 D8	•								

Streams, *continued*

NUMBER, BODY OF WATER	PAGE & GRID	TROUT				BASS		OTHER		
		Brook Trout	Brown Trout	Lake Trout	Rainbow Trout	Smallmouth Bass	Largemouth Bass	Muskellunge	Pike	Walleye
1759 Swift Creek	33 C5	•								
1765 Tank Creek	66 B4	•	•							
1768 Thirtythree Creek	32 E4	•								
1771 Thunder River, North Fork	48 C4	•	•							
1777 Totagatic Flowage	25 E8					•	•			•
1780 Trempealeau River, North Branch	66 A3	•	•							
1786 Trout Creek	84 E4	•	•		•					
1783 Trout Creek	59 F5	•	•							
1792 Turtle-Flambeau Flowage	28 F2							•	•	•
1795 Twenty Mile Creek	26 C3	•	•							
1804 Upper Nemahbin	87 E7						•			•
1810 Walzak Creek	47 A6	•								
1816 Wausaukee River	49 A6	•	•							
1819 Wedde Creek, South Branch	69 F8	•			•					
1822 Whiskey Creek	39 F6	•								
1825 White River, Long Lake Branch	26 C2	•	•							
1828 White River, West Branch	69 E8	•	•		•					
1837 Willow Creek	70 E2	•	•							
1840 Wilson Creek	59 B6	•								
1843 Woods Creek	38 C3	•								

Lakes

NUMBER, BODY OF WATER	PAGE & GRID	BASS		OTHER		
		Largemouth Bass	Smallmouth Bass	Muskellunge	Pike	Walleye
1021 Ballard Lake	29 F7	•	•	•		•
1024 Balsam Lake	40 A4	•			•	•
1039 Beaver Dam Lake	78 F4				•	•
1042 Beckman Lake	92 E1				•	
1045 Big Arbor Vitae Lake	36 B2	•		•		•
1046 Big Cedar Lake	88 A1	•		•	•	•
1048 Big McKenzie Lake	31 B7	•	•	•		•
1054 Big Round Lake	31 F5	•			•	•
1057 Big Sand Lake	29 B7			•	•	•
1063 Black Oak Lake	29 A5	•	•		•	•
1069 Bone Lake	31 F5	•			•	•
1072 Boom Lake	36 E4			•	•	•
1087 Butternut Lake	37 B7		•		•	•
1108 Castle Rock Lake	76 A3	•			•	•
1129 Columbia Lake	70 B2	•	•			•
1135 Crawling Stone Lake	35 B8	•		•		•
1651 Dam Lake	36 C3				•	•
1147 Deer Lake	40 B4	•		•		
1150 Delavan Lake	94 D2		•		•	•
1159 Devil's Lake	85 A5	•	•		•	•
1801 Devils Lake	25 C8				•	•
1168 Eagle Lake	37 B5		•	•		•
1171 East Lake	95 D6				•	
1204 Fence Lake	35 A8		•	•		•
1222 Fox Lake	78 E4				•	•
1234 Green Lake	78 B3	•			•	•
1240 Grindstone Lake	32 B4		•	•		•
1255 High Lake	29 E7			•		•
1273 Island Lake	29 E5			•		•
1280 Kawaguesaga Lake	36 B2			•		•
1291 Kentuck Lake	37 A7			•		•
1300 Lac Courte Oreilles	32 B4		•	•		•
1303 Lac La Belle	87 D7	•			•	•
1306 Lac Vieux Desert	29 A6			•	•	•
1309 Lake Arbutus	67 A6		•	•		•
1312 Lake Chetac	32 D4	•			•	•
1315 Lake Chippewa	33 B6			•		•
1318 Lake DuBay	58 D1				•	•
1321 Lake Geneva	94 E3		•		•	•
1324 Lake Kegonsa	86 F1				•	•
1327 Lake Koshkonong	93 A7				•	•
1363 Lake Mohawksin	46 A1	•	•	•		•
1366 Lake Monona	85 E8	•			•	•
1367 Lake Nebagemon	25 A6				•	•
1369 Lake Noquebay	49 D7	•			•	•
1372 Lake O' the Dalles	40 B3			•	•	
1375 Lake Owen	26 D2			•	•	•

Lakes, *continued*

NUMBER, BODY OF WATER	PAGE & GRID	BASS		OTHER		
		Largemouth Bass	Smallmouth Bass	Muskellunge	Pike	Walleye
1378 Lake Poygan	70 D4			•	•	•
1396 Lake Wausau	58 A2	•	•		•	•
1399 Lake Winnebago	71 F7	•	•		•	•
1402 Lake Wisconsin	85 A6	•	•		•	•
1405 Lake Wissota	55 A5		•		•	•
1423 Little Elkhart Lake	80 B3	•	•		•	•
1441 Little St Germain Lake	36 B3			•	•	•
1453 Long Lake	80 D1	•			•	•
1450 Long Lake	32 E2				•	•
1447 Long Lake	70 D2	•			•	
1456 Loon Lake	27 C6	•	•			•
1459 Lost Land Lake	26 F2			•		•
1465 Lower Post Lake	47 A6	•	•		•	•
1486 Mauthe Lake	80 E1				•	•
1501 Mead Lake	56 C1	•			•	•
1519 Mirror Lake	76 E4	•	•			•
1534 Nagawicka Lake	87 E8	•			•	•
1537 Namekagon Lake	26 D3			•	•	•
1546 Nelson Lake	25 F8	•		•		•
1552 North Lake	87 D8			•	•	•
1555 North Twin Lake	29 B6	•	•			•
1558 Oconomowoc Lake	87 E7			•	•	•
1573 Okauchee Lake	87 D7	•			•	•
1579 Palmer Lake	29 E7	•	•	•		•
1585 Partridge Crop Lake	70 B4			•	•	•
1588 Pelican Lake	47 A6	•		•	•	•
1597 Petenwell Lake	68 E4	•			•	•
1603 Pewaukee Lake	87 E8	•			•	•
1609 Pike Lake	87 B8	•	•			•
1636 Presque Isle Lake	29 D5		•	•		•
1642 Puckaway Lake	78 C2	•			•	•
1654 Red Cedar Lake	32 F3		•		•	•
1675 Rock Lake	86 E4		•		•	•
1678 Round Lake	33 A5		•	•		•
1693 Shadow Lake	70 B2	•			•	•
1696 Shawano Lake	60 C3				•	•
1699 Shell Lake	31 D8		•			•
1741 Squirrel Lake	35 C8	•	•			•
1744 Star Lake	29 F7			•		•
1747 Stormy Lake	29 F8	•		•		•
1756 Swan Lake	77 E8		•			•
1762 Tainter Lake	54 A1		•			•
1774 Tomahawk Lake	31 B8	•		•		•
1789 Trout Lake	36 A2		•	•		•
1798 Twin Valley Lake	84 E3	•		•		•
1807 Upper St Croix Lake	25 C5	•	•		•	•
1813 Wapogasset Lake	40 C4	•			•	•
1831 Whitewater Lake	94 C1	•				•
1834 Wildcat Lake	31 F7	•		•		•
1846 Yellow Lake	31 B5	•			•	•
1849 Yellowstone Lake	91 B7	•		•	•	•

Great Lakes

NUMBER, BODY OF WATER	PAGE & GRID	TROUT				SALMON		
		Brook Trout	Brown Trout	Lake Trout	Rainbow Trout	Chinook Salmon	Coho Salmon	Walleye
1330 Lake Michigan—Algoma	62 E3		•	•	•		•	
1333 Lake Michigan—Kenosha	95 D8		•	•	•	•	•	
1336 Lake Michigan—Kewaunee	73 A7		•	•			•	
1339 Lake Michigan—Manitowoc	73 E6				•			
1342 Lake Michigan—Milwaukee	88 E4		•				•	•
1345 Lake Michigan—Port Washington	88 A4		•		•		•	
1348 Lake Michigan—Racine	95 C8		•	•		•	•	
1351 Lake Michigan—Sheboygan	81 C5		•	•		•	•	
1354 Lake Michigan—Sister Bay	51 D5		•	•				
1357 Lake Michigan—South Milwaukee	95 A8				•	•	•	
1360 Lake Michigan—Two Rivers	73 D6					•	•	
1381 Lake Superior—Bayfield	23 D5	•	•					
1384 Lake Superior—Cornucopia	22 C3		•					
1387 Lake Superior—Saxon Harbor	23 F8			•				
1390 Lake Superior—Superior	20 D3							•
1393 Lake Superior—Washburn	22 E4		•					•

NAME, TOWN	PAGE & GRID	ACRES	DEER	BEAR	SQUIRREL	RABBIT	FURBEARERS	TURKEY	GROUSE	PHEASANT	QUAIL	WOODCOCK	WATERFOWL	HABITAT
Ackley SWA, 12 miles west of Antigo	46 E4	1,118	•	•				•	•	•		•	•	Timber, marsh, openings, flowages
Albany SWA, Albany	92 C3	1,532	•					•	•		•		•	Marsh, potholes, river, timber, cropland
Allenton Marsh SWA, Allenton	87 A8	1,160	•					•	•				•	Farmland
Amberg SWA, 7 miles northwest of Wausaukee	49 A6	1,190	•						•					Coniferous swamp, timbered upland
Amsterdam Sloughs SWA, Webster	31 C5	7,233	•					•	•				•	Marsh, swamp, timbered upland
Augusta SWA, Augusta	55 D7	2,503	•		•	•			•			•	•	Marsh, timber
Avoca Unit–LWSR, Avoca	83 C8	5,743	•					•		•		•	•	Marsh, potholes, timber
Avon Bottoms SWA, 12 miles west of Beloit	93 E5	2,734	•		•	•	•			•			•	River, brush, woodlots, marsh, river bottom, farmland
Badfish Creek SWA, 5 miles southwest of Stoughton	93 A5	1,262	•		•	•		•		•			•	Farmland, marsh, creek, ponds
Bakkens Pond Unit–LWSR, Spring Green	84 D2	2,678	•		•	•		•		•	•	•	•	River, sloughs, marsh, timber
Balsam Branch SWA, Balsam Lake	40 B4	180	•		•	•			•	•			•	Marsh, field, forest
Bean Brook FWA, 5 miles southeast of Springbrook	32 B3	1,728	•						•			•		Stream, timber, marsh
Beaver Brook SWA, Spooner	32 C1	1,964	•						•			•	•	Stream, marsh, timber
Big Beaver Creek SWA, Wheeler	41 E8	572	•		•	•	•		•		•		•	Savanna, stream
Big Creek SFA, Cataract	67 E5	1,316	•				•	•				•	•	Timber, stream, lowland brush
Big Swamp SWA, 6 miles west of Mondovi	54 E1	844	•		•	•								Swamp, marsh, farmland
Blackhawk Lake SRA, 8 miles west of Dodgeville	84 F1	1,486	•		•	•			•	•				Abandoned croplands, lake, timber
Bloomfield SWA, Lake Geneva	94 E4	1,203	•			•				•		•	•	Marsh, lowland timber
Blue River Unit–LWSR, Blue River	83 C7	1,905	•		•	•				•	•	•	•	River, sloughs, marsh, timber
Borst Valley SWA, 7 miles northwest of Independence	65 A8	1,343	•		•	•		•	•	•				Marsh, timber, farmland
Brillion SWA, Brillion	72 E2	4,800	•		•			•		•			•	Marsh, timber, brush
Brooklyn SWA, Belleville	92 B3	2,534	•		•	•	•			•	•		•	Marsh, timber, cropland, stream
Buckhorn SWA, New Lisbon	76 A3	1,643	•		•	•		•	•			•	•	Wetlands, meadow
Buena Vista Marsh SWA, Plover	69 B7	12,700	•						•			•	•	Prairie
Cadiz Springs SRA, 5 miles west of Monroe	92 E1	625	•			•				•	•	•	•	Marsh, timber, lake, cropland
Cherokee Marsh SFA, Madison	85 D8	1,183	•		•	•				•			•	Marsh, timber, cropland
Chief River SWA, 15 miles east of Hayward	33 A6	1,183	•						•					Coniferous swamp, timbered upland
Chimney Rock SWA, 12 miles north of Independence	54 F4	634	•		•	•			•	•				Marsh, timber, farmland
Clam River FWA, Bashaw	31 D7	2,323	•						•					Timber, stream
Clover Valley SWA, Whitewater	94 B1	531	•		•	•	•			•		•		Marsh, timber
Colburn SWA, 13 miles northeast of Friendship	69 E6	4,965	•			•							•	Marsh, timber, brush
Collins Marsh SWA, Reedsville	72 E3	4,200	•					•		•			•	Marsh, timber, brush
Coulee Experimental Forest, 5 miles south of Bangor	74 B3	3,000	•		•				•					Upland timber
Crex Meadows SWA, Grantsburg	30 C2	30,000	•	•	•	•	•		•			•	•	Grass marsh, prairie, timbered upland
Cylon Marsh SWA, Deer Park	41 D5	500	•	•	•	•	•	•	•	•			•	Marsh, farmland
Cylon SWA, Deer Park	41 D5	2,342	•	•	•	•	•	•	•	•	•		•	Meadow, hardwoods
Danbury SWA, Danbury	31 A5	2,866	•	•	•	•	•		•			•	•	Sand barrens, timber
Deansville SWA, 5 miles east of Sun Prairie	86 C2	1,970	•		•	•	•	•		•			•	Marsh, timber
Deer Creek SWA, Leeman	60 E2	1,490	•			•			•	•			•	Marsh
Dell Creek SWA, 6 miles northeast of Reedsburg	76 E4	2,557	•		•	•			•			•		Stream, timber
Deppe SWA, Borth	70 E4	430	•		•	•		•		•			•	Marsh, grasslands
Dewey Marsh SWA, 9 miles north of Stevens Point	58 D2	6,000	•		•	•			•				•	Marsh, brush, timber
Dike 17 SWA, 15 miles east of Black River Falls	67 C7	3,100	•						•				•	Marsh, wet prairie
Douglas County SWA, Solon Springs	25 D5	4,000	•						•					Open land, brush, timber
Dunnville SWA, 5 miles south of Downsville	53 D8	3,294	•		•	•	•	•		•			•	Marsh, river bottom, farmland
Eau Galle River SWA, Elmwood	53 C7	236	•		•	•		•						Forest, river bottom
Eldorado SWA, 4 miles northwest of Fond du Lac	79 B6	6,381	•		•	•		•		•		•	•	Brush and grass marsh, timber
Emmons Creek SFA, 11 miles northeast of Almond	70 C1	1,500	•		•				•					Stream, brush, timber
Fish Lake SWA, Grantsburg	30 D2	14,000	•		•	•	•	•	•				•	Grass marsh, timbered upland
French Creek SWA, 7 miles northeast of Portage	77 D8	3,450	•		•			•	•	•			•	Marsh, timber
Gardner Swamp SWA, 5 miles northeast of Brussels	62 C2	1,180	•		•	•		•	•				•	Marsh, timbered lowland, stream
George W Mead SWA, 6 mi W of Knowlton	58 D1	33,000	•	•	•	•		•	•	•		•	•	River, marsh, brush, timber
Germania SWA, 9 miles north of Montello	78 A1	2,334	•		•	•		•		•			•	Marsh, river, brush, flowage, woodlots
Goose Lake SWA, Deerfield	86 E3	2,300	•		•	•				•			•	Lakes, marsh, timber, cropland
Grand River Marsh SWA, Kingston	78 C1	6,958	•		•	•		•		•			•	Marsh, farmland, wood lots, river
Grassy Lake SWA, Doylestown	86 A2	695	•		•	•		•		•			•	Marsh, farmland, timber
Green Bay West Shore SWA–Little Tail Unit, Suamico	61 D7	293	•		•	•		•					•	Lake, forest, marsh
Green Bay West Shore SWA–Long Tail Unit, Suamico	61 E7	434	•		•	•							•	Lake, marsh
Green Bay West Shore SWA–Pecor Point Unit, Pensaukee	61 B8	130	•		•	•							•	Lake, marsh, forests
Green Bay West Shore SWA–Tibbet-Suamico Unit, Little Suamico	61 D7	307	•		•	•		•					•	Lake, marsh
Green Bay West Shores SWA–Oconto Marsh Unit, Oconto	61 B8	928	•							•	•	•	•	Lake, timber, marsh
Green Bay West Shores SWA–Peats Lake Unit, Green Bay	61 B6	317	•		•	•							•	Marsh, timber
Green Bay West Shores SWA–Pensaukee Unit, Pensaukee	61 C7	370	•	•									•	Marsh, timbered upland and lowland
Green Bay West Shores SWA–Peshtigo Harbor Unit, 5 miles southeast of Peshtigo	62 A1	4,894	•		•	•		•		•			•	River delta marsh
Green Bay West Shores SWA–Sensiba Unit, 6 mi north of Green Bay	61 E7	570	•		•	•		•					•	Marsh, timber
Hay Creek SWA, Sand Creek	42 E2	387	•	•	•	•		•					•	Wetlands, woodlands
Hay Creek–Hoffman Lake SWA, 8 miles northeast of Park Falls	35 A5	13,800	•	•					•			•	•	Upland timber, conifers, stream, lake, swamp
Hay River SWA, Wheeler	42 F1	120	•	•	•	•		•					•	Wetlands, marsh, forest
Helena Marsh Unit–LWSR, Spring Green	84 D3	615	•		•	•		•				•	•	River, sloughs, marsh, timber
Hinkson Creek SFA, Poynette	85 A8	220	•		•	•		•					•	Prairie, savanna
Holland SWA, Greenleaf	72 C2	536	•			•		•		•			•	Timber, brush marsh, farmland
Honey Creek SWA, Burlington	95 C5	1,023	•		•	•	•	•		•			•	Marsh, upland, grass, timber, lowland brush
Hook Lake SWA, Oregon	85 F8	1,100	•		•	•				•			•	Forest, bog, meadow
Horicon Marsh SWA, Horicon	79 F6	10,962	•		•	•	•			•			•	Marsh, upland timber, farmland
Jackson Marsh SWA, Jackson	88 B2	2,312	•		•	•		•	•			•	•	Marsh, lowland conifers

NAME, TOWN	PAGE & GRID	ACRES	DEER	BEAR	SQUIRREL	RABBIT	FURBEARERS	TURKEY	GROUSE	PHEASANT	QUAIL	WOODCOCK	WATERFOWL	HABITAT
Jefferson Marsh SWA, Jefferson	87 F5	3,000	•					•	•		•		•	Wetlands, bog
Jennings Creek SWA, Rio	78 F2	530	•		•	•	•	•				•	•	Timber, marsh
Joel Marsh SWA, Turtle Lake	41 B6	1,192	•		•								•	Marsh, brush, grass, woodlots
Kickapoo River SWA–Bell Center Unit, Gays Mills	83 B5	1,370	•				•	•		•			•	Marsh, swamp, upland
Kickapoo River SWA–Wauzeka Unit, Wauzeka	82 D4	5,697	•		•		•	•	•				•	Upland timber, bottom lands
Kiel Marsh SWA, Kiel	80 A2	843	•		•	•	•	•				•	•	Brush, marsh, timber, open water
Killsnake SWA, 5 miles east of Chilton	72 F2	7,000	•			•		•	•	•			•	Marsh, brush, cedar swamp
Kimberly-Clark SWA, 13 miles northwest of Phillips	34 D2	7,670	•	•					•	•				Timber, brush, marsh, creek
Kissick Swamp SWA, Hayward	32 A3	941	•						•			•		Swamp, timbered uplands
Knapp Creek SWA, Port Andrews	83 C6	5,000	•		•	•			•		•	•	•	Creek, brush, timber, farmland
Koshkonong SWA, Fort Atkinson	93 A8	800	•						•	•			•	Marsh, lake
La Crosse River SFA, Tomah	67 F6	300	•				•	•				•	•	Meadow, river bottom
Lake Butte des Morts SWA, Omro	71 E5	265	•										•	Marsh, meadow
Lake Mills SWA, Lake Mills	86 E3	3,300	•			•	•	•		•			•	Lakes, marsh, timber, farmland
Lake Noquebay SWA, 8 miles northeast of Crivitz	49 C8	1,300	•						•				•	Marsh, timber, uplands
Lakes Coulee SWA, Blair	66 C1	800	•		•	•	•	•	•	•				Wetlands
Lambs Creek SWA, Cedar Falls	53 A8	750	•	•	•	•		•	•	•			•	Stream, timber, marsh
Lawrence Creek FWA, Westfield	77 A7	961	•		•			•						Stream, timbered upland
Liberty Creek SWA, 5 miles northeast of Albany	92 C4	400	•				•						•	Marsh, brush, cropland, stream
Lightning Creek SWA, Almena	41 B7	329	•					•					•	Marsh, stream bottom
Lima Marsh SWA, Lima Center	93 B8	2,048	•			•	•	•		•			•	Marsh, timber, farmland
Little Rice SWA, 6 miles northwest of Crandon	37 F7	1,900	•					•					•	Lake, marsh
Lodi Marsh SWA, Lodi	85 B7	1,100	•		•	•		•		•			•	Marsh, cropland, timber, stream
Lone Rock Unit–LWSR, Lone Rock	84 C1	1,500	•		•	•							•	Timber, marsh, brush, river, sloughs
Loon Lake SWA, 6 miles northeast of Turtle Lake	41 A7	3,123	•						•				•	Timber, wetland, pothole
Mack SWA, Shiocton	71 A7	1,358	•			•			•	•		•		Timber, marsh, farmland
Maine SWA, Leeman	60 F2	750	•						•	•				Marsh, timber
Mazomanie Unit–LWSR, Mazomanie	85 C5	3,550	•		•		•				•	•	•	Marsh, potholes, timber, river, stream
McKenzie Creek SWA, Clam Falls	31 E6	5,497	•						•			•	•	Stream, timbered upland, lake
McMillan Marsh SWA, Spencer	57 C5	6,500	•			•			•			•	•	Marsh, timbered lowland
Meadow Valley SWA, Valley Junction	67 E8	58,000	•		•	•	•	•	•				•	Marsh, timber, lakes, open fields
Mecan River SFA, Richford	69 F7	6,630	•						•				•	Spring pond, marsh, fields, timber
Mud Lake SWA, 6 miles northeast of Bailey's Harbor	51 E5	2,290	•			•	•		•				•	Lake, timbered lowland, marsh, stream
Mud Lake SWA, Reeseville	86 C4	4,500	•		•	•	•	•		•			•	Lake, marsh, farmland
Mud Lake SWA, Rio	86 A1	2,262	•		•	•	•	•					•	Marsh, potholes, timber
Muddy Creek SWA, Elk Mound	54 B2	4,100	•		•	•		•					•	Marsh, farmland, wood lots, stream
Mukwa SWA, New London	71 A5	1,291	•			•			•			•	•	Marsh, brush, farmland
Mullet Creek SWA, 13 miles east of Fond du Lac	80 C1	2,200	•		•	•	•		•			•	•	Farmland, marsh, timber
Navarino SWA, 9 miles south of Shawano	60 E2	15,000	•			•			•			•	•	Marsh, timbered ridges, river sloughs
New Auburn SWA, New Auburn	42 D3	1,175	•			•			•				•	Marsh, timbered upland
New Munster SWA, New Munster	95 E5	1,220	•		•	•	•	•		•		•	•	Marsh, timber, farmland, flowage
New Wood SWA, 19 miles northwest of Merrill	45 C8	4,635	•						•			•		Cedar swamp, timbered upland
North Bend Bottoms SWA, North Bend	66 E3	1,453	•	•			•	•	•			•	•	River, lowland timber, potholes
Otter Creek SWA, Wheeler	42 E1	1,040	•	•	•	•	•	•					•	Forest, oak barrens
Outagamie SWA, Shiocton	60 F2	1,000	•						•	•		•		Marsh, timber
Paradise Marsh SWA, 6 miles north of Fall River	78 F3	1,283	•		•	•	•	•			•			Marsh, potholes, stream
Paul J Olson SWA, Rudolph	58 F1	3,000	•		•				•					Timber, brush, grassland
Pershing SWA, Gilman	44 D1	7,900	•			•			•			•	•	Brush, timber, marsh
Peshtigo Brook, 10 miles northeast of Suring	48 E4	2,370	•		•				•					Swamp, timbered ridges
Peter Helland SWA, Pardeeville	78 F1	3,432	•		•	•	•	•		•			•	Wetlands, uplands, forest
Peters Marsh SWA, 10 miles northeast of Antigo	47 C6	1,681	•	•		•	•	•	•			•	•	Timber, openings, brushland, ponds
Pine Island SWA, 5 mi W of Portage	77 E6	5,165	•		•			•	•	•			•	Marsh, timber, river
Pine River SFA, Wild Rose	70 D1	1,155	•			•			•			•		Stream, timber, clearings
Potato Creek SWA, 6 miles south of Weyerhauser	42 C4	984	•					•				•		Marsh, timbered upland, flowages
Powell Marsh SWA, 10 miles north of Lac du Flambeau	28 F4	4,096	•										•	Marsh, lakes
Poygan Marsh SWA, Poy Sippi	70 E3	2,995	•										•	Marsh, stream
Prince's Point SWA, Whitewater	94 A1	2,000	•					•		•			•	Marsh, potholes, timber, farmland
Rat River SWA, 8 mi west of Menasha	71 C6	4,042	•				•						•	Stream, marsh, timber
Rice Beds Creek SWA, 11 miles southeast of Milltown	41 A6	3,181	•					•	•				•	Marsh, timbered upland
Richard Bong SRA, 8 miles southeast of Burlington	95 D6	4,568			•	•	•	•		•				Farmland, potholes, timber, grassland, marsh
Ridgeville SWA, Norwalk	75 B7	400	•					•	•			•	•	Meadow
Rock Falls SWA, Rock Falls	54 D2	268	•		•	•		•					•	Open prairie, mature forest
Rocky Run SFA, Poynette	77 F8	710	•					•		•			•	Marsh, timber, cropland, stream
Rome Pond SWA, Rome	87 F6	2,500	•		•	•		•		•			•	River, marsh, potholes, timber, farmland
Rowan Creek SFA, Poynette	85 A8	650	•		•		•	•	•				•	Wetlands, upland forest
Rulland's Coulee SFA, Cashton	74 C4	325	•					•	•			•	•	Meadows, woodlands
Sand Creek FWA, 105 miles southwest of Bashaw	31 D7	1,526	•						•					Timber, stream
Sandhill SWA, Babcock	68 C2	9,150	•		•			•					•	Marsh, timber
Sawyer Creek FWA, Shell Lake	31 D8	744	•						•					Stream, springs, marsh, timbered upland
Scuppernong RHA, Eagle	94 A3	589	•			•	•	•		•				Marsh, potholes, stream, lowland timber
Shaw Marsh SWA, Beaver Dam	86 A4	976	•					•					•	Marsh
Sheboygan Marsh SWA, Elkhart Lake	80 B2	14,000	•		•	•	•	•		•			•	Marsh, swamp, lowland forests
Silvernail SWA, Exeland	33 E8	1,040	•	•										Marsh
South Beaver Creek SWA, Buckholz Corners	66 E2	1,000	•	•					•				•	Marsh, stream, upland timber
Spring Creek SWA, 5 miles northeast of Catawba	34 F4	960	•	•					•			•	•	Marsh, timbered upland, coniferous swamp

Continued on page 96

Recreation Areas

NAME, LOCATION	PAGE & GRID	ACREAGE AND/OR MILES	ADMINISTRATION	CAMPING	BOATING	FISHING	SWIMMING	HIKING	BIKING	PICNICKING	SNOWMOBILING	CROSS-COUNTRY SKIING	INTERPRETIVE OPPORTUNITIES
400 State Trail, Reedsburg	76 E3	22 miles	WDNR	●	●		●	●	●	●		●	
Ahnapee State Trail, Sturgeon Bay	62 C4	48 miles	WDNR	●	●		●	●	●	●	●		
Amnicon Falls State Park, Amnicon Falls	21 F5	825 acres	WDNR		●		●		●			●	●
Apostle Islands National Lakeshore, Red Cliff	23 C5	42,160 acres	NPS		●	●	●		●			●	●
Aztalan State Park, Aztalan	86 E4	172 acres	WDNR		●	●	●		●		●	●	●
Badger State Trail, Shorewood Hills	85 E7	40 miles	WDNR				●	●		●			
Bearskin State Trail, Minocqua	36 B1	243 miles	WDNR		●		●	●	●	●		●	●
Belmont Mound State Park, Leslie	91 B5	274 acres	WDNR				●	●	●				
Big Bay State Park, La Pointe	23 D6	2,350 acres	WDNR	●	●	●	●		●		●	●	●
Big Foot Beach State Park, Lake Geneva	94 E3	272 acres	WDNR	●	●	●	●		●		●	●	●
Black River State Forest, Black River Falls	67 C5	67,070 acres	WDNR	●	●	●	●	●	●	●	●	●	●
Blue Mound State Park, Blue Mounds	84 E4	1,153 acres	WDNR	●			●	●	●	●		●	●
Brule River State Forest, Winneboujou	25 A7	40,882 acres	WDNR	●	●	●	●	●	●	●	●	●	●
Brunet Island State Park, Cornell	43 D6	1,225 acres	WDNR	●	●	●	●	●	●			●	●
Buckhorn State Park, Kelly	76 A3	6,990 acres	WDNR	●	●	●	●	●		●		●	●
Buffalo River State Trail, Fairchild	55 E8	36 miles	WDNR					●	●		●	●	
Cadiz Springs State Recreation Area, Browntown	92 E1	644 acres	WDNR	●	●	●	●		●			●	●
Capital City State Trail, Monona	85 E8	17 miles	WDNR	●				●					
Capital Springs State Park & Recreation Area, Monona	85 E8	3,000 acres	WDNR	●	●	●		●	●	●		●	●
Cattail State Trail, Amery	41 C5	18 miles	WDNR					●	●		●	●	
Chequamegon-Nicolet National Forest, Fifield	26 E4	1,520,000 acres	USFS	●	●	●	●	●	●	●	●	●	●
Chippewa Moraine State Recreation Area, Island Lake	42 D4	3,272 acres	WDNR	●	●	●		●		●		●	●
Chippewa River State Trail, Eau Claire	54 C4	26 miles	WDNR		●			●	●		●	●	
Copper Culture Mounds State Park, Oconto	61 B7	42 acres	WDNR		●	●		●					
Copper Falls State Park, Mellen	27 C6	2,676 acres	WDNR	●	●	●	●	●	●	●		●	●
Council Grounds State Park, Merrill	46 D1	509 acres	WDNR	●	●	●	●	●	●	●		●	●
Devil's Lake State Park, Crawford Crossing	85 A5	9,217 acres	WDNR	●	●	●	●	●	●			●	●
Eisenbahn State Trail, Eden	79 D8	25 miles	WDNR					●	●		●	●	
Elroy-Sparta State Trail, Elroy	76 C1	32 miles	WDNR	●				●	●		●	●	●
Flambeau River State Forest, Oxbo	34 D1	90,147 acres	WDNR	●	●	●	●	●	●	●	●	●	●
Fox River State Trail, Green Bay	72 C2	25 miles	WDNR					●	●		●	●	
Friendship State Trail, Brillion	72 D2	4 miles	WDNR					●	●		●	●	
Gandy Dancer State Trail North, Boylston	20 F3	15 miles	WDNR					●	●		●	●	
Gandy Dancer State Trail South, Saint Croix Falls	40 B3	47 miles	WDNR					●	●		●	●	
Glacial Drumlin State Trail East, Jefferson Junction	87 E5	29 miles	WDNR		●		●	●	●	●		●	●
Glacial Drumlin State Trail West, Cottage Grove	86 E1	21 miles	WDNR		●		●	●	●	●			
Governor Dodge State Park, Dodgeville	84 E2	5,350 acres	WDNR	●	●	●	●	●	●	●	●	●	●
Governor Knowles State Forest, Lind	30 D2	32,500 acres	WDNR	●	●		●		●	●	●	●	●
Governor Nelson State Park, Pheasant Branch	85 D8	422 acres	WDNR		●	●	●	●		●		●	●
Governor Thompson State Park, Athelstane	49 C5	2,800 acres	WDNR	●	●	●	●	●	●	●		●	
Great River State Trail, Holmen	74 A1	21 miles	WDNR	●	●			●	●		●	●	
Green Circle State Trail, Stevens Point	58 F2	31 miles	WDNR					●	●			●	
Hank Aaron State Trail, Wauwatosa	88 E3	12 miles	WDNR					●	●				
Harrington Beach State Park, Lake Church	80 F4	715 acres	WDNR	●	●	●	●	●	●	●	●	●	●
Hartman Creek State Park, Cobb Town	70 B1	1,417 acres	WDNR	●	●	●	●	●	●	●	●	●	●
Havenwoods State Forest, Glendale	88 D3	237 acres	WDNR					●	●	●		●	●
Heritage Hill State Historical Park, Allouez	72 A2	54 acres	WDNR							●			
High Cliff State Park, Menasha	71 D8	1,187 acres	WDNR	●	●	●	●	●	●	●	●	●	●
Hillsboro State Trail, Hillsboro	76 D1	4 miles	WDNR					●	●		●	●	
Hoffman Hills State Recreation Area, Rusk	54 A1	707 acres	WDNR					●	●	●		●	●
Horicon National Wildlife Refuge, LeRoy	79 E6	21,000 acres	USFWS			●		●	●			●	●
Interstate Park, Saint Croix Falls	40 B3	1,330 acres	WDNR	●	●	●	●	●	●	●		●	●
Kettle Moraine State Forest—Lapham Peak Unit, Delafield	87 E8	1,006 acres	WDNR	●				●	●	●		●	●
Kettle Moraine State Forest—Loew Lake Unit, Plat	87 C8	1,086 acres	WDNR		●	●		●			●		
Kettle Moraine State Forest—Northern Unit, Campbellsport	80 E1	29,268 acres	WDNR	●	●	●	●	●	●	●	●	●	●
Kettle Moraine State Forest—Pike Lake Unit, Pike Lake	87 B8	678 acres	WDNR		●	●	●	●	●	●	●	●	●
Kettle Moraine State Forest—Southern Unit, Palmyra	94 A3	22,300 acres	WDNR	●	●	●	●	●	●	●	●	●	●
Kinnickinnic State Park, River Falls	52 B2	1,239 acres	WDNR		●	●	●	●		●		●	
Kohler-Andrae State Park, Weedens	81 D5	988 acres	WDNR	●		●	●	●	●	●		●	●
La Crosse River State Trail, Sparta	75 A5	22 miles	WDNR	●		●		●	●		●		
Lake Kegonsa State Park, Kegonsa	86 F1	343 acres	WDNR	●	●	●	●	●	●	●		●	●
Lake Wissota State Park, Anson	55 A5	1,062 acres	WDNR	●	●	●	●	●	●	●	●	●	●
MacKenzie Environmental Education Center, Poynette	85 A8	500 acres	WDNR					●		●			●
Mascoutin Valley State Trail, Ripon	78 B4	11 miles	WDNR					●	●		●	●	
Menominee River State Recreation Area, Kremlin	39 E8	1,962 acres	WDNR	●	●	●		●			●	●	
Merrick State Park, Czechville	65 D6	320 acres	WDNR	●	●	●		●		●		●	●
Military Ridge State Trail, Dodgeville	84 F2	40 miles	WDNR	●				●	●		●	●	●
Mill Bluff State Park, Camp Douglas	76 A1	1,258 acres	WDNR	●			●		●	●		●	●
Mirror Lake State Park, Dellwood	77 E5	2,179 acres	WDNR	●	●	●	●	●	●	●		●	●
Mountain-Bay State Trail, Weston	58 B3	83 miles	WDNR					●	●		●	●	
Natural Bridge State Park, Leland	84 B4	530 acres	WDNR					●	●	●		●	●
Necedah National Wildlife Refuge, Cloverdale	68 E2	43,656 acres	USFWS		●	●		●				●	●
Nelson Dewey State Park, Turkey River	89 C7	756 acres	WDNR	●				●		●		●	●
New Glarus Woods State Park, Cass-ville	92 B2	431 acres	WDNR	●				●	●	●		●	●
Newport State Park, Rowleys Bay	51 D6	2,373 acres	WDNR	●	●	●		●	●	●		●	●
Nicolet State Trail, Gillett	60 B4	89 miles	WDNR					●	●		●	●	
Northern Highland-American Legion State Forest, Boulder Junction	29 F6	232,000 acres	WDNR	●	●	●	●	●	●	●	●	●	●
Oconto River State Trail, Oconto	61 B8	8 miles	WDNR					●	●		●	●	
Old Abe State Trail, Norma	55 A5	20 miles	WDNR					●	●		●	●	
Pattison State Park, Black River	24 A3	1,476 acres	WDNR	●		●	●	●	●	●		●	●
Pecatonica State Trail, Calamine	91 C6	10 miles	WDNR					●	●		●	●	
Peninsula State Park, Fish Creek	51 E5	3,776 acres	WDNR	●	●	●	●	●	●	●	●	●	●
Perrot State Park, Trempealeau	65 F8	1,270 acres	WDNR	●	●	●	●	●	●			●	●
Peshtigo River State Forest, Athelstane	49 C5	9,200 acres	WDNR	●	●	●	●	●	●	●	●	●	
Point Beach State Forest, Two Rivers	73 D6	2,903 acres	WDNR	●	●	●	●	●	●	●	●	●	●
Potawatomi State Park, Idlewild	62 B3	1,225 acres	WDNR	●	●	●		●	●	●	●	●	●
Red Cedar State Trail, North Menomonie	53 B8	14.5 miles	WDNR					●	●		●	●	●
Rib Mountain State Park, Rib Mountain	58 A2	1,528 acres	WDNR					●		●			
Richard Bong State Recreation Area, Brighton	95 D6	4,515 acres	WDNR	●	●	●	●	●	●	●	●	●	●
Roche-A-Cri State Park, Friendship	69 F5	604 acres	WDNR	●		●		●		●		●	●
Rock Island State Park, Washington	51 B8	912 acres	WDNR	●	●	●	●	●		●			●
Rocky Arbor State Park, Wisconsin Dells	77 D5	244 acres	WDNR	●				●					●
Saunders State Trail, Boylston	20 F3	8 miles	WDNR					●	●		●	●	
St Croix National Scenic Riverway, Saint Croix Falls	40 B3	252 miles	NPS	●	●	●	●	●				●	●
Straight Lake State Park, Luck	31 F5	1,800 acres	WDNR	●	●	●		●		●			
Sugar River State Trail, New Glarus	92 B2	24 miles	WDNR	●				●	●		●	●	
Tomorrow River State Trail, Plover	69 A7	29 miles	WDNR					●	●		●	●	
Tower Hill State Park, Spring Green	84 D3	77 acres	WDNR	●	●	●		●		●			●
Trempealeau National Wildlife Refuge, West Prairie	65 F7	6,446 acres	USFWS		●	●	●	●	●			●	●
Tuscobia State Trail, Lymantown	34 B4	74 miles	WDNR					●	●		●	●	
Upper Mississippi River National Wildlife and Fish Refuge, La Crosse	74 B1	240,000 acres	USFWS	●	●	●	●	●				●	●
White River State Trail, Elkhorn	94 D3	19 miles	WDNR					●	●		●	●	
Whitefish Dunes State Park, Jacksonport	63 A5	863 acres	WDNR		●	●	●	●		●		●	●
Wild Goose State Trail, Fond du Lac	79 C7	34 miles	WDNR					●	●		●	●	
Wild Rivers State Trail, Tuscobia	32 F2	104 miles	WDNR					●	●				
Wildcat Mountain State Park, Ontario	75 D7	3,643 acres	WDNR	●	●	●		●		●	●	●	●
Willow River State Park, Burkhardt	40 F2	2,891 acres	WDNR	●	●	●	●	●	●	●	●	●	●
Wiouwash State Recreation Trail, Oshkosh	71 E6	41 miles	WDNR					●	●		●	●	
Wyalusing State Park, Wyalusing	82 F3	2,628 acres	WDNR	●	●	●		●	●	●		●	●
Yellowstone Lake State Park, Yellowstone	91 B7	968 acres	WDNR	●	●	●	●	●	●	●	●	●	

NUMBER, NAME, LOCATION	PAGE & GRID	RV SITES	TENTING
4399 9 Mile All Sport Resort, Langlade	48 D1	65	●
4000 Ahnappe River Trails Campground, Algoma	62 E3	72	●
4003 Alana Springs Campground, Richland Center	83 B8	35	●
4012 Apostle Islands Area Campground, Pureair	23 D5	63	●
4015 Apple Creek Campground, Sniderville	72 B1	155	●
4018 Aqualand Campground, Sister Bay	51 E5	150	●
4021 Arbor Vitae Campground, Arbor Vitae	36 B2	114	●
4024 Arrowhead RV Campground, Plainville	76 D4	358	●
4025 Badgerland Campground, Kegonsa	86 F1	109	●
4030 Baraboo Hills Campground, West Baraboo	77 F5	157	●
4033 Bass Lake Campground, Lyndon Station	76 D4	70	●
4039 Beantown Campground, Baileys Harbor	51 F5	78	●
4042 Bear Lake Campground & Resort, Manawa	70 A3	182	●
4045 Benson's Campground, Dundee	80 D1	250	●
4054 Blackhawk Camping Resort, Milton	93 B7	490	●
4058 Blue Lake Campground, Davis Corners	77 C6	100	●
4060 Blue Top Resort, Fremont	70 C4	60	●
4063 Bluebird Springs Campground, Holiday Heights	74 B2	148	●
4069 Bonanza Camping Resort, Wisconsin Dells	77 E5	111	●
4071 Boulder Creek Campground, Bagley	89 A7	167	●
4073 Breezy Hill Campground, Marblehead	79 D8	98	●
4075 Buckatabon Lodge & Lighthouse Inn, Eagle River	37 A5	61	●
4078 Buffalo Lake Camping Resort, Montello	77 B8	45	●
4082 Camp 10 Campground LLC, Reedsville	72 D3	89	●
4084 Camp Holiday, Boulder Junction	29 F5	230	●
4087 Camp Namekagon RV Park & Campground, Stanberry	32 A3	34	●
4090 Camping in the Clouds, Florence	39 B5	51	●
4096 Cedar Springs RV Park & Campground, Kelly	76 A3	60	●
4099 Chain-O-Lakes Resort & Campground, Eagle River	37 B6	200	●
4102 Chapparal Campground & Resort, Wonewoc	76 D2	187	●
4105 Chetek River Campground, Chetek	42 C2	100	●
4108 Christian's Campground, Enterprise	47 A5	25	●
4109 Circle K Campground, Palmyra	94 A2	99	●
4111 Circle R Campground, Paukotuk	79 A6	125	●
4114 Coloma Camperland, Coloma	69 F7	74	●
4123 Country House Motel & RV Park, Spooner	32 C1	21	●
4126 Country Roads Motorhome & RV Park, Dellwood	77 E5	100	●
4129 Country View Campground, Caldwell	95 B5	159	●
4132 Cozy Inn Motel & RV Campground, Biron	69 A5	17	●
4133 Crane Berry, Babcock	68 C2	40	●
4135 Crazy Horse Campground, Brodhead	92 D4	197	●
4141 Crystal Lake Campground, Roxbury	85 B6	100	●
4145 Deep Lake Campground, Brooks	77 C6	62	●
4150 Deerhaven Campground, King	70 B2	84	●
4153 Dell Pines Campground, Dellwood	77 E5	151	●
4159 Devil's River Campground, Cooperstown	72 C4	129	●
4162 Diamond Lake Family Campground, Loomis	49 E8	78	●
4165 Door County KOA, Brussels	62 C2	250	●
4171 Duck Creek Campground, Wyocena	77 F8	134	●
4174 East Side Campground, Nobleton	32 E2	28	●
4177 Edge-O-Dells Resort, Plainville	77 D5	78	●
4186 Evergreen Campsites Inc, Wild Rose	70 D2	150	●
4189 Featherstone RV Park, Birchwood	32 E3	24	●
4192 Flambeau Lodge & Campground, Ladysmith	33 F8	10	●
4198 Fond du Lac East/Kettle Moraine KOA, Graham Corners	80 C1	340	●
4201 Forest Pond Campground, Argonne	37 A7	12	●
4204 Fox Hill RV Park & Campground, Pecks Corners	77 F5	120	●
4205 Fremont RV Campground, Fremont	70 C4	283	●
4207 Frontier Bar & Campground, Cedar	27 A7	45	●
4210 Frontier Wilderness Campground, Egg Harbor	50 F4	240	●
4213 Gala Resort & Campground, Readfield	70 C4	82	●
4214 Glacier Valley Campground, Pardeeville	78 E2	140	●
4216 Grand Valley Campground, Kingston	78 D2	221	●
4219 Great River Harbor, West Newton	65 C5	120	●
4222 Green Lake Campground, Green Lake	78 B3	370	●
4225 Happy Acres Kampground, Paddock Lake	95 D6	202	●
4226 Happy Ours RV Park, Chittamo	25 D6	70	●
4231 Harbour Village Resort, Carlsville	62 A4	210	●
4234 Hawk's Resort, Bear Lake	42 C4	10	●
4237 Hayward KOA, Hayward	25 F8	159	●
4240 Heaven's Up North Family Campground, Lakewood	48 C3	116	●
4246 Hickory Hills Campground, Albion	93 A7	277	●
4249 Hickory Oaks Campground, Oshkosh	71 E6	29	●
4255 Highland Park Campground, Spooner	31 C8	48	
4258 Hiles Pine Lake Campground, Hiles	37 E7	88	●
4261 Hi-Pines Campground, Eagle River	37 A5	145	●
4264 Hixton/Alma Center KOA, Alma Center	66 A4	101	●
4265 HO-Chunk RV Resort, Lyndon Station	76 C4	144	●
4267 Hoeft's Resort & Campground, Beechwood	80 E2	180	●
4270 Holiday Shores Camp-Resort, Plainville	77 D5	500	●
4271 HTR Door County, Egg Harbor	50 F4	160	●
4273 Hucklberry Acres Campground, New London	71 B5	176	●
4276 Indian Shores Camping Resort, Lake Tomahawk	36 C2	263	●
4279 Indian Trails Campground, Pardeeville	77 E8	333	●
4282 Iola Pines Campgrounds, Iola	59 F6	75	●
4291 Kalbus' Country Harbor, Point Comfort	79 A7	90	
4303 Kewaunee RV Park & Campground, Kewaunee	73 A7	74	●
4306 Keyes Lake Campground, Ridgetop	38 B4	41	●
4309 Kilby Lake Campground, Mecan	77 B8	119	●
4187 Kinney Lake Campground, Hunting	59 E7	560	●
4312 Lake Arrowhead Campground, Marquette	78 C2	240	●
4318 Lake DuBay Shores Campground, Knowlton	58 D2	200	●
4321 Lake George Campsite, Malvern	36 F4	35	●
4324 Lake Hilbert Campground, Fence	38 D4	105	●
4327 Lake Joy Campground, Belmont	91 B5	244	●
4330 Lake Lenwood Beach & Campground, Barton	88 A1	132	●
4333 Lake Mason Campground, Big Spring	77 D6	180	●
4336 Lake of the Woods Campground, Dakota	69 F8	300	●
4339 Lake Pepin Campgrounds, Pepin	64 A3	200	●
4340 Lakefront RV Park, Woodruff	36 B2	170	●
4342 Lakeland Camping Resort, Charlie Bluff	93 B7	682	●
4343 Lakeside Fire Campground, New Rome	68 C4	218	●
4345 Lakeview Campground, Kloten	71 F8	156	●
4348 Leon Valley Campground, Leon	75 A5	150	●
4352 Little Creek Campground & Cabins, Fairchild	55 E8	55	●
4354 Log Cabin Resort & Campground, Trego	32 B1	30	●
4360 Lost Falls Campground, Fall Hall Glen	66 D4	52	●
4363 Lured in Lodge & Campground, Bear Lake	42 C4	27	●
4366 Lynn Ann's Campground, Saint Germain	36 B3	90	●
4369 Madison Campground, Keyeser	85 C1	92	●
4371 Maple Bear Campground, Irma	46 A2	60	●
4372 Maple Heights Campground, Lakewood	48 C2	114	●
4375 Maple View Campground, Norman	73 B6	100	●
4378 McCaslin Mountain Campground, Lakewood	48 B4	110	●
4384 Merry Mac's Camp'n, Merrimac	85 A6	222	●
4385 Milton KOA, Newville	93 B7	264	●
4386 Moen Lake Campground, Rhinelander	36 E4	91	●
4390 Moon Lake Resort, Clayton	41 C7	45	●
4393 Moonlite Trails Campground, New Miner	68 D3	39	●
4396 Neshonoc Lakeside Campground, West Salem	74 A3	284	●
4408 Northern Exposure Resort & Campground, Sumner	42 B2	67	●
4411 Northern Lure Resort & Campground, Glidden	27 E6	19	●
4414 Northforest Campground, Crescent Corner	46 A3	152	●
4417 Oakdale KOA, Oakdale	75 A8	61	●
4420 Oakwood Bar, Restaurant & Campground, Saxeville	70 D2	153	●
4423 Ox Creek Resort, Mecan	77 C8	30	●
4429 Parkland Village Campground, Vaudreuil	67 C5	80	●
4432 Patricia Lake Campground, Minocqua	36 B1	100	●
4433 Pearl Lake RV Campground, Redgranite	70 E2	200	●
4435 Pelican Lake Campground, Pelican Lake	37 F5	100	●
4438 Peshtigo River Campground, Crivitz	49 D7	115	●
4441 Pettibone Resort, La Crosse	74 B1	163	●
4442 Pettit's Lakeview Campground & Bar, Newville	93 B7	91	●
4444 Pilgrims Campground, Fort Atkinson	86 F4	89	●
4447 Pine Grove Campground, Leopolis	59 C8	263	●
4450 Pine Harbor Campground, Lake Wissota	55 A5	26	●
4453 Pineland Camping Park, Big Flats	69 E5	198	●
4459 Plymouth Rock Camping Resort, Elkhart Lake	80 B3	690	●
4462 Pride of America Camping Resort, Wyocena	77 F8	372	●
4474 Red Barn Campground, Beaver Brook	32 D1	66	●
4477 Ridgewood on the River, Meehan	69 A6	113	●
4480 River Bay Camping Resort & Marina, Plainville	77 D5	270	●
4483 River Forest Rafts Campground, Markton	48 E2	52	●
4486 River Road RV Campground, Stanberry	32 A3	24	●
4492 River's Edge Park, Thornapple	43 B6	18	●
4489 Rivers Edge Campground, Casimir	58 E2	252	●
4495 Rock Lake Lodge & Campground, Eagleton	43 D5	117	●
4498 Rolling Thunder RV Park & Campground, Madge	32 D2	30	●
4499 Rustic Timbers, Egg Harbor	50 F4	240	●
4501 Rustic Woods, Little Hope	70 C2	180	●
4504 Sandy Hill Campground, Ludington	55 C7	32	●
4507 Scenic Ridge Campground, Heart Prairie	94 C1	200	●
4510 Scenic View Bar & Campground, Hertel	31 C7	40	●
4513 Shady Acres Campsite, Bolt	72 B4	21	●
4516 Shady Oaks Campground, Markesan	78 C3	82	●
4519 Shady Rest Campground, Haugen	32 E1	79	●
4520 Shangri-La Campground, Plainville	76 D4	220	●
4522 Sherwood Forest Camping & RV Park, Wisconsin Dells	77 D5	162	●
4523 Silver Cliff Camp, Athelstane	48 B4	40	●
4525 Silver Springs Campsites, Doylestown	78 F2	300	●

NUMBER, NAME, LOCATION	PAGE & GRID	RV SITES	TENTING
4528 Six Lakes Resort and RV Park, Chetek	42 C3	170	
4531 Sky High Camping Resort, Dekorra	77 F7	224	●
4532 Sleepy Dragon Campground, Rio	86 A1	135	●
4534 Smokey Hollow Campground, Harmony Grove	85 A7	236	●
4542 SpringLake Campground, Cherokee	57 B6	193	●
4546 St Joseph Resort, Necedah	68 F3	40	●
4549 Stand Rock Campground, Wisconsin Dells	77 D5	237	●
4552 Stoney Creek RV Resort, Osseo	55 F6	172	●
4558 Terrace View Campsites, Heafford Junction	36 F2	45	●
4456 The Playful Goose Campground, Horicon	87 A6	140	●
4561 Thornapple River Campground, Ladysmith	33 F7	25	●
4563 Three Lakes Campground, Three Lakes	37 C6	125	●
4564 Tilleda Falls Campgrounds, Tilleda	59 C8	46	●
4567 Timber Trail Camp Resort, Young America	80 F1	131	●
4570 Timber Trail Campground, Bruemmerville	62 E3	107	●
4573 TJ's Timberline Resort & Campground, Bear Lake	42 C4	15	●
4579 Tom's Campground, Dodgeville	84 F3	60	●
4576 Tomorrow Wood Campground, Hancock	69 E7	170	●
4582 Tranquil Timbers Camping Resort, Sturgeon Bay	62 B3	276	●

NUMBER, NAME, LOCATION	PAGE & GRID	RV SITES	TENTING
4585 Tranquil Vista Campground, Pembine	39 F6	25	●
4588 Triangle Farm Campground, Orihula	70 D4	80	●
4591 Tunnel Trail Campground, Hoffman Corners	75 B8	80	●
4594 Twin Springs Resort Campground, Rusk	53 A8	90	●
4600 Viking Village Campground & Resort, Stoughton	86 F1	71	
4603 Vista Royalle Campground, Bancroft	69 B7	264	●
4606 Wagon Trail Campground, Rowleys Bay	51 D6	145	●
4607 Wannabee Campground, Lake Delton	77 E5	120	●
4609 Washington Island Camping Retreat, Detroit Harbor	51 B7	94	●
4615 Waupaca S'more Fun Campground, Waupaca	70 B2	108	●
4618 Weaver's Resort & Campground, Pelican Lake	47 A5	47	●
4621 West Bay Camping Resort, Roosevelt	36 E4	45	●
4630 Whispering Pines Campground, Council Bay	66 F1	195	●
4633 Whitetail Bluff Camp and Resort, Cassville	90 C1	151	●
4636 Whitetail Ridge Campground & RV Park, Sarona	32 E1	116	●
4639 Wild West Campground & Corral, Blaine	70 B1	54	●

NUMBER, NAME, LOCATION	PAGE & GRID	RV SITES	TENTING
4642 Wilderness Campgrounds, Dalton	77 D8	360	●
4645 Wildlife Bar & Campground, Norrie	59 A5	150	●
4648 Wildwood Campground, Iron River	22 F1	25	●
4651 Wildwood Resort, Wickware	42 C2	97	●
4654 Willow Mill Campsite, Rio	78 F1	220	●
4655 Winding River Campground, New Lisbon	76 A2	85	●
4657 Wisconsin Dells KOA, Wisconsin Dells	77 D5	129	●
4658 Wisconsin Riverside Resort, Spring Green	84 D3	140	●
4659 Wishing Well RV Park, Koshkonong Mounds	93 A8	300	●
4660 Wolf River Trips & Campground, Ostrander	70 B4	232	●
4666 Yogi Bear's Jellystone Park Camp-Resort, Caledonia	95 B7	334	●
4672 Yogi Bear's Jellystone Park Camp-Resort, Sturgeon Bay	62 B3	275	●
4675 Yogi Bear's Jellystone Park Camp-Resort, Warrens	67 E7	600	●
4678 Yogi Bear's Jellystone Park Camp-Resort, Wisconsin Dells	77 E5	246	●
4681 Yukon Trails Camping, Lyndon Station	76 C4	214	●

Family Outings

AMERICAN FAMILY FIELD – Milwaukee – 88 E3 2001 ballpark built for the Milwaukee Brewers of baseball's National League. Features convertible roof.

APOSTLE ISLANDS CRUISE SERVICE – Bayfield – 23 C5 Narrated sightseeing cruises through Apostle Islands in Lake Superior. Trips may include stops on Stockton or Raspberry Islands. Sites include cliffs, caves and lighthouses.

APOSTLE ISLANDS NATIONAL LAKESHORE – Manitou Island – 23 B6 Guided tours of historic fish camp. One of 45 archaeological sites in Apostle Islands. Believed occupied during fur trading era by Woodland Indians. Other interests include Old Bayfield County Courthouse, now Visitor Center, constructed from locally quarried brownstone.

BARLOW PLANETARIUM – Menasha – 71 C7 State-of-the-art Digistar II/Sky-Skan technology provides changing planetarium and sky shows. Science gallery features changing exhibits and interactive computer kiosks that focus on space and other science topics.

BAY BEACH AMUSEMENT PARK – Green Bay – 61 F7 Midway features Ferris wheel, merry-go-round, tilt-a-whirl and scrambler. Children's wading pool.

BLUE HERON LANDING – Horicon – 79 F6 Narrated tour of inner Horicon Marsh aboard pontoon boat.

CAMP FIVE LOGGING MUSEUM – Laona – 38 F1 Tour begins with Lumberjack Special steam train ride to Camp Five Farm. Museum features logging lore. Audio-visual presentation. Blacksmith shop, animal barn and corral. Surrey and pontoon boat rides.

CENTER FOR THE VISUAL ARTS – Wauksau – 58 A2 Permanent collections include paintings, sculpture, decorative arts. Galleries house changing exhibits.

CHARLES A GRIGNON HOME – Kaukauna – 72 C1 Guided tour of 1830s Greek Revival house exhibiting split-lathe method of construction with interior walls covered with plaster and marble dust. Carved details on doors, window frames and cherry staircase rail.

CHARLES ALLIS ART MUSEUM – Milwaukee – 88 E4 Tudor mansion houses personal collection of industrialist Charles Allis. Landscapes by 19th-century French and American artists. Chinese, Japanese and Korean ceramics.

CHAZEN MUSEUM OF ART – Madison – 85 E8 Large museum maintains extensive collections of European and American paintings, sculpture and photography. Various other permanent and temporary exhibits.

CHIPPEWA VALLEY MUSEUM – Eau Claire – 54 C3 Local history exhibits include Woodland Native Americans, area exploration, trapping, logging, agriculture and industrial growth. Working crank telephones and ice cream parlor.

CIRCUS WORLD MUSEUM – Baraboo – 77 F5 Original winter quarters of Ringling Brothers Circus (1884–1918). Complex encompasses thirty buildings including library and big top. Performances in season. Collection of circus wagons.

DISCOVERY WORLD – Milwaukee – 88 E3 Lakefront family museum with interactive exhibits relating to science and technology. Fresh water and salt water aquariums. Public sails aboard replica 19th-century schooner *S/V Denis Sullivan* during summer.

EAA AVIATOR MUSEUM – Oshkosh – 71 F6 Large collection of rare and unique aircraft. Museum traces development of aviation from beginning moments in flight to today's high-tech composite aircraft. Air Adventure and Junior Aviator Theaters. Pioneer Airport features 1920–1930s flying paraphernalia and seasonal aircraft fly-bys.

FAIRLAWN MANSION & MUSEUM – Superior – 20 E3 Former residence of Superior's second mayor and lumber baron Martin Pattison. Victorian mansion houses exhibits on maritime commerce, Native American lore and local history.

FAWN DOE ROSA WILDLIFE EDUCATION PARK – St. Croix Falls – 40 B3 Animal park featuring deer and other large animals including coyote and grizzly bear. Small animals in petting zoo.

FIRST CAPITOL – Belmont – 91 B5 Site of capital of Wisconsin Territory before official move to Madison. Tours of restored Council House and Supreme Court House.

FISERV FORUM – Milwaukee – 88 E3 Built in 2018. Serves as home court for the Milwaukee Bucks of the NBA. Seats over 17,000. Also hosts games for Marquette University, concerts and various other sporting events.

FORT CRAWFORD MUSEUM – Prairie du Chien – 82 E2 Relics of 19th-century medicine. Displays include Native American herbal remedies, drug store, dentist and physicians offices. Pharmacy features 1890s prescriptions and hand-cut glass container used by 16th-century English chemists.

FORTS FOLLE AVOINE HISTORICAL PARK – Yellow Lake – 30 B4 Living-history park features reconstructed 1802-1804 Northwest Company and XY Company fur trading posts and Ojibwe village. Fur trade and Native American archaeological exhibits.

GREAT RIVER ROAD – Prescott – 52 D2 Signed route paralleling Mississippi River. Winds through picturesque villages and along base of towering bluffs. Waysides, scenic overlooks and historic plaques line route. 250 miles.

H H BENNETT STUDIO & MUSEUM – Wisconsin Dells – 77 D5 Studio of early photographer H. H. Bennett restored to 1908 appearance. Exhibits focus on Bennett's life and prolific career, science of photography and regional history.

HAGGERTY MUSEUM OF ART – Milwaukee – 88 E3 Over 6,000 works representing Renaissance, Baroque and Modern paintings; sculpture, prints and photography, decorative arts, Asian and tribal arts.

HENRY VILAS ZOO – Madison – 85 E8 28-acre zoo with over 650 animals, birds, amphibians and fish. Children's zoo. Camel rides.

HERITAGE HILL STATE HISTORICAL PARK – Allouez – 72 A2 Living-history museum with costumed interpreters. 22 buildings containing original and reconstructed period pieces. Bark chapel, fur trader's cabin, sugaring house and commercial buildings.

HISTORIC ROGERS STREET FISHING VILLAGE – Two Rivers – 73 D6 Site of early Native American and French Canadian fishing village. Museum houses fishing and boating artifacts. Kahlenberg marine diesel engine and fishing tug. Lighthouse.

HOARD HISTORICAL MUSEUM & NATIONAL DAIRY SHRINE – Fort Atkinson – 93 A8 Housed in former home of Frank and Luella Hoard. 16 exhibit rooms feature Black Hawk War exhibit and displays of birds, toys, dolls and local Native American artifacts. Rotating exhibits. Self-guided, multimedia tour outlines past, present and future of dairy industry. Extensive collection of dairy artifacts and memorabilia

THE HOUSE ON THE ROCK – Spring Green – 84 E2 Modern architectural marvel situated on chimney-like rock. Designed and built by Alex Jordan. World's largest indoor carousel. Unique exhibits housed in various settings including Infinity Room, Doll House Building, Oriental Room and Music of Yesterday Museum.

INTERNATIONAL CRANE FOUNDATION – Baraboo – 77 E5 Center dedicated to preservation and study of cranes. Audio-visual presentations and chick-hatching display. Many species of adult cranes on display in pens. Nature trails. Guided and self-guided tours.

JOHN MICHAEL KOHLER ARTS CENTER – Sheboygan – 81 C5 Visual and performing arts center housed in restored 19th-century building. Extensive collection of prehistoric Indian artifacts. Changing exhibits by contemporary artists.

THE KALAHARI RESORT – Wisconsin Dells – 77 E5 Largest indoor water park in America. Water coaster, wave pool, family raft ride and lazy river. Substantial outdoor section includes slalom race slides and kidszone.

KENOSHA PUBLIC MUSEUM – Kenosha – 95 E8 Natural history and art museum. Anthropology, geology and zoology displays. Oriental art and artifacts. Wisconsin folk pottery.

LA CROSSE QUEEN – La Crosse – 74 B1 Mississippi River cruises aboard paddle wheeler.

LAURA INGALLS WILDER WAYSIDE – Pepin – 53 F6 Birthplace of Laura Ingalls Wilder, author of Little House books. Replica of log cabin from *Little House in the Big Woods*. Picnic area.

LAMBEAU FIELD – Green Bay – 61 F6 Open-air football stadium built in 1957 for the Green Bay Packers of the NFL. Names for team founder, player and coach Curly Lambeau.

LEIGH YAWKEY WOODSON ART MUSEUM – Wausau – 58 A2 Museum features art inspired by nature. Famous Birds in Art collection displays variety of artistic styles. Grounds cover four acres and include formal English Garden and Margaret Woodson Fisher Sculpture Gallery.

LINCOLN PARK ZOO – Manitowoc – 73 E5 Small zoo featuring native animals in natural settings. Bear, wolves, cougar and deer. Expanded animal exhibits during summer season.

LITTLE WHITE SCHOOLHOUSE – Ripon – 78 B4 Birthplace of Republican Party in 1854. Party founding triggered by passing of Kansas–Nebraska bill extending slavery beyond limits set by Missouri Compromise.

LOGAN MUSEUM OF ANTHROPOLOGY – Beloit College – 93 F7 Extensive collection of ethnological and archaeological materials from Europe, Central and South America and North Africa. Displays on physical anthropology and Old Stone Age.

MACKENZIE CENTER – Poynette – 85 A8 Conservation and natural history museum. Native wildlife exhibits, 19th-century cabin with logging displays, pictures and mounted specimens of plants and animals. Nature trails and arboretum.

MADELINE ISLAND HISTORICAL MUSEUM – La Pointe – 23 D5 Former site of American Fur Company trading post. Accessible by Madeline Island Ferry. Single building containing four pioneer log structures. Fur company building, jail, barn and Old Sailor's Home. Displays and artifacts relating to history of Chequamegon region.

MADISON CHILDREN'S MUSEUM – Madison – 85 E8 Hands-on exhibits for wide range of ages. Mazes, puzzles and games. Computer display. Toddler's Nest explores sight, sound, touch and motion. Changing exhibits.

MADISON MUSEUM OF CONTEMPORARY ART – Madison – 85 E8 Changing exhibits of Oriental, European and American painting, sculpture and photography.

MARSH HAVEN NATURE CENTER – Waupun – 79 D5 Nature center situated on northern edge of Horicon Marsh, resting and feeding area for spring and fall migrating waterfowl, including Canada geese, ducks, swans, cranes and heron. Marsh's ecology, history and wildlife explored through displays, exhibits, self-guided nature trails and outdoor programs. Observation tower overlooks marsh.

MILTON HOUSE – Milton – 93 B7 Original stagecoach inn, restored to 1840s condition, when it was part of the underground railroad. Secret tunnel still intact.

MILWAUKEE ART MUSEUM – Milwaukee – 88 E3 20th-century building designed by renowned architect Eero Saarinen. 19th- and 20th-century European and American art by Degas, Toulouse-Lautrec, Miro, Picasso, O'Keefe and Warhol. Decorative arts, Haitain art and works by architect Frank Lloyd Wright.

MILWAUKEE COUNTY ZOO – Milwaukee – 88 E2 190 acres of exotic animals exhibited in five continental groupings. Natural habitat settings show prey and predator in close proximity. Highlights include Lowland Gorillas and rare white tiger. Miniature train and Zoomobile rides. Children's zoo.

MILWAUKEE PUBLIC MUSEUM – Milwaukee – 88 E3 Highlights include natural history exhibits and lifestyle displays of various cultures. Diorama features life-size dinosaur models. Fine and decorative arts collection.

THE MINING MUSEUM & ROLLO JAMISON MUSEUM – Platteville – 90 C4 Mining Museum traces development of lead and zinc mining in Upper Mississippi Valley. Exhibits include dioramas, artifacts and photographs. Guided tour through 1845 Bevans lead mine. Rides available in 1931 locomotive and ore cars. In adjacent museum, collector Rollo Jamison accumulated over 20,000 everyday items. Exhibits include turn-of-20th-century carriages, farm implements, tools, kitchen utensils and musical instruments.

MT OLYMPUS WATER AND THEME PARK – Wisconsin Dells – 77 E5 Theme park includes six roller coasters, 37 water slides, kiddie areas, wave pool and go-karts.

NATIONAL RAILROAD MUSEUM – Green Bay – 61 F6 National Railroad Museum preserves over 65 locomotives and cars, railroad memorabilia and archives. Collection includes Rock Island Aerotrain, Joseph Lister Hospital Car and Union Pacific Big Boy. 20-minute ride on restored Barney and Smith coach. Costumed guides.

NEVILLE PUBLIC MUSEUM – Green Bay – 61 F7 Six galleries housing art, history and science exhibits. Highlights include Transparent Anatomical Mannikin and On the Edge of the Inland Sea, an exhibit tracing 10,000 years of natural history and civilization in northeast Wisconsin. Art collection includes paintings, sculpture and decorative arts.

NOAH'S ARK – Wisconsin Dells – 77 E5 Largest waterpark in US. Numerous large and innovative waterslides, two wave pools, two lazy rivers, four children's water-play areas, bumper boats and 18-hole miniature golf.

OCTAGON HOUSE MUSEUM – Hudson – 52 A2 Eight-sided dwelling built in 1855. Period furnishings from St. Croix County families. Garden and carriage houses. Doll collection. Guided tours.

OLD WORLD WISCONSIN – Eagle – 94 A3 Outdoor living museum representing Danish, Finnish, German, Norwegian, Irish, Bohemian and American cultures. Original buildings of immigrant settlers. Log cabins, farms, shops, town hall and church. Costumed interpreters perform daily chores and seasonal activities. Livestock and food crops.

ONEIDA NATION MUSEUM – Oneida – 72 A1 Displays feature history of League of the Iroquois—spiritual life, politics and craftsmanship. Reconstructed stockaded village including bark longhouse and medicinal herb garden. Demonstrations on tomahawk throwing, corn grinding, Native American games and other seasonal activities.

ORIGINAL WISCONSIN DUCKS – Wisconsin Dells – 77 E5 Seven-mile tours on Wisconsin River and over land in original World War II amphibious vehicles.

OSHKOSH PUBLIC MUSEUM – Oshkosh – 71 F6 1908 English-style mansion, home of Oshkosh businessman Edgar Sawyer. Exhibits and dioramas illustrate exploration, settlement and development of Lake Winnebago Region. Displays include fine, folk and decorative arts, textiles, toys, natural history specimens, Native American artifacts and other local history items. 1895 Apostles Clock.

THE PABST MANSION – Milwaukee – 88 E3 Flemish Renaissance Revival Mansion built for Captain Frederick Pabst, founder of Pabst Brewery.Cultural Museum hosts exhibits on the turn of the century.

PAINE ART CENTER & ARBORETUM – Oshkosh – 71 F6 1927 Tudor-style mansion houses period rooms, 19th- and 20th-century paintings, sculpture, Oriental rugs, Chinese decorative arts and collection of Greek and Russian icons. 15-acre arboretum contains formal English garden, rose and alpine gardens, native and exotic trees and shrubs.

PANTHER INTAGLIO MOUND – Fort Atkinson – 93 A8 Only known intaglio effigy mound remaining in world. Carved below ground level for ceremonial purposes by Effigy Mound Culture about 1000 AD. Discovered in 1850 by Increase A. Lapham.

PEBBLE HOUSE – Port Washington – 88 A4 Gatehouse for Port Washington Power Plant of Wisconsin Electric Power Company. Built in 1848 by blacksmith Edward Dodge with pebbles collected from Lake Michigan. Black basalt, pink and gray granites, flints and quartzites alternately layered on exterior.

PENDARVIS – Mineral Point – 91 A6 Group of restored miner's homes furnished with antiques and lead mining artifacts. Log and limestone houses built during 1830s and 1840s resembling former homes in Cornwall, England.

PINECREST HISTORICAL VILLAGE – Manitowoc – 72 E4 Buildings range from late 1800s to early 1900s. Moved from original locations to village site. Cabins, houses, sawmill, church, bank, smokehouse and barn. Group tours by appointment.

RACINE ART MUSEUM – Racine – 95 C8 Modern Facility exhibits contemporary crafts including ceramic, glass, wood and metal art.

RACINE ZOO – Racine – 95 C8 28-acre park on shores of Lake Michigan. More than 350 mammals, birds and reptiles. Big cats, wading birds, primates, hoofed animals, penguins, and petting zoo.

RAHR–WEST ART MUSEUM – Manitowoc – 73 E5 Victorian mansion houses numerous collections. 19th-century American paintings and furniture, Chinese ivory carvings, Boehm porcelains, art glass, prehistoric relics and antique dolls.

SCHLITZ AUDUBON CENTER – Milwaukee – 88 D4 Varied terrain including river and floodplain, Lake Michigan shoreline, bluff and ravines, deciduous woodlands, open fields and ponds. Nature trails include specially designed wildlife observation points. Interpretive center.

ST JOAN OF ARC CHAPEL – Milwaukee – 88 E3 Medieval French chapel shipped to US in 1927 stone by stone. Dedicated to St. Joan of Arc. Featuring Gothic altar and Joan of Arc Stone. First reconstructed on Long Island, New York, and again at Marquette University in 1965.

STATE CAPITOL – Madison – 85 E8 1906–1917 granite Beaux Arts-style structure serves as Wisconsin's third capitol building. Guided tours of rotunda, Governor's Conference Room, State Supreme Court room, and Senate and Assembly Chambers. Interior features 43 varieties of stone, decorative murals, glass mosaics and hand-carved furniture. Museum and observation deck.

STONEFIELD – Nelson Dewey State Park – 89 C7 Replica of 1890s rural farming community on former plantation of Nelson Dewey, Wisconsin's first governor. Buildings include State Agricultural Museum, Nelson Dewey House, general store and railroad depot.

SWISS HISTORICAL VILLAGE – New Glarus – 92 B2 Fourteen buildings describe Swiss immigration to New Glarus. Buildings include log church and cabin, blacksmith shop, cheese factory, schoolhouse and general store. Extensive flower gardens. Guided tours.

TALIESIN & FRANK LLOYD WRIGHT VISITOR CENTER – Spring Green – 84 D3 Guided tour of renowned architect Frank Lloyd Wright's Hillside Home School. Tour explores theater, drafting studio, Dana Gallery and Robert's Room.

TIMBAVATI WILDLIFE PARK – Wisconsin Dells – 77 E5 Wildlife park and petting zoo that specializes in more than 400 exotic animals and 75 species such as Toucan, Arctic Fox, Kudu and Tamarin. Park also features safari train, camel rides and pig races.

TOMMY BARTLETT SHOW AND EXPLORATORY – Wisconsin Dells – 77 E5 Waterskiing and hang gliding demonstration. Trampoline and sway pole acrobats. Comedy juggler. Robot-guided exploratory tours. More than 175 hands-on scientific exhibits.

UWSP MUSEUM OF NATURAL HISTORY – Stevens Point – 58 F2 Interactive exhibits interpreting geologic time and distances in outer space. Mammal, bird and fish displays. Mineral and rock exhibit.

VILLA LOUIS – Prairie du Chien – 82 E2 Former home of Hercules Dousman of American Fur Company. Original structure built on Native American burial mound. Victorian mansion filled with hand-painted china, Waterford crystal chandeliers, valuable paintings and rare books.

VILLA TERRACE DECORATIVE ARTS MUSEUM – Milwaukee – 88 E4 1923 Italian-style villa overlooking Lake Michigan. Exhibits decorative arts including period furnishings and porcelains.

WADE HOUSE – Greenbush – 80 C2 Restored inn built in 1851. Costumed interpreters performing seasonal tasks, making candles and soap, gardening and blacksmithing.

WESLEY M. JUNG CARRIAGE MUSEUM – Greenbush – 80 C2 State carriage museum. Over 100 restored carriages. Working wagons include butcher's carts, grocery wagons, street sprinkler and fire-fighting equipment.

WILDERNESS RESORT – Wisconsin Dells – 77 E5 Scenic resort features eight theme based waterparks including thrill rides, waterslides, lazy and wild rivers, swimming pools and children's area. Overnight and day-use accommodations.

WILDERNESS ZOO & RECREATION PARK – Hayward – 32 A4 35-acre recreational park featuring wild and domestic animals, petting zoo and western town.

WILDWOOD ZOO – Marshfield – 57 E6 60-acre park featuring over 200 animals and birds from North America Grizzly bears, cougar, American Bison and timber wolves. Aviary. Petting zoo.

WILDWOOD WILDLIFE PARK & NATURE CENTER – Minocqua – 36 B1 Wildlife park with over 100 varieties of native animals and fowl. Tame deer herd, animal nursery, otter colony, beaver pond and exotic birds. Nature boardwalk and boat rides.

WISCONSIN AUTOMOTIVE MUSEUM – Hartford – 87 B8 Antique and classic cars from 1902 to early sixties. Kissels, Fords, Auburns, Buicks, Pierce Arrows and Fire Engines. Industrial and farm engines.

WISCONSIN HISTORICAL MUSEUM – Madison – 85 E8 Permanent exhibit explores Wisconsin Woodland Indian life from prehistoric times to 20th century. Temporary exhibits rotating every six months on first floor.

WISCONSIN LOGGING MUSEUM – Eau Claire – 54 C3 Authentically re-created 1890s logging camp. Bunkhouse, cook shanty, blacksmith shop and barn housing antique tools and equipment.

WISCONSIN MARITIME MUSEUM – Manitowoc – 73 E5 Great Lakes maritime history displays including sailing ships, modern ships and maritime artifacts. Model ship display and workshop. Complete tour of USS *Cobia*, World War II submarine.

WISCONSIN VETERANS MUSEUM – Madison – 85 E8 Exhibits, artifacts and dioramas illustrate Wisconsin military history and veterans' activities from the Civil War to the Persian Gulf War. Military aircraft and ship models also on display. Changing exhibits.

WOODLAND DUNES NATURE CENTER – Manitowoc – 73 D6 Over 100 species of nesting birds spotted each year. Narrow tongue of land forms portion of natural border between two distinct areas of natural growth. Northern and southern species of birds and plants found here. Bird-banding station. Self-guided nature trail through cattail marsh.

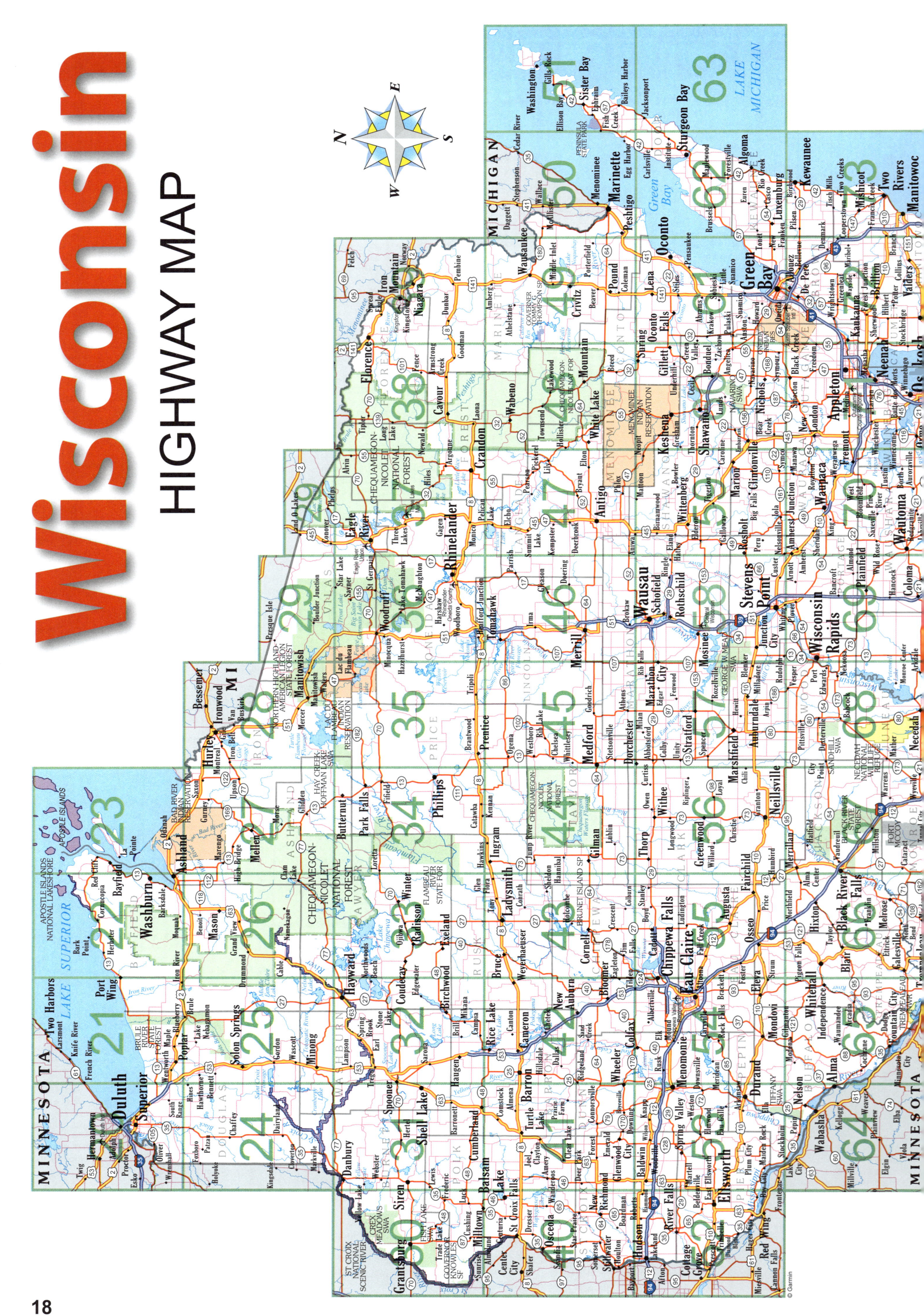

Wisconsin
HIGHWAY MAP

Grid numbers refer to detailed map pages

Scale 1:1,315,000

1 inch represents 20.75 miles
1 centimeter represents 13.15 kilometers

miles 0 6 12 18 24 30 36 48

kilometers 0 12 24 36 48 60 72 84

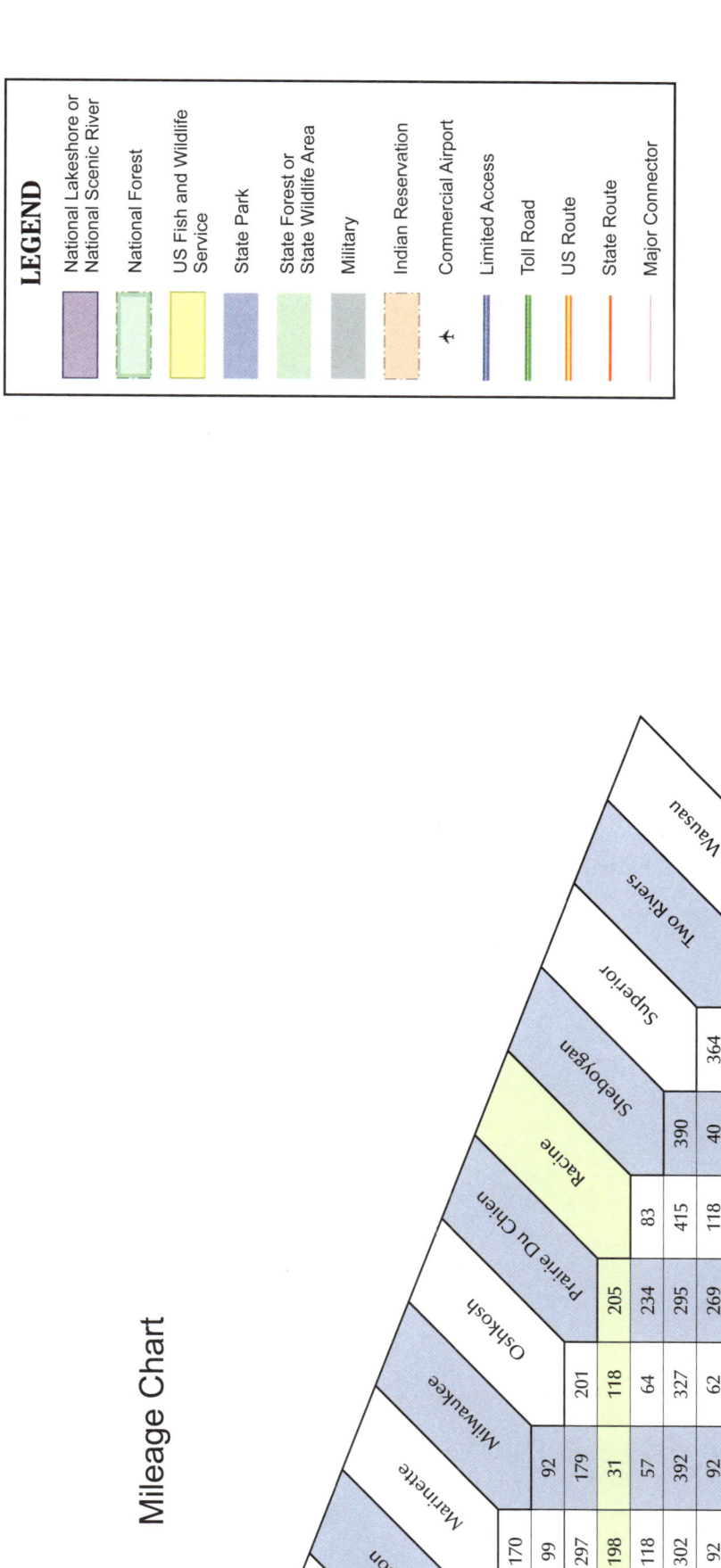

LEGEND

	National Lakeshore or National Scenic River
	National Forest
	US Fish and Wildlife Service
	State Park
	State Forest or State Wildlife Area
	Military
	Indian Reservation
←	Commercial Airport
	Limited Access
	Toll Road
	US Route
	State Route
	Major Connector

Mileage Chart

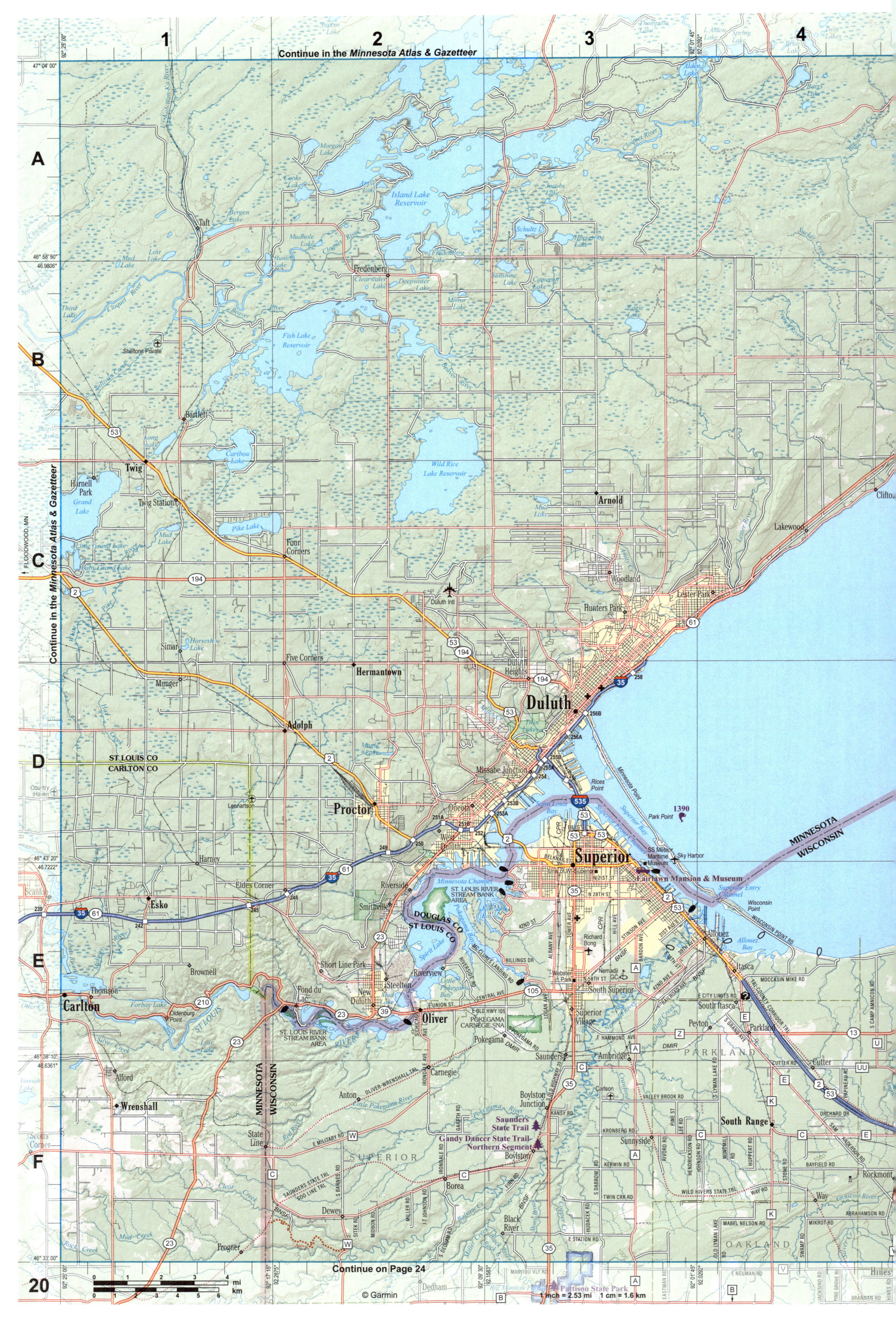

Continue on Page 24

© Garmin

1 inch = 2.53 mi   1 cm = 1.6 km

20

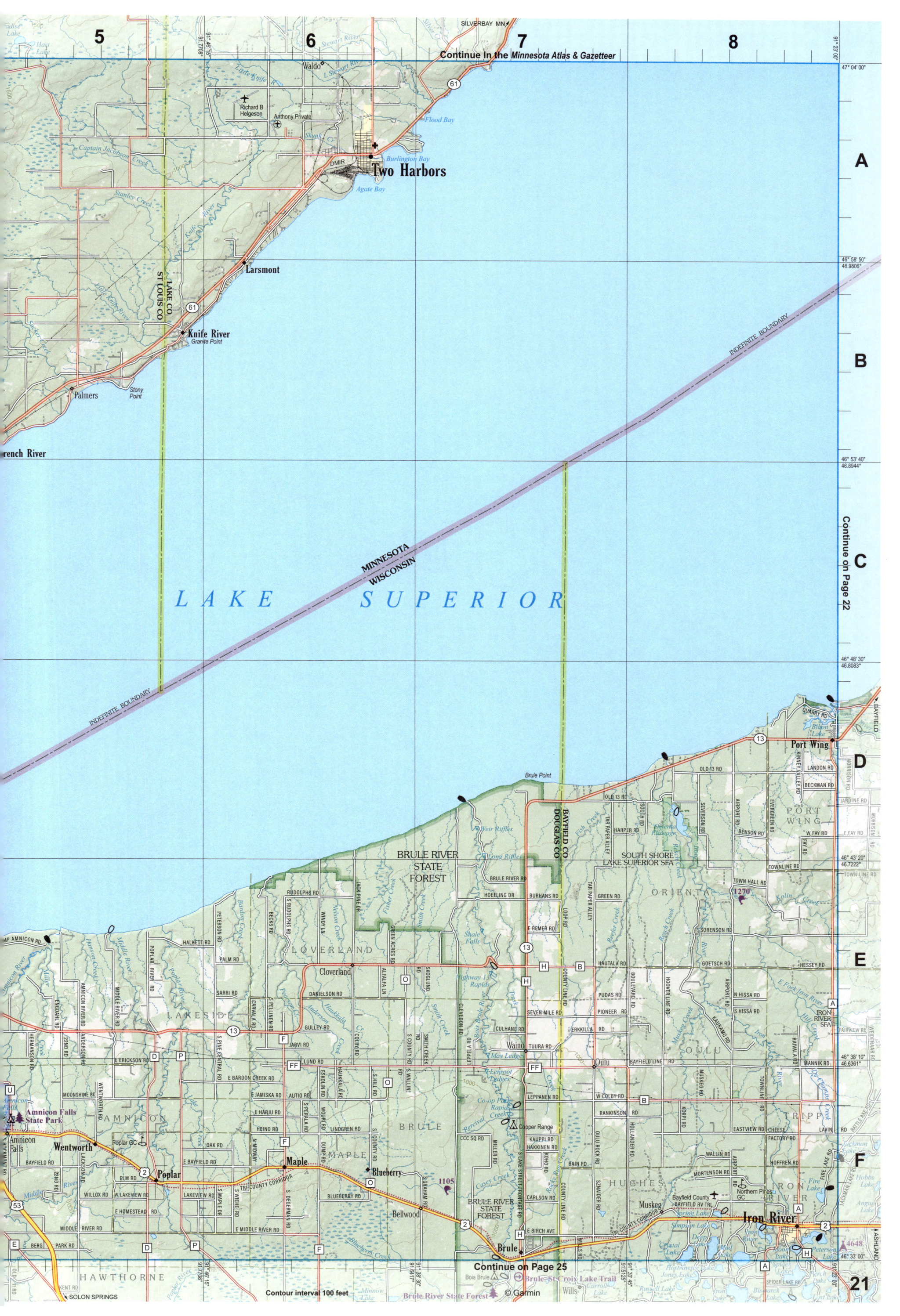

SILVERBAY MN

Continue In the *Minnesota Atlas & Gazetteer*

47° 04' 00"

61

Waldo

Richard B
Helgeson
Anthony Private

Flood Bay

Skunk

Burlington Bay

DMIR

Two Harbors

Agate Bay

A

46° 58' 50"
46.9806°

61

Larsmont

INDEFINITE BOUNDARY

B

61

Knife River
Granite Point

Palmers

Stony
Point

French River

46° 53' 40"
46.8944°

MINNESOTA
WISCONSIN

L A K E   S U P E R I O R

Continue on Page 22

C

46° 48' 30"
46.8083°

INDEFINITE BOUNDARY

QUARRY RD

BAYFIELD

Bibon
Lake

13

Port Wing

Brule Point

KINNEY ALLEY RD

LANDON RD

BECKMAN RD

MORRISON RD

OLD 13 RD

D

P O R T
W I N G

EVERGREEN RD

Weir Riffles

BRULE RIVER
STATE
FOREST

Long Riffles

Fish Creek

TAR PAPER ALLEY

HARPER RD

SOUTH RD

SEVERSON RD

AIRPORT RD

BENSON RD

TOWNLINE RD

OLD 13 RD

46° 43' 20"
46.7222°

TOWN LINE RD

BURHANS RD

GREEN RD

SOUTH SHORE
LAKE SUPERIOR SFA

O R I E N T A

TOWN HALL RD

1270

Solin

E Fork Iron River

W FAY RD

E FAY RD

RUDOLPHS RD

JACK PINE DR

BRULE RIVER DR

HOELING DR

E REMER RD

13

B

HAUTALA RD

HOOVER LINE RD

GOETSCH RD

HESSEY RD

CAMP AMNICON RD

Amnicon
River

Middle River

Bardon Creek

Barnes Creek

PETERSON RD

BECKS RD

PALM RD

WINDY LN

Nelson Creek

GREEN ACRES RD

Shale
Falls

Highway 13 Rapids

PUDAS RD

H

L O V E R L A N D

HALKETT RD

POPLAR
RIVER RD

S RUDOLPHS RD

Cloverland

ALFALFA LN

SKOGLUND RD

COUNTY LINE RD

PIONEER RD

AIRPORT RD

N HISSA RD

S HISSA RD

IRON
RIVER SFA

E

SARRI RD

DANIELSON RD

CHWALA RD

S PELLINEN RD

GULLEY RD

Smith Creek

S COUNTY RD

SMITH CREEK RD

LEPPELA RD

CULHANE RD

TUURA RD

SEVEN MILE RD

ERKKILA RD

Waino

O U L U

BAYFIELD LINE RD

KAHAMO RD

RAVINA RD

46° 38' 10"
46.6361°

FAIRVIEW RD

WEBERMAN RD

L A K E S I D E

ENGDAHL RD

22ND RD

HERMANSON RD

ANDERSSON RD

MIDDLE RIVER RD

13

S PINE CENTRAL RD

ABVI RD

F

LUND RD

FF

E BARDON CREEK RD

COEBURG RD

MAUNULA RD

S WALLIN

LEPPANEN RD

W COLBY RD

Oulu

B

MANNIK RD

TOWNLINE

NORKOL RD

T R I P P

E ERICKSON RD

P

MOONSHINE RD

WENTWORTH RD

U

Amnicon
Falls

**Amnicon Falls
State Park**

A M N I C O N

E JAMISKA RD

E HARJU RD

HEINO RD

AUTIO RD

WOJURE RD

ESKOLA RD

S PERALA RD

LINDGREN RD

B R U L E

S COUNTY RD

KAUPPI RD

OULU ROCK RD

BAIN RD

RANKINSON RD

EASTVIEW RD

HOLLANDER RD

S ZNIDER RD

WALLIN RD

MORTENSON RD

EASTVIEW RD

KORPI RD

FACTORY RD

H U G H E S

LAVIN

Northern Pines GC

E Fork
Iron
River

Iron
River

F

Amnicon
Falls

Wentworth

BAYFIELD RD

23RD RD

2

LACKSON RD

ELM RD

Poplar

WILLOX RD

Poplar GC

E BAYFIELD RD

OAK RD

DUMP RD

MILLER RD

CCC SQ RD

Copper Range

S LAKE STREET FRONTAGE RD

HAKKINEN RD

KOHO RD

Maple

M A P L E

Blueberry

1105

BAYFIELD COUNTY

BAYFIELD HWY TRL

Muskeg

HOFFREN RD

FIRE LANE RD

Hobbs
Lake

53

WILLOX RD

S MAPLE RD

W LAKEVIEW RD

LAKEVIEW RD

TRI COUNTY CORRIDOR

S DECORMAN RD

Casey Creek

SIGMAN RD

2

Bellwood

BLUEBERRY RD

E HOMESTEAD RD

BRULE RIVER
STATE
FOREST

CARLSON RD

E BIRCH AVE

TRI COUNTY CORRIDOR

Iron River

2

A

46° 33' 00"

4648

ASHLAND

E BERG RD

PARK RD

MIDDLE RIVER RD

E MIDDLE RIVER RD

E

P

Brule

Bois Brule

H

Simpson Lake

Spring Lake

Spider Lake RD

H

Peterson
Lake

H A W T H O R N E

SOLON SPRINGS

Contour interval 100 feet

91° 46' 15"

91° 41' 15"

Continue on Page 25

Brule–St. Croix Lake Trail

Brule River State Forest

© Garmin

91° 37' 30"

91° 33' 30"

91° 28' 45"

91° 25' 00"

L A K E   S U P E R I O R

Continue on Page 21

APOSTLE ISLANDS
NATIONAL LAKESHORE

Sand Island
APOSTLE
ISLANDS
NATIONAL
LAKESHORE

Herbster

Cornucopia

Port Wing
Boreal Forest SNA

BAYFIELD

BELL

CLOVER

PORT WING

ORIENTA

WASHBURN

BAYVIEW

Washburn

CHEQUAMEGON-NICOLET

NATIONAL FOREST

Barksdale

TRIPP

BARKSDALE

Ashland

Moquah

Iron
River

PILSEN

EILEEN

KEYSTONE

© Garmin

1 inch = 2.53 mi   1 cm = 1.6 km

22

Continue in the *Minnesota Atlas & Gazetteer*

Anstad Bay

A P O S T L E   I S L A N D S

Outer
Island

Devils
Island
Devils Island
Shoal

North Twin
Island

Rocky Island
South
Twin Island
Rocky Island
South Twin
Island

Bear Island Shoal
York Island Shoals

Bear
Island

Otter Island
Otter Island

Ironwood
Island
Ironwood Island

Cat
Island
Cat Island

Outer Island
Sand Point

A

47° 04' 00"

46° 58' 50"
46.9806°

York
Island

A P O S T L E   I S L A N D S   N A T I O N A L   L A K E S H O R E

int Detour
Eagle Bay

Raspberry
Island

Marina Shoal

Clay Banks

Apostle Islands
National Lakeshore

Manitou Island
Manitou Island

Trout Point

Balancing Rock

Gull Island Shoal

B

Raspberry
Bay
Raspberry Point

INDEFINITE BOUNDARY

Frog
Bay

RUSSELL

Oak Island

Stockton   Island

Stockton Island

EMIL RD

Petit Cache
PETERSON HILL RD
BLUEBERRY RD
ROWLEY RD
OLD COUNTY HWY K

RED CLIFF
INDIAN
RESERVATION

Red Cliff
Point

Red Cliff
Bay

PAGEANT

BISHOP LN

Oak Island

Quarry Point

Quarry
Bay

Presque Isle
Bay
Presque Isle Point

Gull Island

Hermit Island

Steamboat Point

Michigan Island

C

46° 53' 10"

Red Cliff

BRADUM RD

TURNER RD

TOWN LINE RD

Buffalo Bay
Buffalo Bay

Roys Point

Basswood
Island

WEST   CHANNEL

NORTH   CHANNEL

Devils Cauldron

School House RD

Amnicon
Bay

BAD RIVER
INDIAN RESERVATION

Amnicon Point

CHIPPEWA TRL

BETZOLD RD
OLSON RD
J
J
13

J
I
Apostle Highlands
GC
4012

Bayfield
Dalrymple Park
Apostle Islands National Lakeshore
Apostle Islands Cruise Service

N SHORE DR
BENJAMIN BLVD
BIG BAY RD

LA
POINTE

Madeline   Island

Big Bay Town Park

D

46° 48' 00"

BAY RD

Pureair
1381

Point De Froid

Pikes Bay

H
Madeline Island Hist Museum
La Pointe

FERRY

Sunset
Bay

BLACK SHANTY RD
HAGEN RD
HAINES RD

Big
Bay

Big Bay Point

Big Bay
State Park

L A K E   S U P E R I O R

ASHLAND CO
IRON CO

mo
Van Tassells

H
H
Madeline Island

CHEBOMNICON RD

Chebomnicon
Bay

Madeline Island
Golf Club

S SHORE DR

Grants Point

SOUTH   CHANNEL

46° 43' 20"
46.7222°

Houghton Point

Long Island

AINL

Chequamegon Point

INDEFINITE BOUNDARY

E

CHEQUAMEGON
BAY

Oak Point

46° 38' 10"
46.6361°

Lake Park
2
TOLL RD

LAKE PARK RD
JOHNSON RD
REYNOLA RD

Wood Creek Slough

BAD RIVER
INDIAN RESERVATION

Honest John
Lake

Hanging
Swamp

WISCONSIN
MICHIGAN

505

F

Hidgkins Park
A
WOODBURN LN
MCDONALD RD
BEAR TRAP RD
ODANA RD

Odanah

BRICK RD

MAPLE ST

MADIGAN RD

Marble Point

Newago Creek

SAXON

Oronto Bay

Saxon Harbor
1387

122

3
OLD AIRPORT RD

GINGLES

White River

PEARCE RD

SANBORN

2
GRAVEYARD CREEK RD

ASHLAND CO
IRON CO

Saxon Harbor
Park
A

BERG RD

Continue on Page 27

Birch   GURNEY

Contour interval 100 feet

© Garmin

23

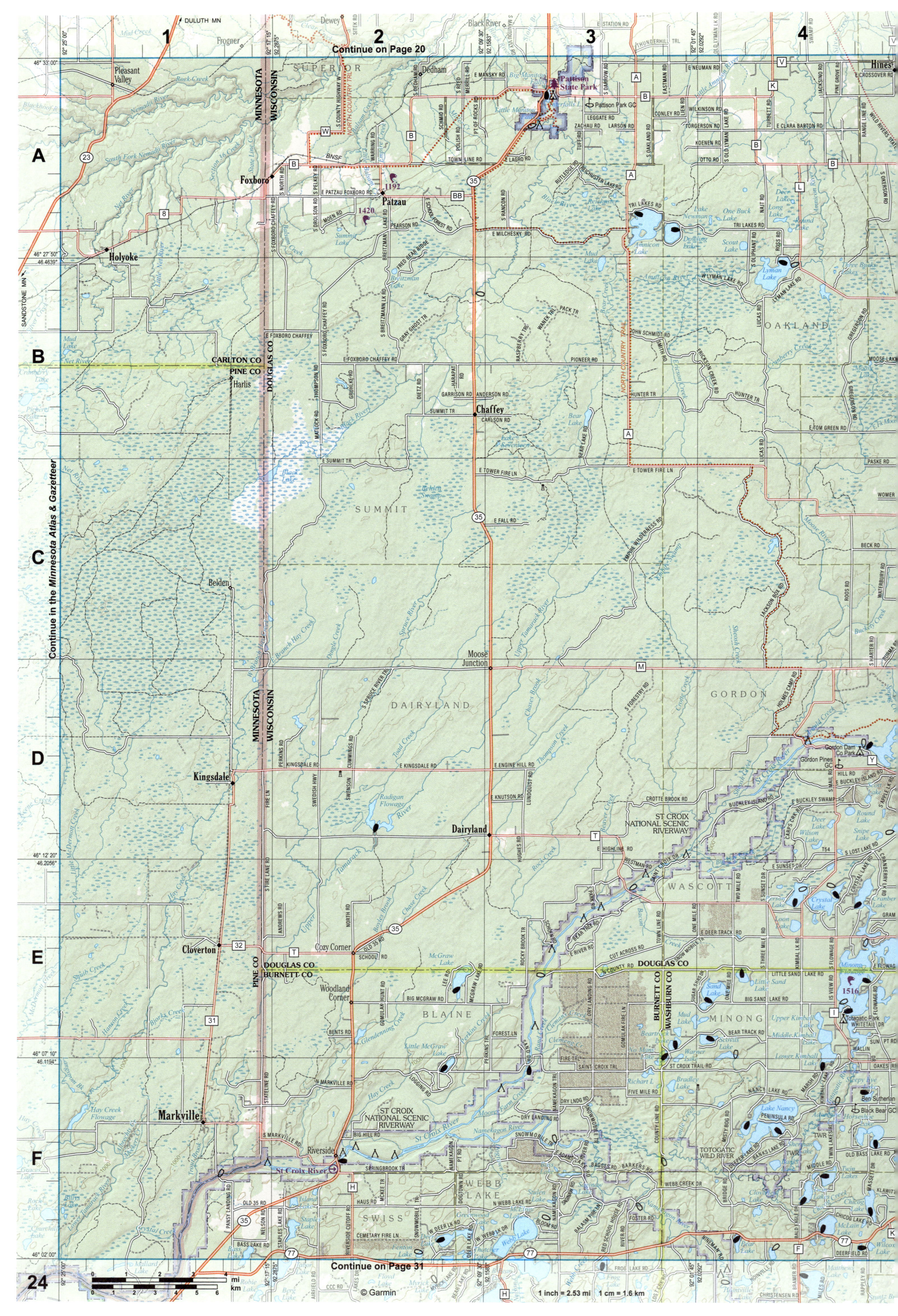

Continue on Page 31

Continue in the *Minnesota Atlas & Gazetteer*

© Garmin

1 inch = 2.53 mi   1 cm = 1.6 km

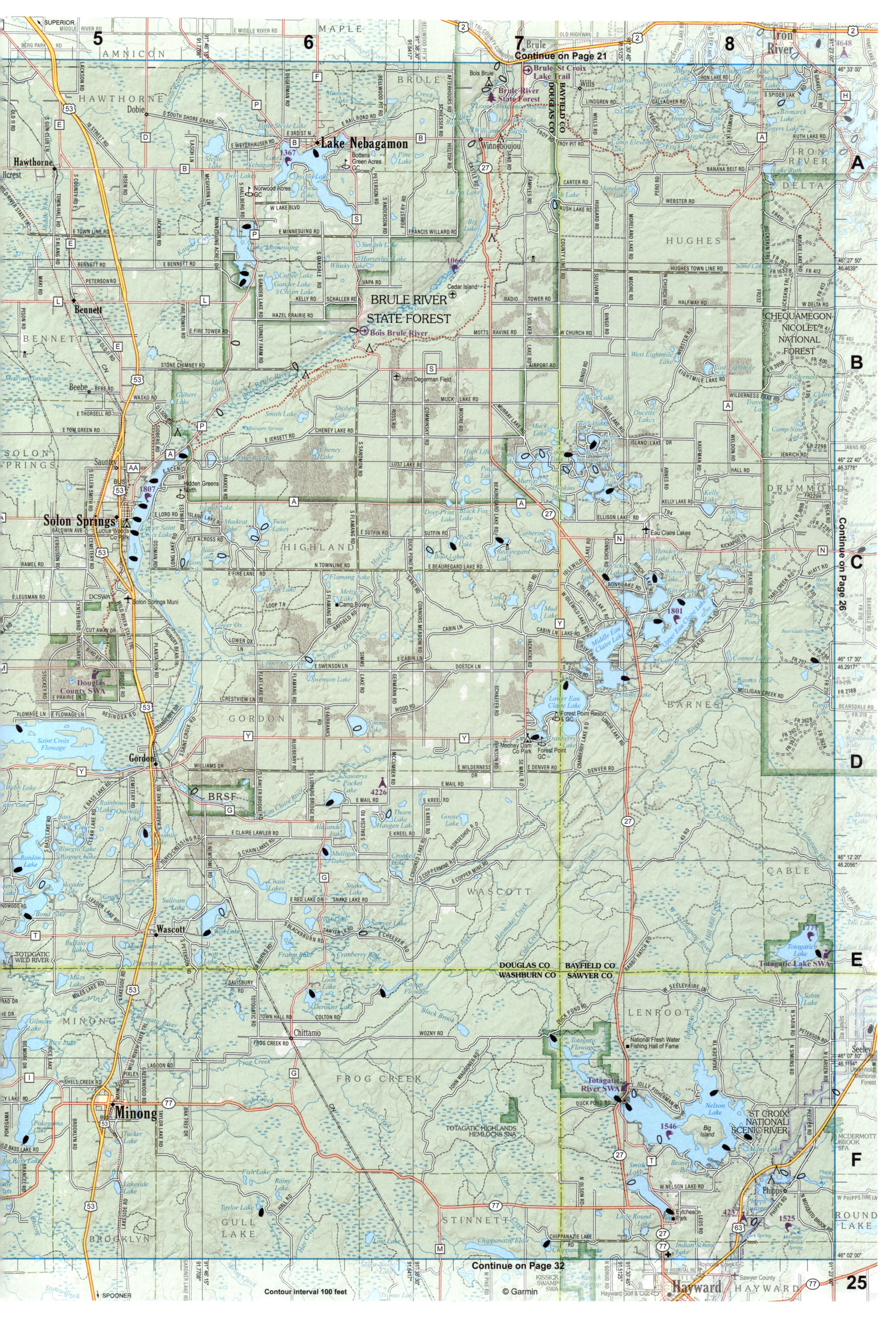

BRULE RIVER
STATE FOREST

Bois Brule River

BRULE RIVER
STATE FOREST

CHEQUAMEGON-
NICOLET
NATIONAL
FOREST

Lake Nebagamon

Hawthorne

Bennett

Beebe

Solon Springs

Gordon

BRSF

Wascott

Minong

HIGHLAND

GORDON

WASCOTT

BARNES

DRUMMOND

CABLE

LENROOT

STINNETT

BROOKLYN

GULL
LAKE

Continue on Page 26

DOUGLAS CO   BAYFIELD CO
WASHBURN CO   SAWYER CO

Totagatic Lake SWA

National Fresh Water
Fishing Hall of Fame

Totagatic
River SWA

ST CROIX
NATIONAL
SCENIC
RIVER

Phipps

Seeley

Chittamo

FROG CREEK

TOTAGATIC HIGHLANDS
HEMLOCKS SNA

Contour interval 100 feet

© Garmin

HAYWARD

25

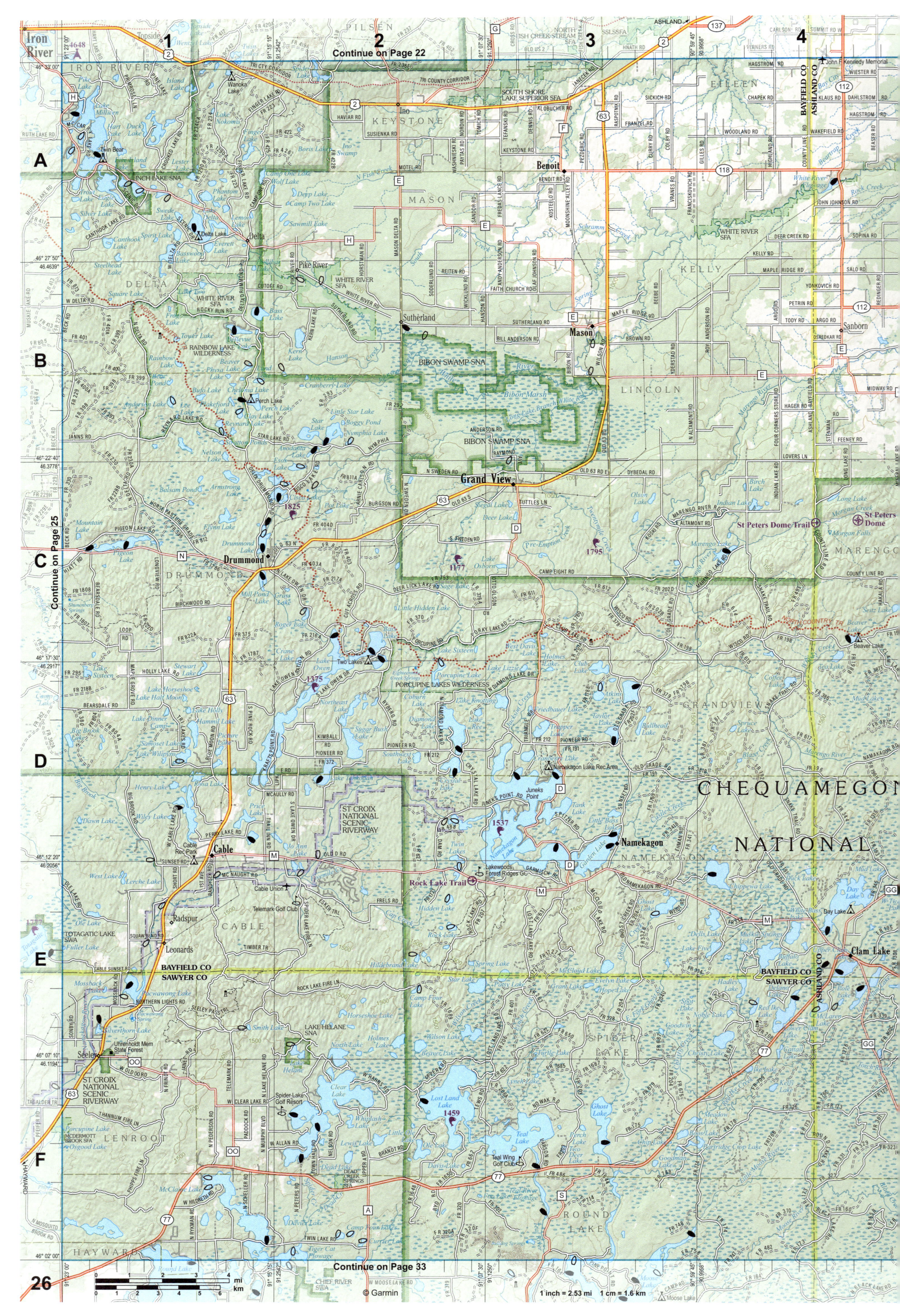

Continue on Page 25

1 inch = 2.53 mi   1 cm = 1.6 km

© Garmin

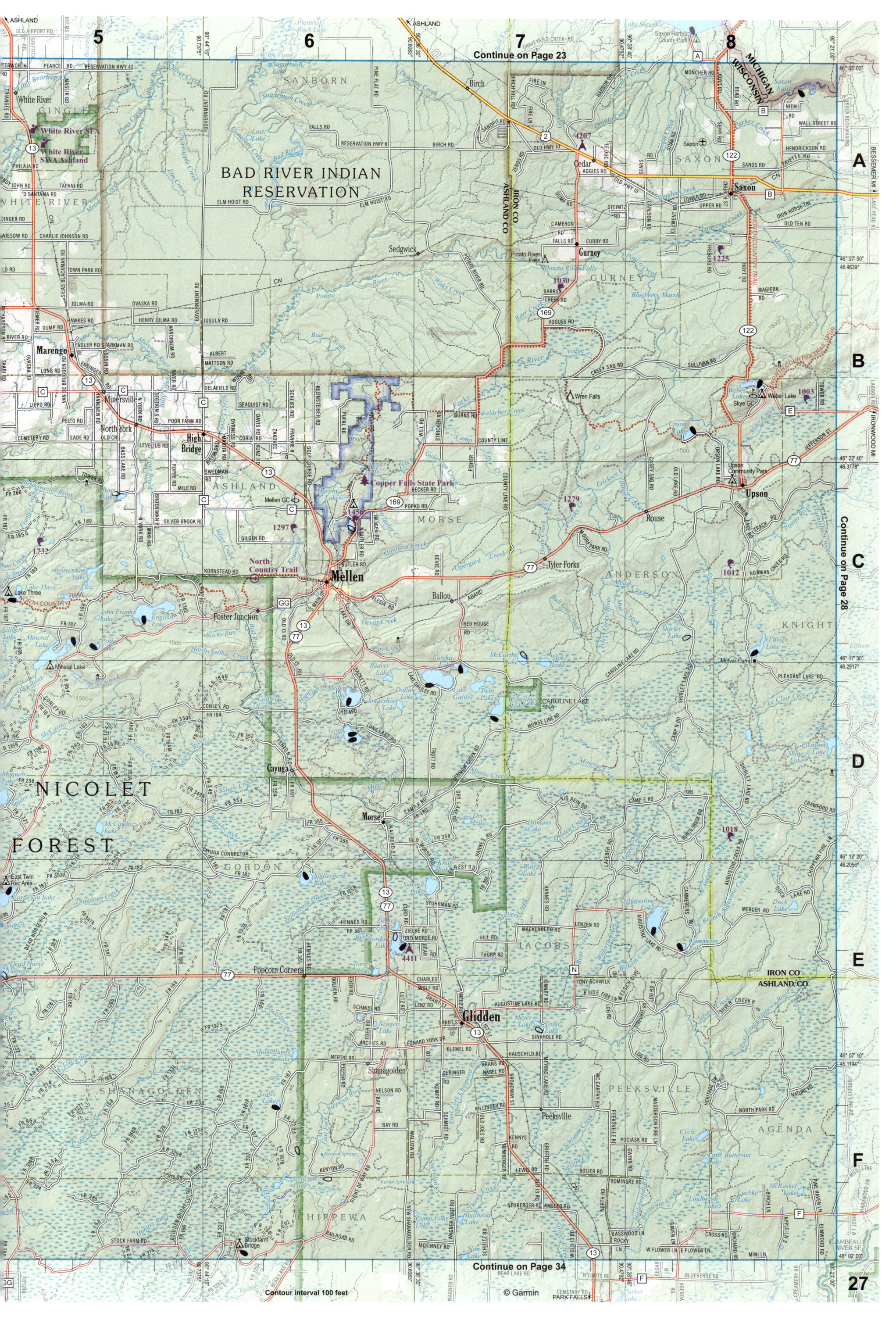

Continue on Page 28

Contour interval 100 feet

© Garmin

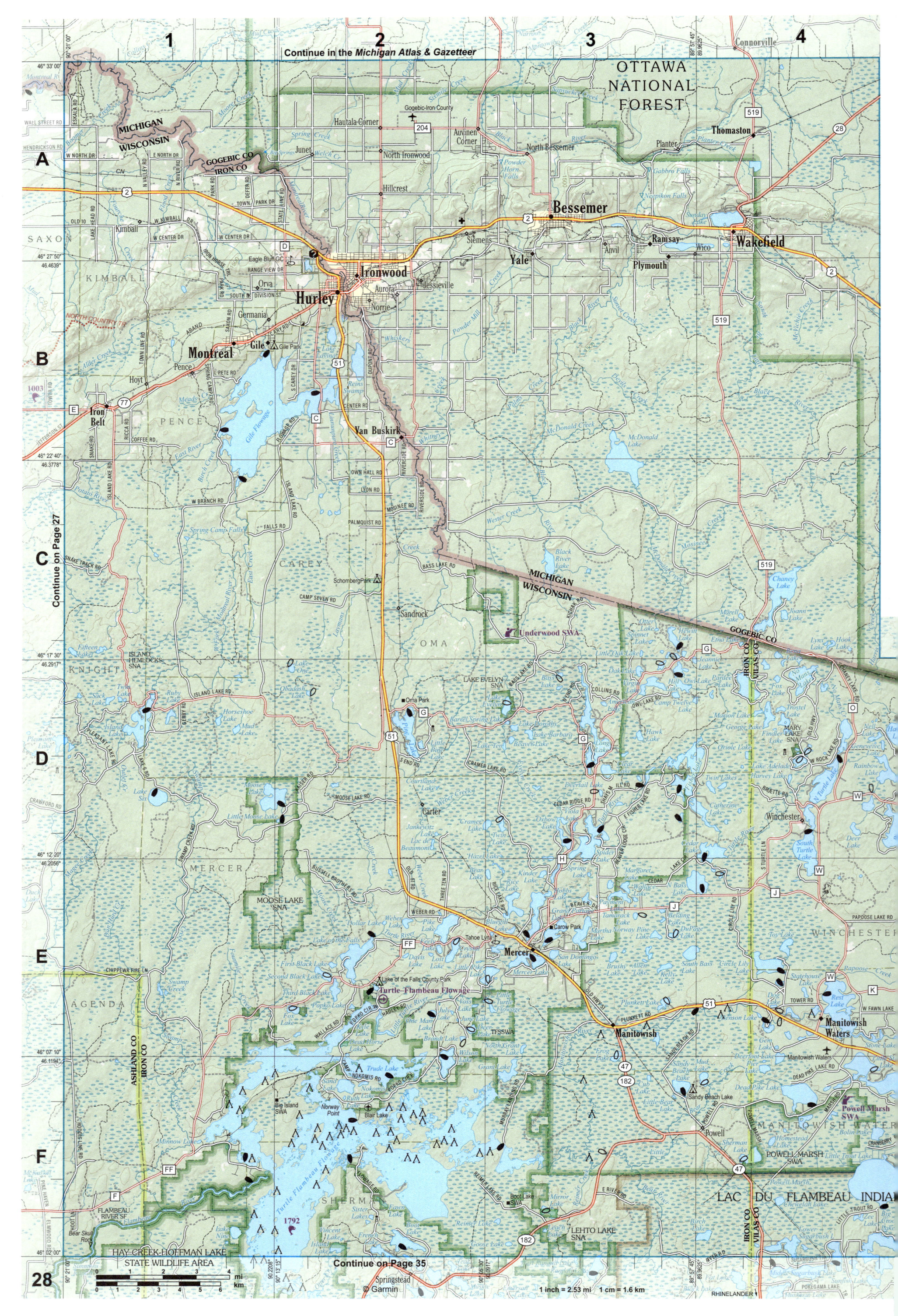

OTTAWA
NATIONAL
FOREST

MICHIGAN
WISCONSIN

GOGEBIC CO
IRON CO

A

SAXON

KIMBALL

Thomaston

Bessemer

Ramsay

Wakefield

Yale

Anvil

Plymouth

Wico

Ironwood

Orva

Hurley

Aurora

Jessieville

Germania

Norrie

B

Montreal

Gile

Gile Park

Pence

Hoyt

PENCE

Iron
Belt

Van Buskirk

E

McDonald Creek

McDonald
Lake

C

CAREY

Schomberg Park

Sandrock

MICHIGAN
WISCONSIN

Chaney
Lake

GOGEBIC CO
IRON CO

OMA

Underwood SWA

KNIGHT

Island Lake
SNA

Island
Hemlocks
SNA

Lake Evelyn
SNA

Orma Park

Mary
Lake

O

Winchester

D

Carter

MERCER

MOOSE LAKE
SNA

J

WINCHESTER

W

Mercer

PAPOOSE LAKE RD

K

E

ASHLAND CO
IRON CO

AGENDA

Turtle-Flambeau Flowage

Lake of the Falls County Park

Manitowish

Manitowish
Waters

Powell
Marsh
SWA

POWELL MARSH
SWA.

Powell

MANITOWISH WATER

F

Big Island
SWA

Norway
Point

Blair Lake

SHERM

FLAMBEAU
RIVER SF

1792

LEHTO LAKE
SNA

LAC DU FLAMBEAU INDIAN

HAY-CREEK-HOFFMAN LAKE
STATE WILDLIFE AREA

1 inch = 2.53 mi   1 cm = 1.6 km

Continue on Page 27

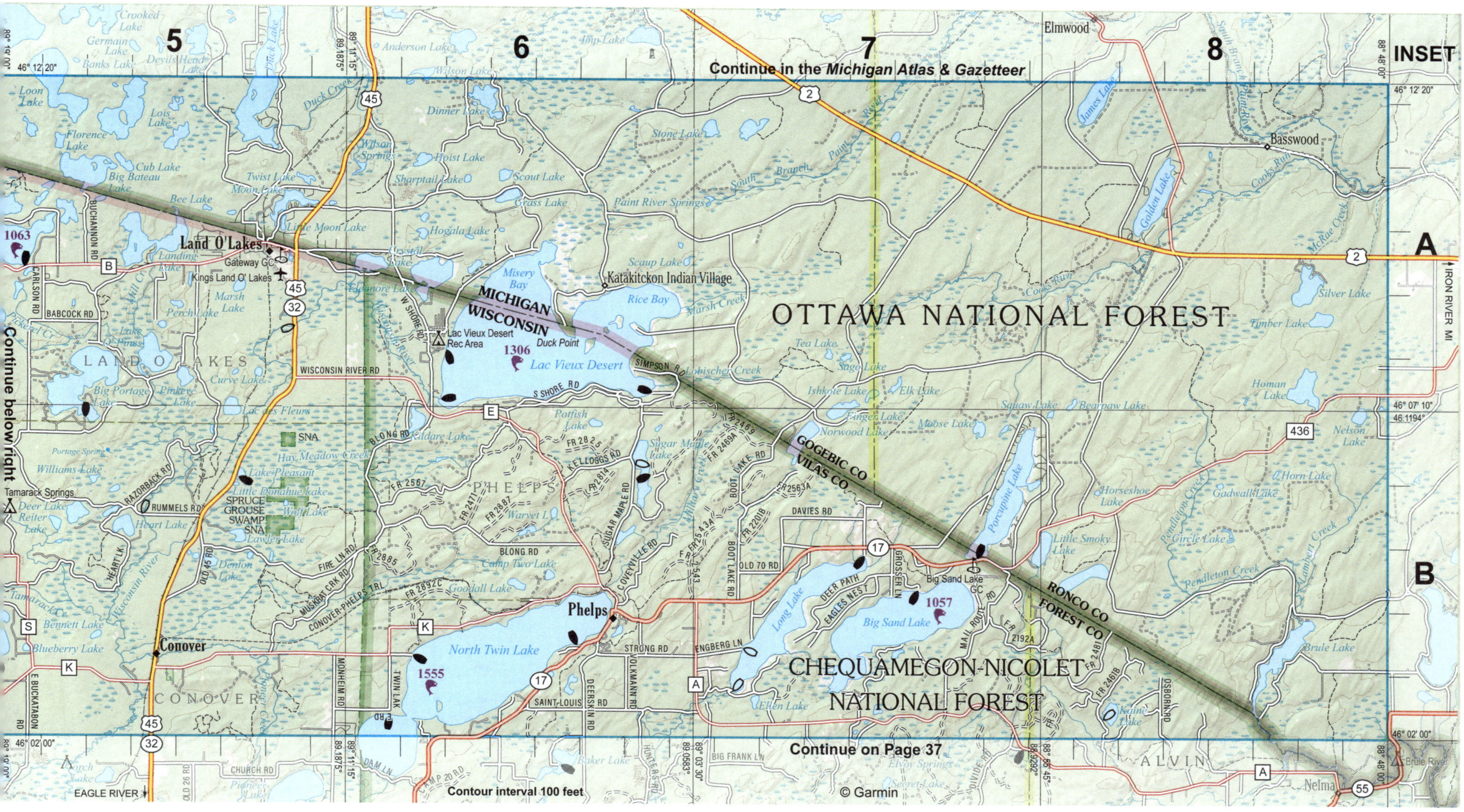

Elmwood

Continue in the *Michigan Atlas & Gazetteer*

Basswood

OTTAWA NATIONAL FOREST

Land O'Lakes

MICHIGAN
WISCONSIN

Katakitekon Indian Village

Lac Vieux Desert
Rec Area

Lac Vieux Desert

Duck Point

GOGEBIC CO.
VILAS CO.

Phelps

Conover

North Twin Lake

Big Sand Lake

RONCO CO.
FOREST CO.

CHEQUAMEGON-NICOLET
NATIONAL FOREST

ALVIN

Nelma

Continue on Page 37

Contour interval 100 feet

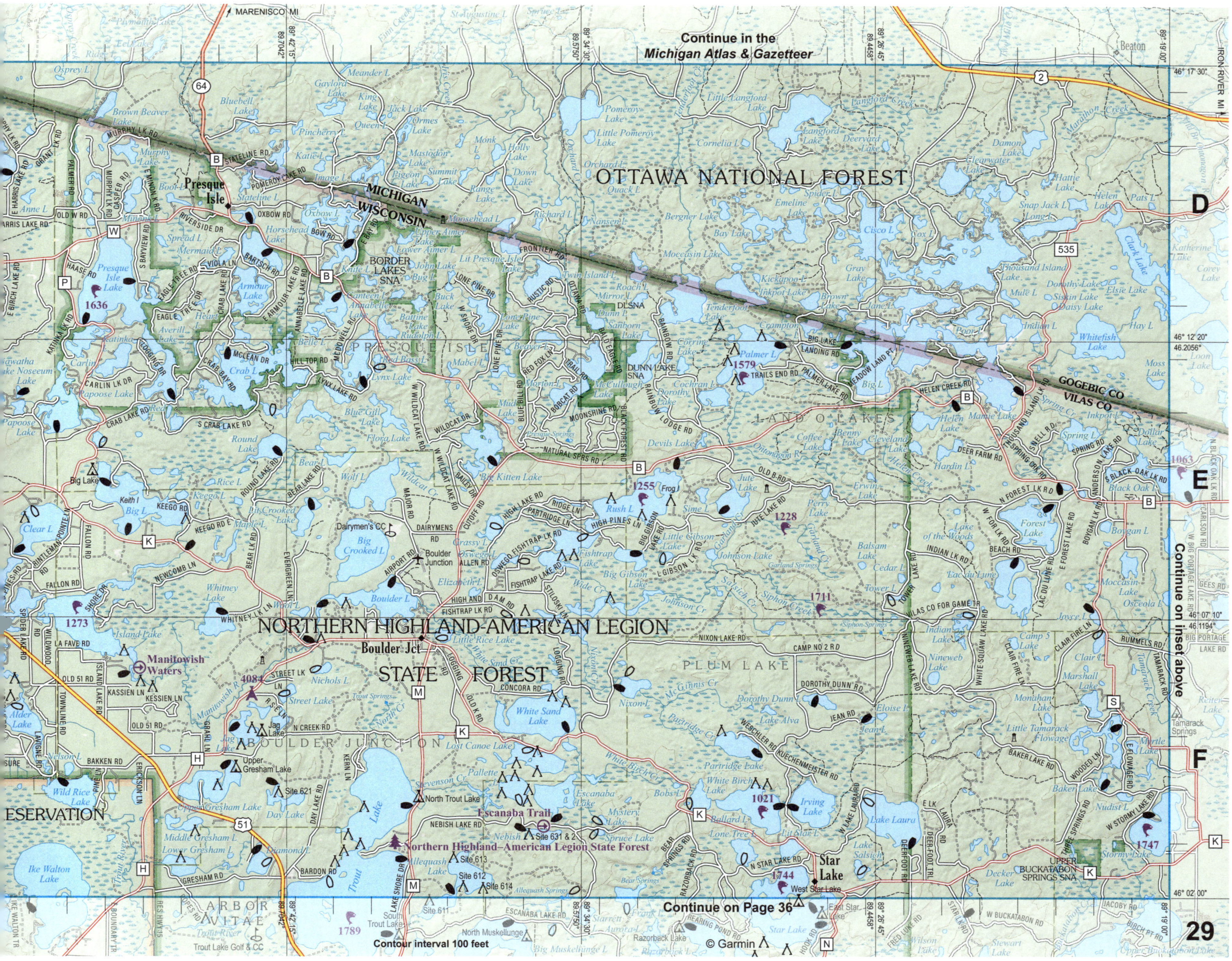

© Garmin

MARENISCO MI

Continue in the
Michigan Atlas & Gazetteer

Beaton

OTTAWA NATIONAL FOREST

Presque Isle

MICHIGAN
WISCONSIN

BORDER
LAKES
SNA

PRESQUE ISLE

LAND O'LAKES

GOGEBIC CO.
VILAS CO.

Manitowish Waters

NORTHERN HIGHLAND-AMERICAN LEGION

Boulder Jct.

STATE FOREST

BOULDER JUNCTION

PLUM LAKE

RESERVATION

Escanaba Trail

Northern Highland–American Legion State Forest

Star
Lake

UPPER
BUCKATABON
SNA

ARBOR
VITAE

Continue on Page 36

Contour interval 100 feet

© Garmin

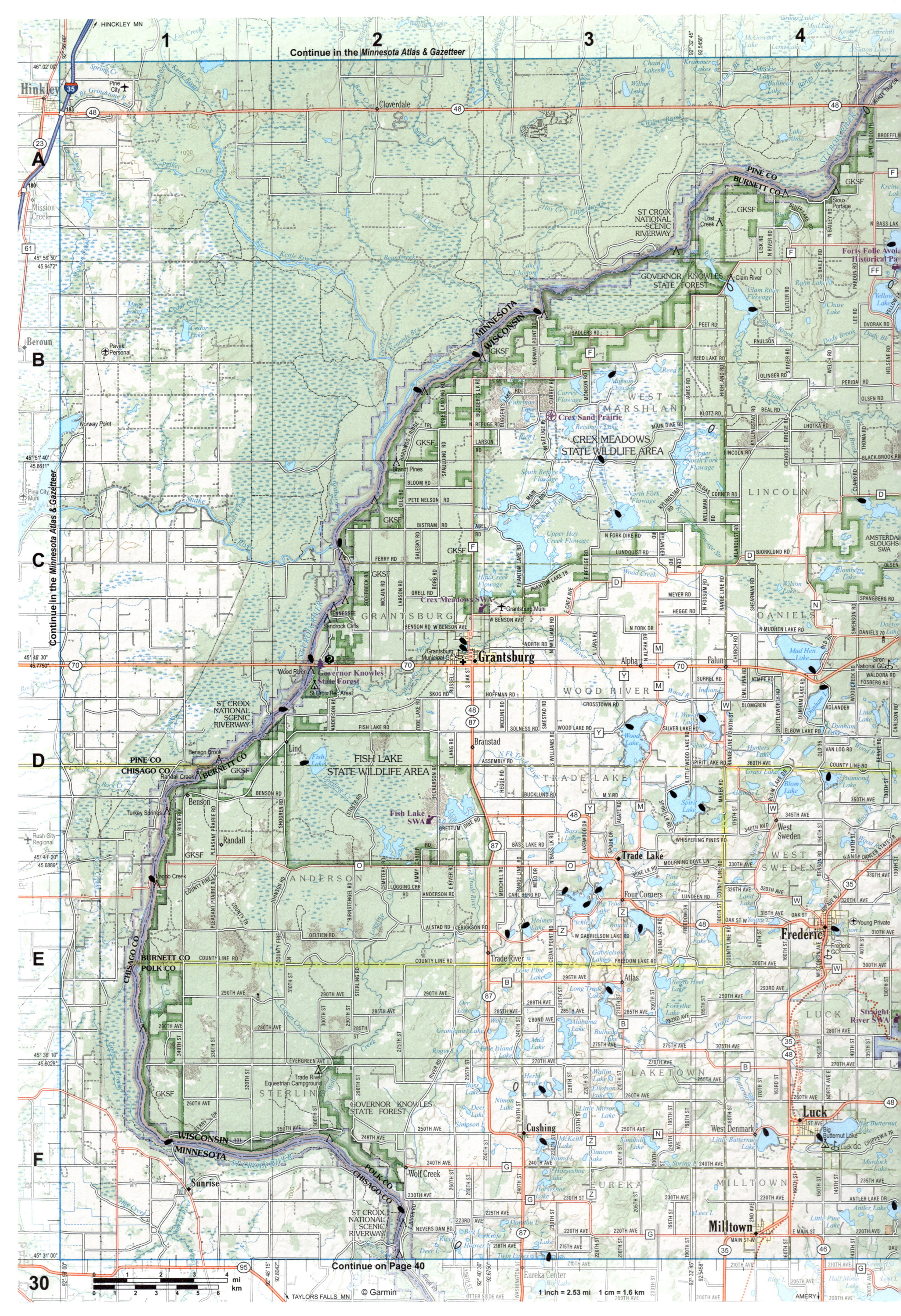

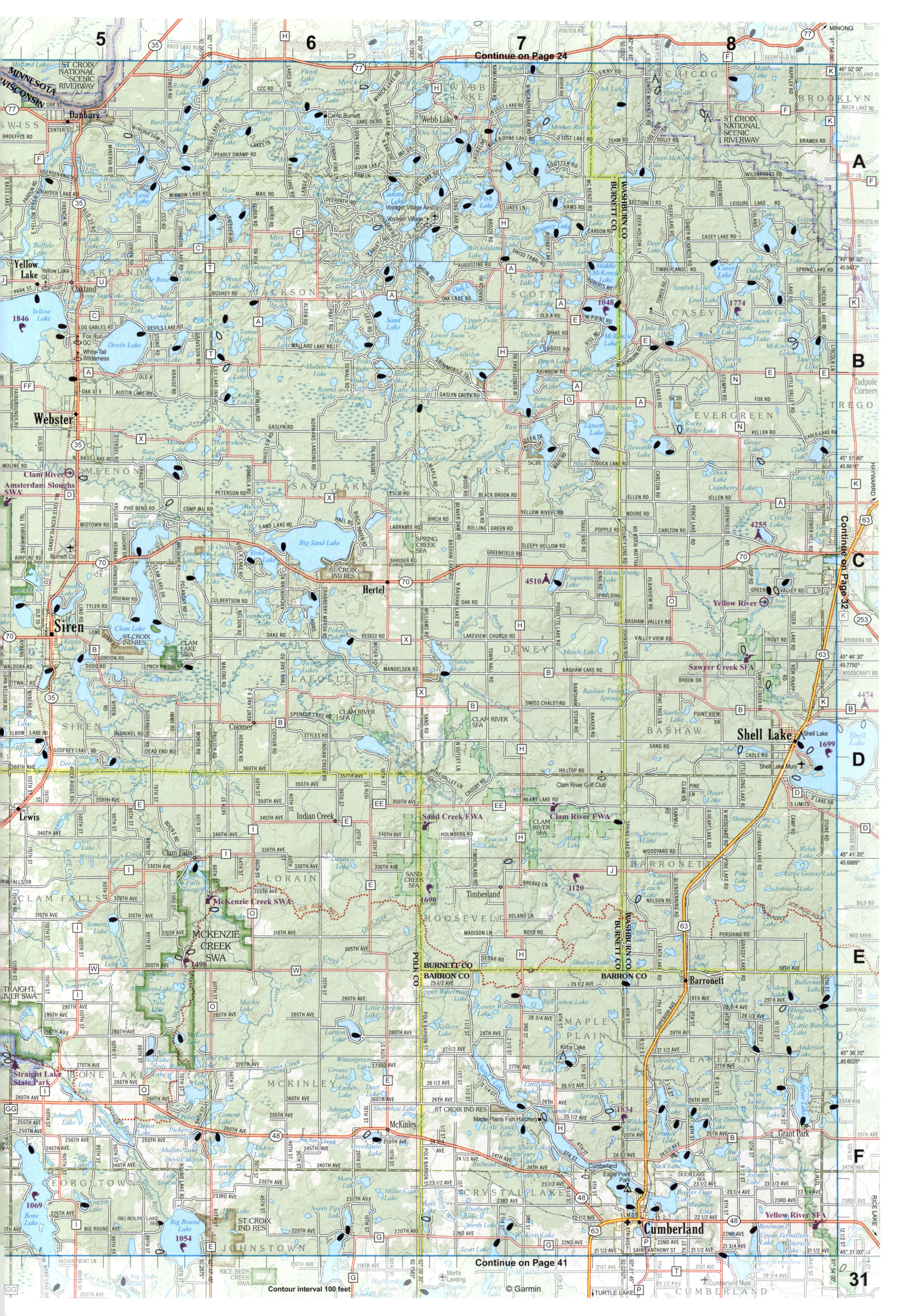

Continue on Page 24

Continue on Page 32

Continue on Page 41

Contour interval 100 feet

© Garmin

31

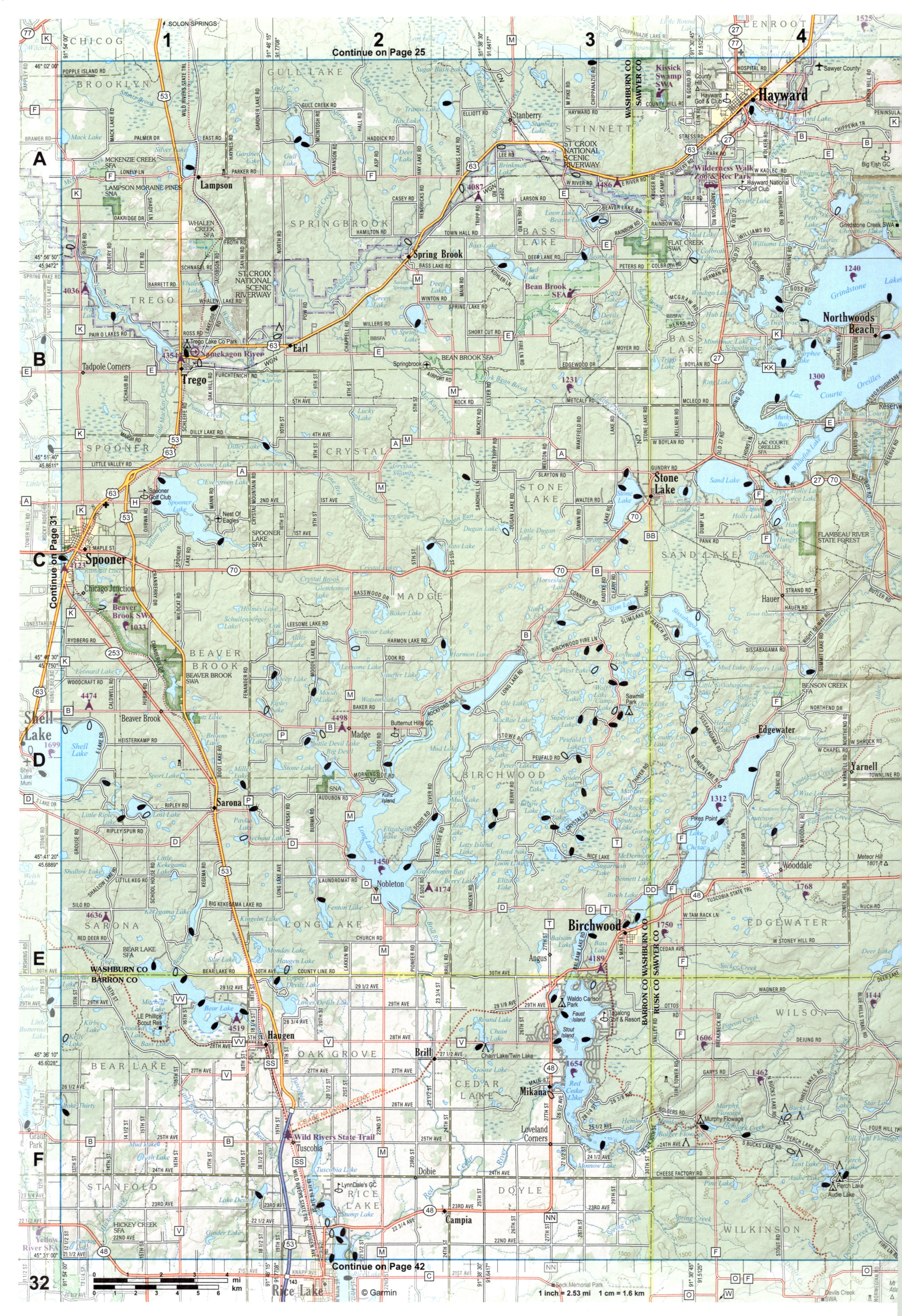

Continue on Page 25

Continue on Page 31

Continue on Page 42

32

1 inch = 2.53 mi 1 cm = 1.6 km

© Garmin

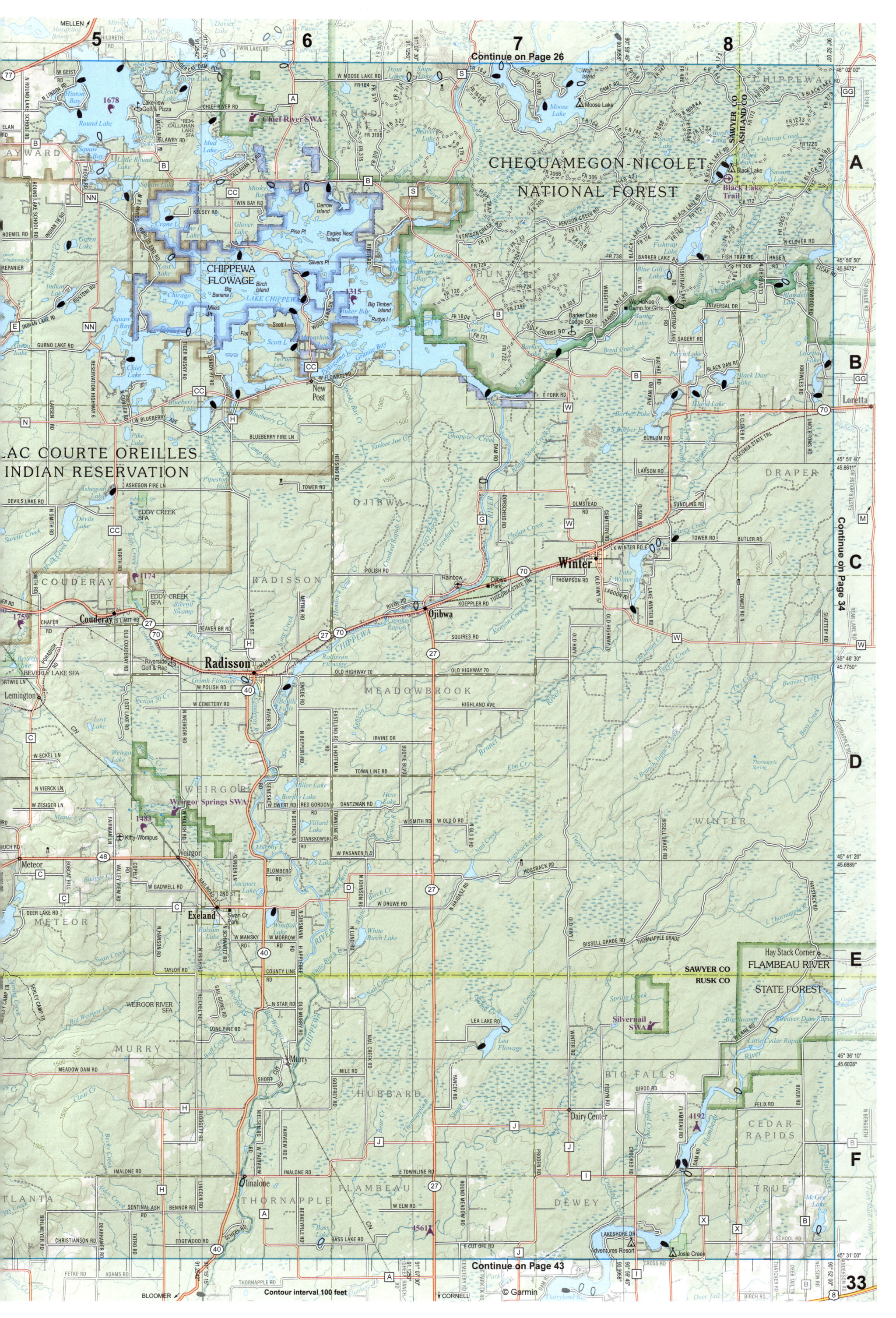

CHEQUAMEGON-NICOLET

NATIONAL FOREST

LAC COURTE OREILLES
INDIAN RESERVATION

CHIPPEWA
FLOWAGE

OJIBWA

RADISSON

COUDERAY

Couderay

Radisson

Ojibwa

Winter

MEADOWBROOK

WEIRGOR

Weirgor Springs SWA

Meteor

Weirgor

Exeland

METEOR

WINTER

DRAPER

Loretta

Continue on Page 34

SAWYER CO
RUSK CO

FLAMBEAU RIVER

Hay Stack Corner

STATE FOREST

Silvernail SWA

MURRY

Murry

HUBBARD

Dairy Center

Big Falls

CEDAR
RAPIDS

DEWEY

TRUE

Imalone

THORNAPPLE

FLAMBEAU

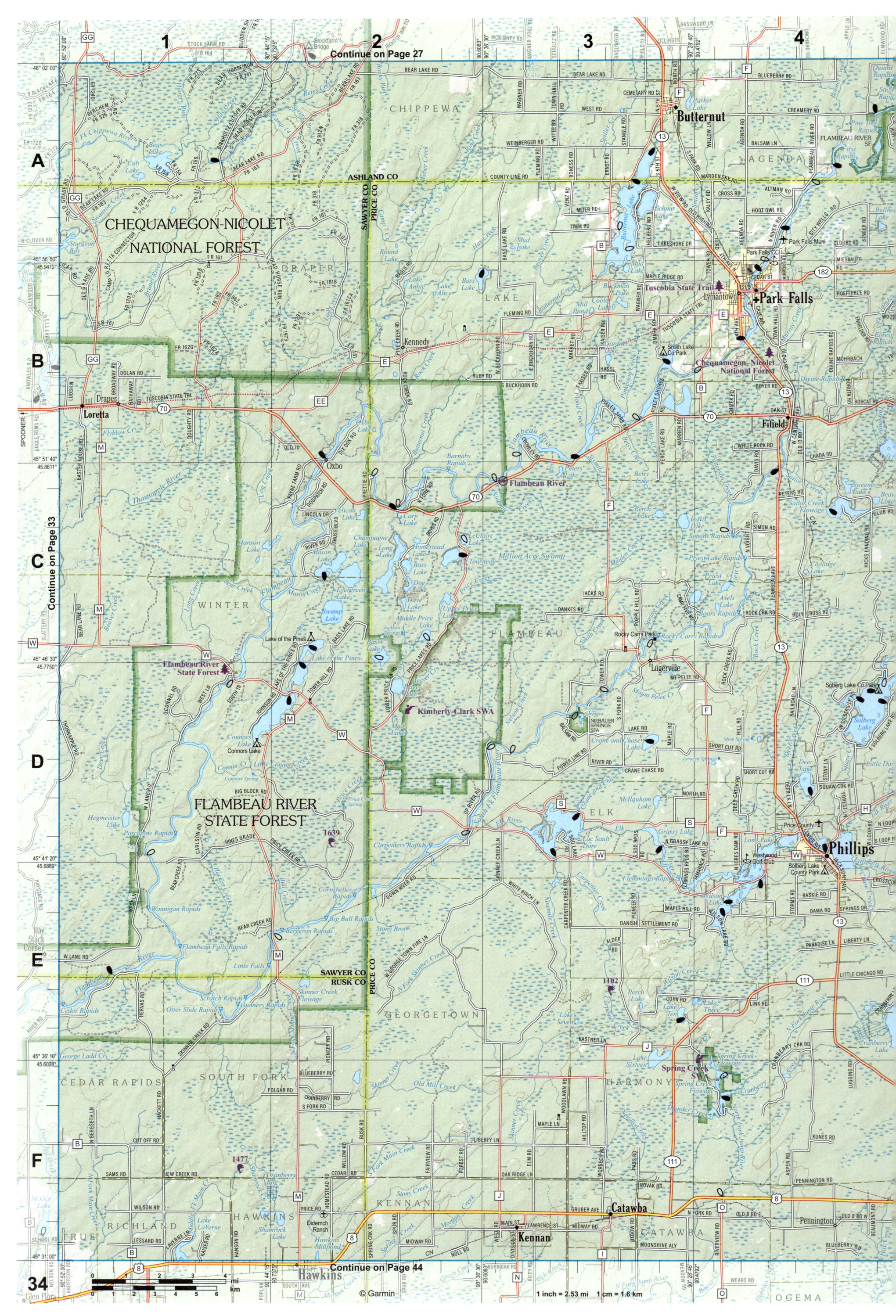

Continue on Page 27

Continue on Page 33

CHEQUAMEGON-NICOLET
NATIONAL FOREST

Butternut

Park Falls

Tuscobia State Trail

Chequamegon-Nicolet
National Forest

Fifield

Draper
Loretta

Oxbo

Flambeau River

WINTER

FLAMBEAU

Flambeau River
State Forest

Lake of the Pines

Kimberly-Clark SWA

FLAMBEAU RIVER
STATE FOREST

ELK

Lugerville

Phillips

Solberg Lake Co Park

SAWYER CO
RUSK CO

GEORGETOWN

Spring Creek

HARMONY

CEDAR RAPIDS

SOUTH FORK

HAWKINS

RICHLAND

KENNAN

CATAWBA

Catawba

Kennan

Continue on Page 44

34

© Garmin

1 inch = 2.53 mi   1 cm = 1.6 km

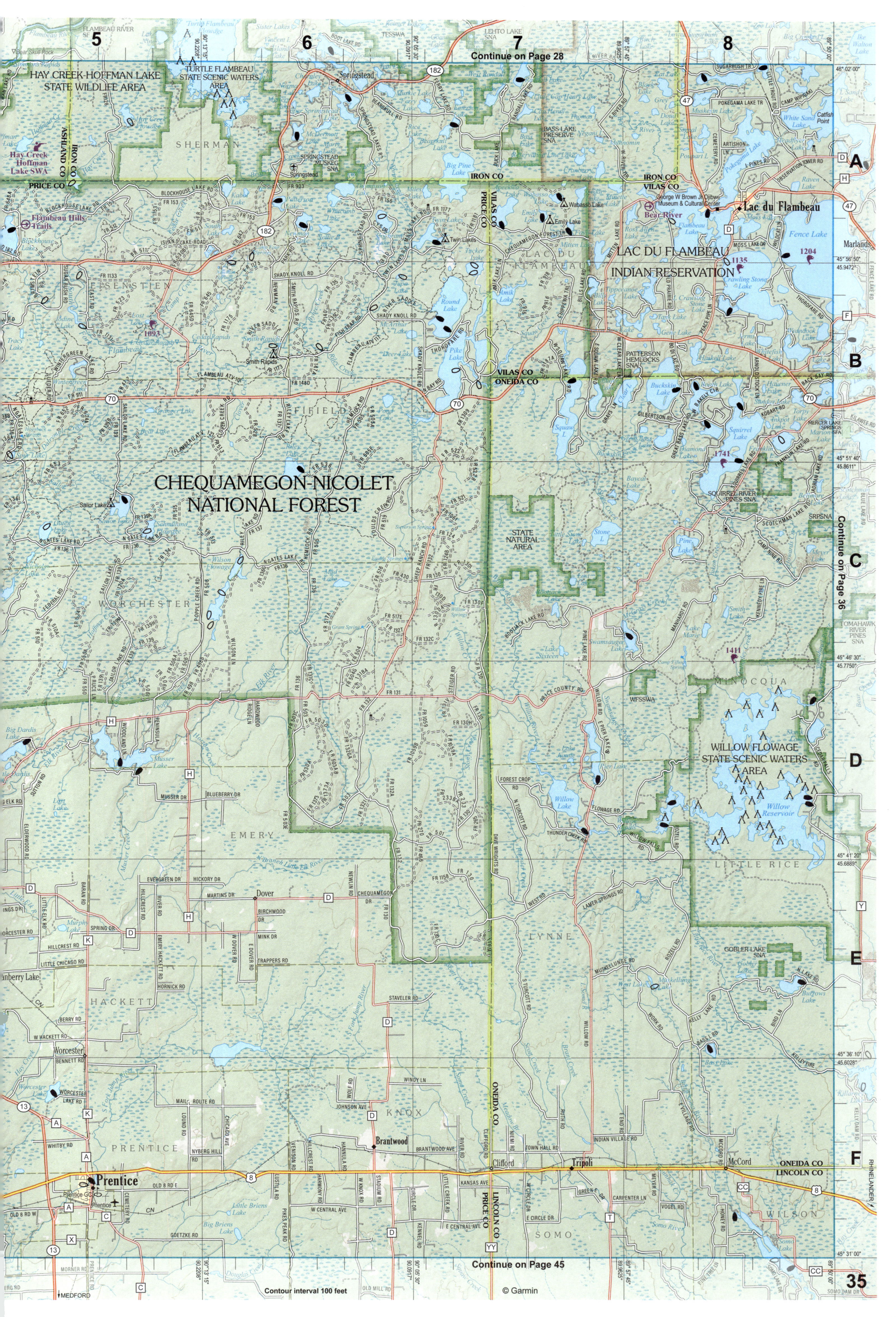

Continue on Page 28

CHEQUAMEGON-NICOLET
NATIONAL FOREST

HAY CREEK-HOFFMAN LAKE
STATE WILDLIFE AREA

TURTLE FLAMBEAU
STATE SCENIC WATERS
AREA

LAC DU FLAMBEAU
INDIAN RESERVATION

Lac du Flambeau

WILLOW FLOWAGE
STATE SCENIC WATERS
AREA

Continue on Page 36

Continue on Page 45

Contour interval 100 feet

© Garmin

35

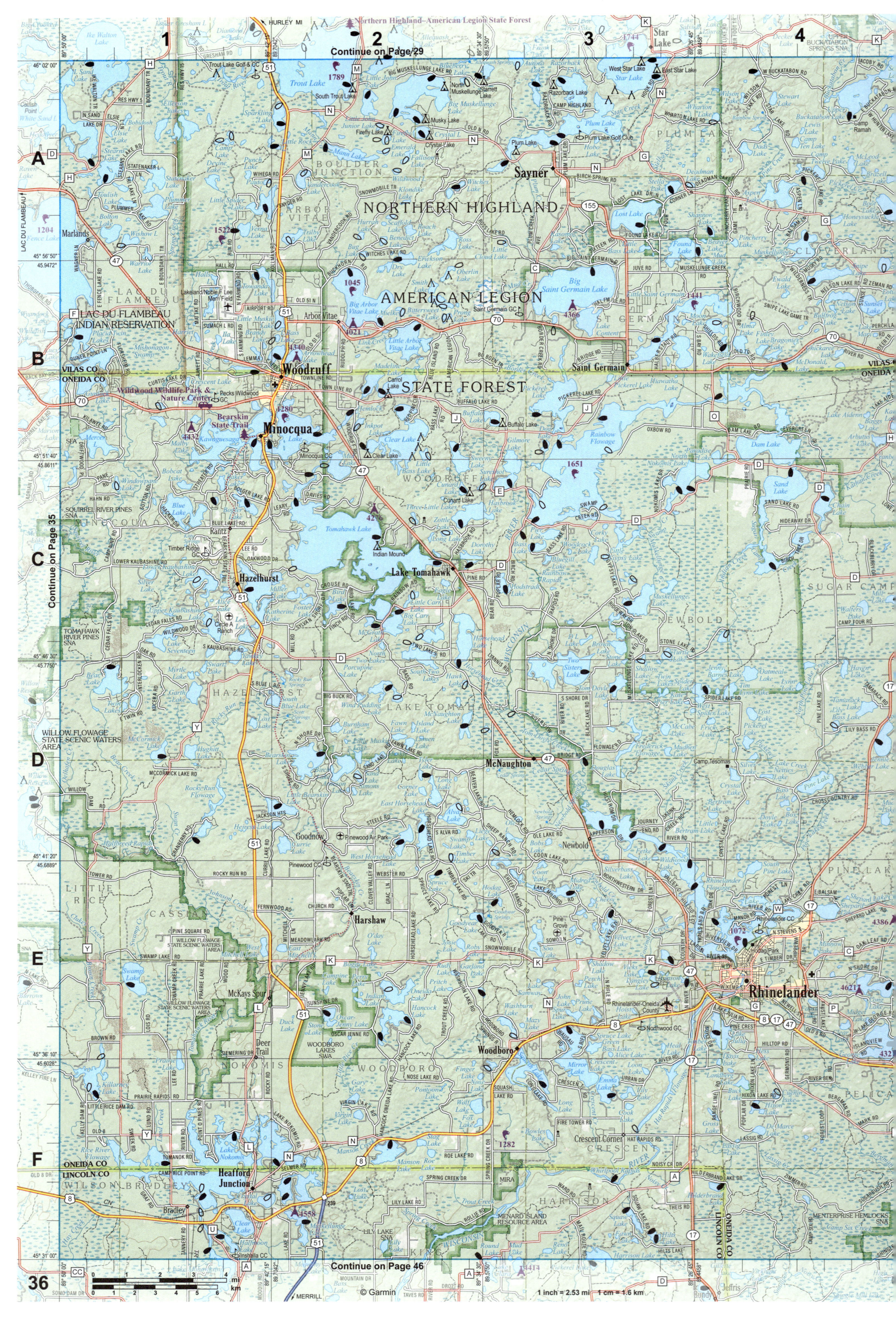

Continue on Page 35

© Garmin

1 inch = 2.53 mi   1 cm = 1.6 km

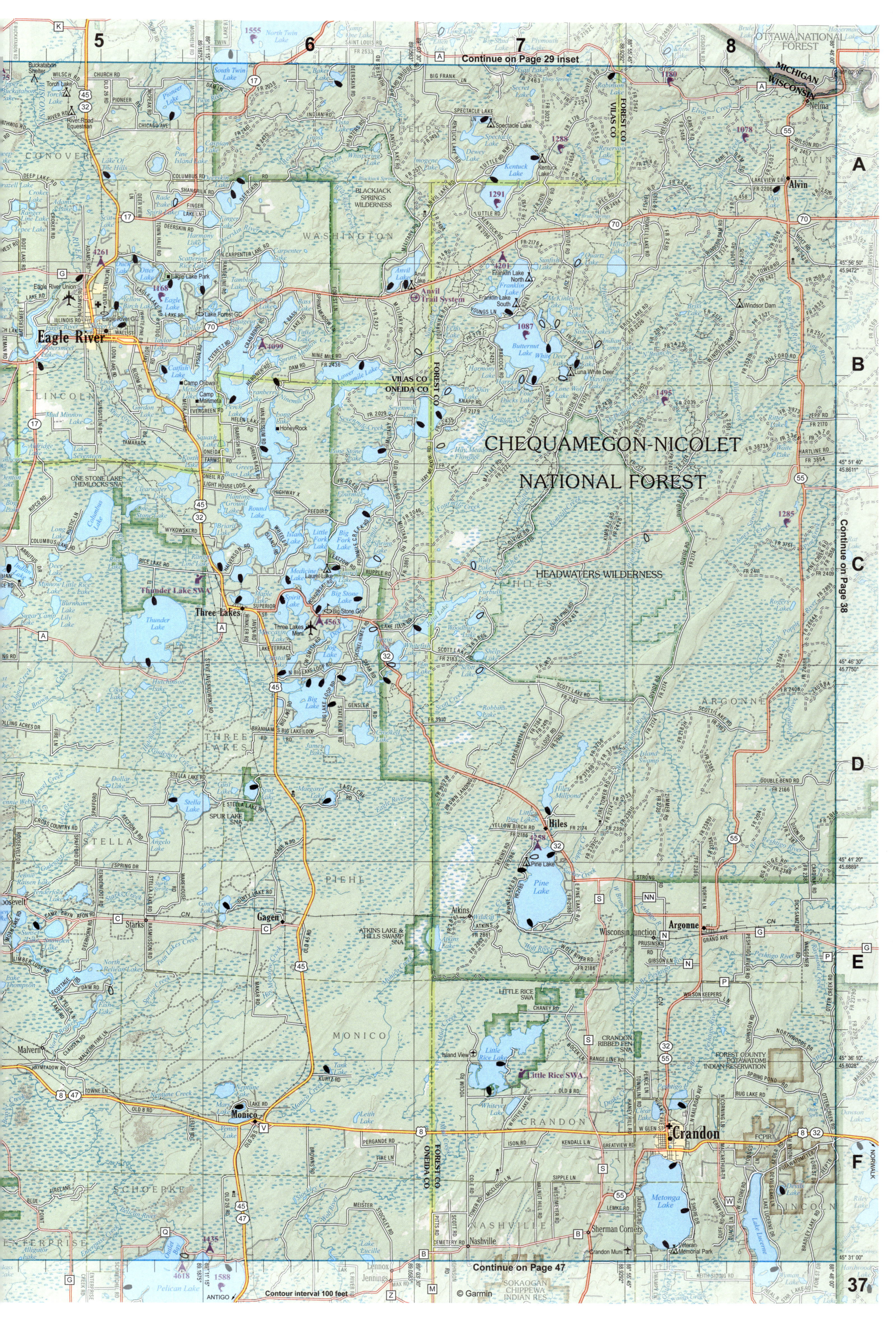

CHEQUAMEGON-NICOLET

NATIONAL FOREST

Continue on Page 38

Contour interval 100 feet

© Garmin

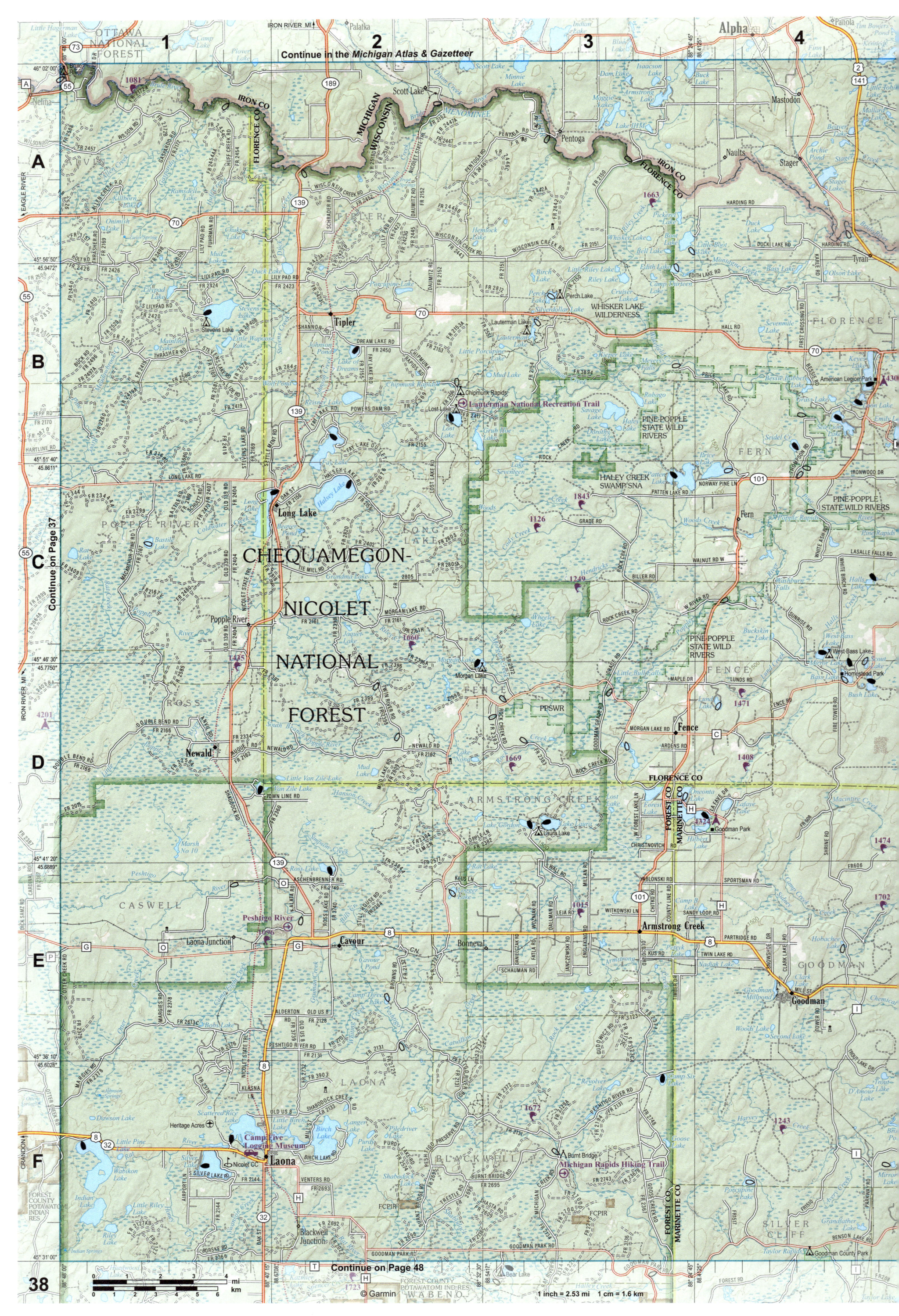

Continue in the *Michigan Atlas & Gazetteer*

Continue on Page 37

Alpha

OTTAWA NATIONAL FOREST

IRON CO

MICHIGAN / WISCONSIN

Pentoga

Naults

Stager

FLORENCE CO

WHISKER LAKE WILDERNESS

Tipler

Lauterman National Recreation Trail

Chipmunk Rapids

PINE-POPPLE STATE WILD RIVERS

FLORENCE

FERN

HALEY CREEK SWAMP SNA

Long Lake

CHEQUAMEGON-

NICOLET

NATIONAL

FOREST

Popple River

Fern

PINE-POPPLE STATE WILD RIVERS

West Bass Lake

Homestead Park

FENCE

Morgan Lake

PPSWR

Fence

Newald

FLORENCE CO

ROSS

Goodman Park

MARINETTE CO

FLORENCE CO

Laura Lake

Armstrong Creek

CASWELL

Peshtigo River

Laona Junction   Cavour   Bonneval   Armstrong Creek   GOODMAN

Goodman

LAONA

Heritage Acres

Camp Five Logging Museum

Nicolet CC   Laona

BLACKWELL

Burnt Bridge

Michigan Rapids Hiking Trail

Blackwell Junction

FOREST COUNTY POTAWATOMI INDIAN RES

SILVER CLIFF

Goodman County Park

WABENO

FOREST CO

MARINETTE CO

FCPIR

Continue on Page 48

© Garmin

1 inch = 2.53 mi   1 cm = 1.6 km

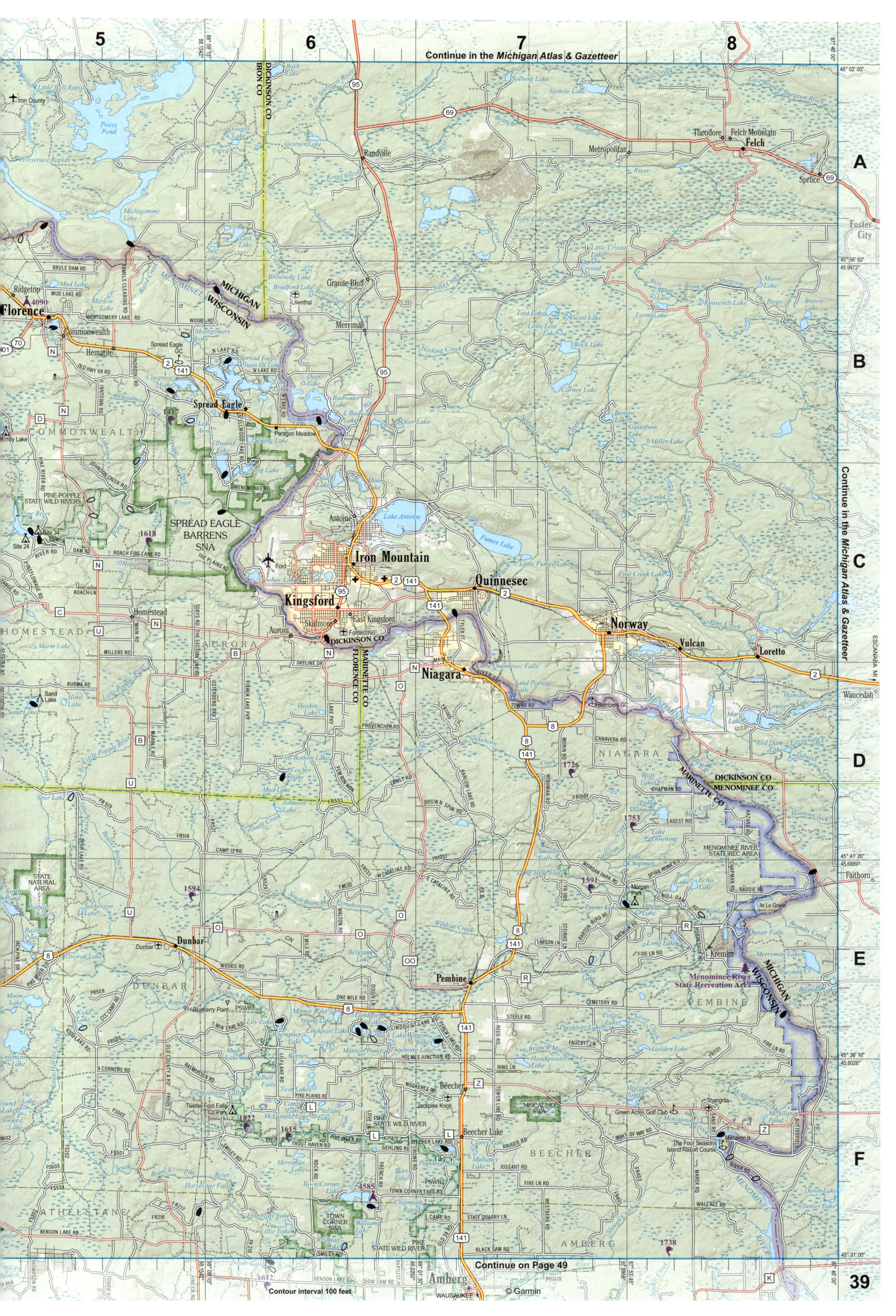

Continue on Page 49

Contour interval 100 feet

© Garmin

39

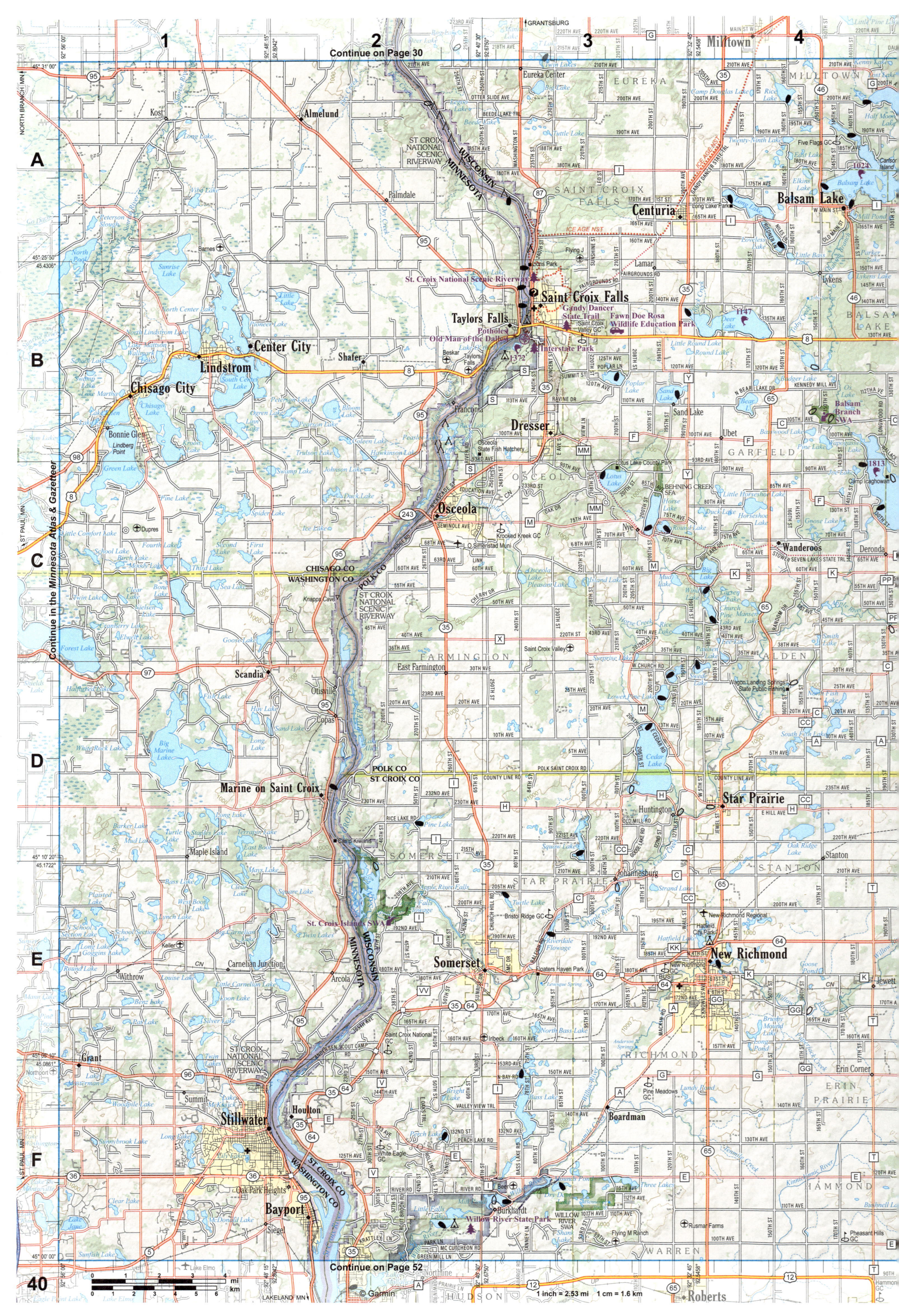

Continue in the *Minnesota Atlas & Gazetteer*

1 inch = 2.53 mi
1 cm = 1.6 km

© Garmin

Continue on Page 42

Contour interval 100 feet

© Garmin

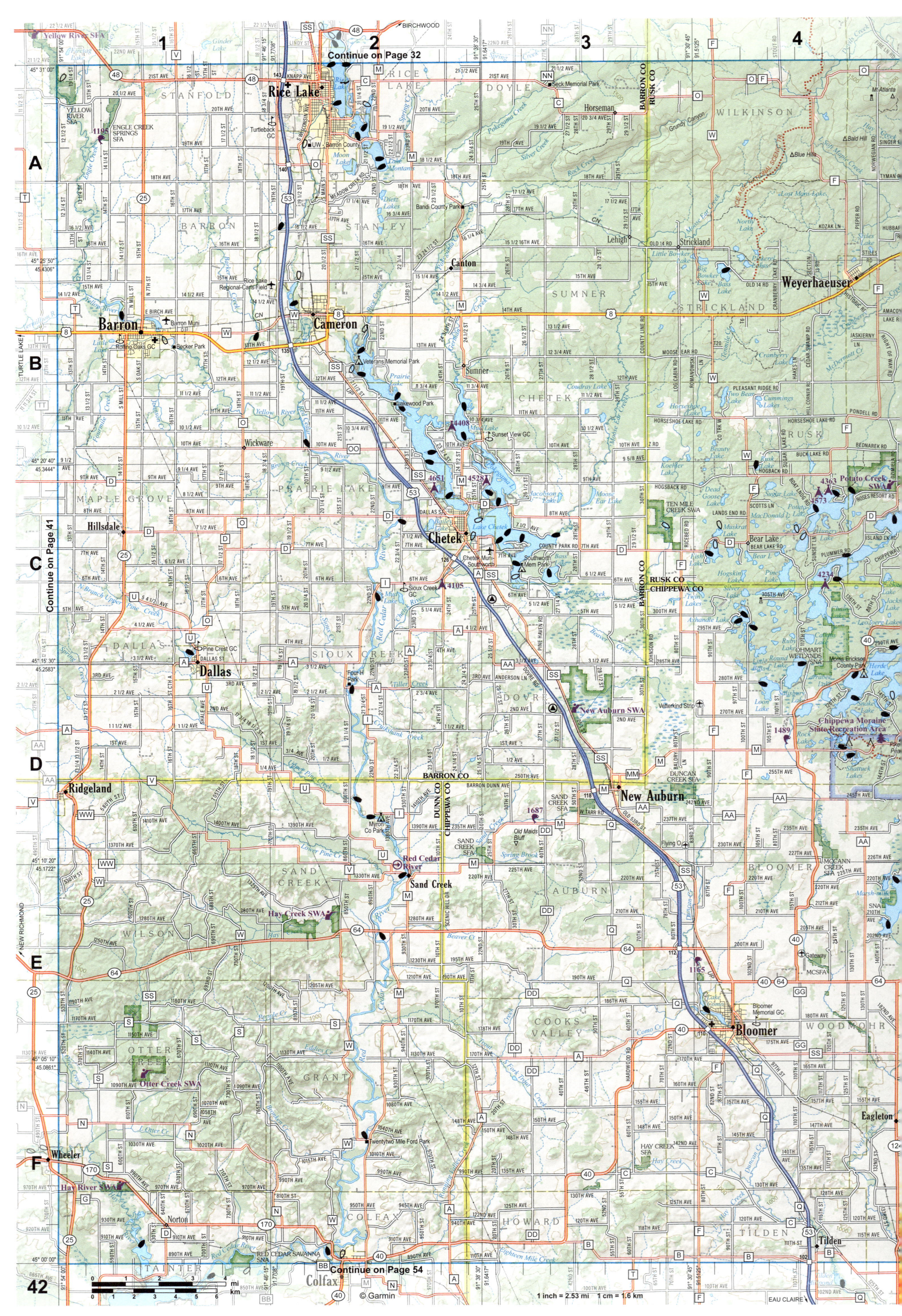

Continue on Page 41

© Garmin

1 inch = 2.53 mi   1 cm = 1.6 km

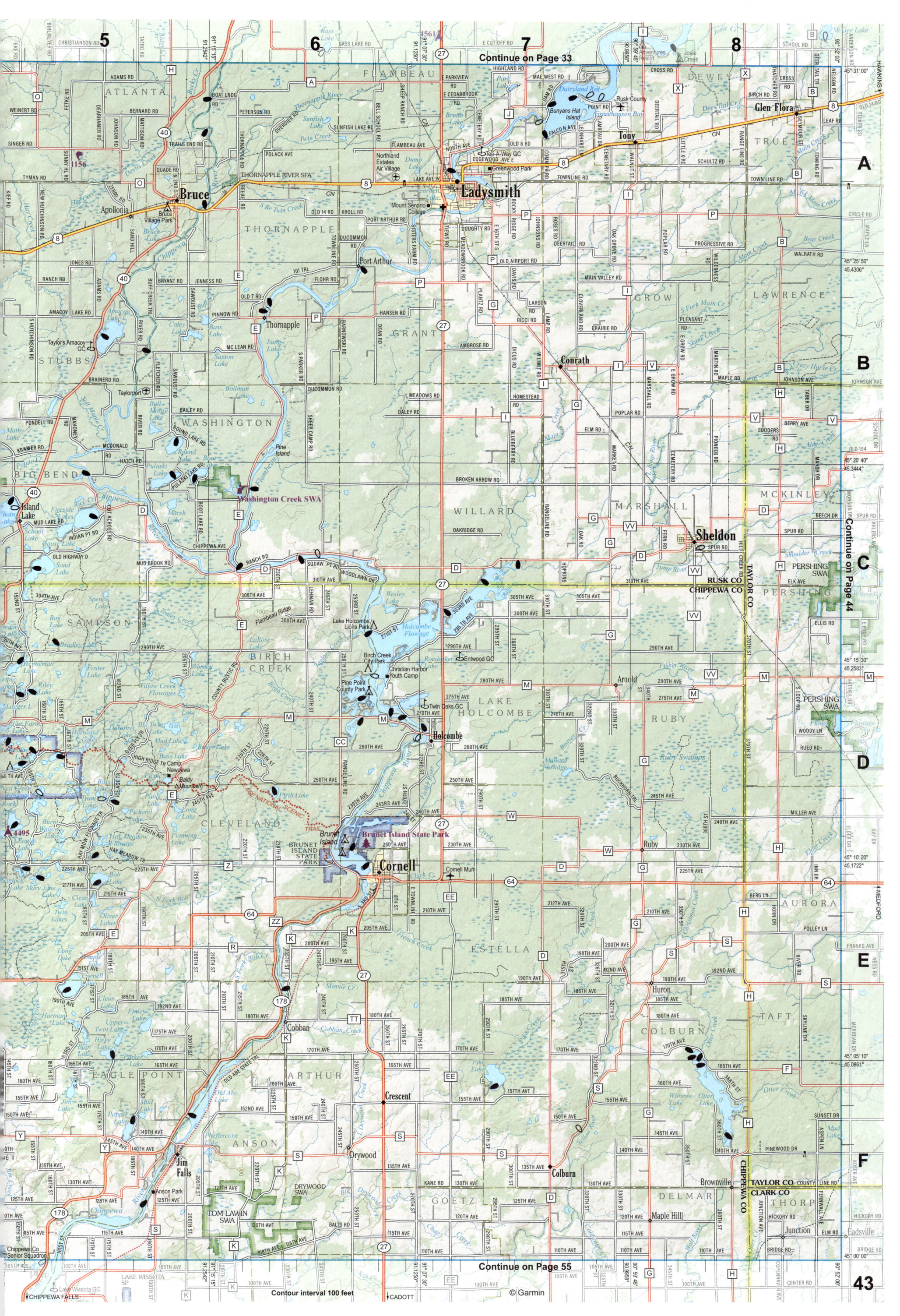

Continue on Page 33

Continue on Page 44

Continue on Page 55

Contour interval 100 feet

© Garmin

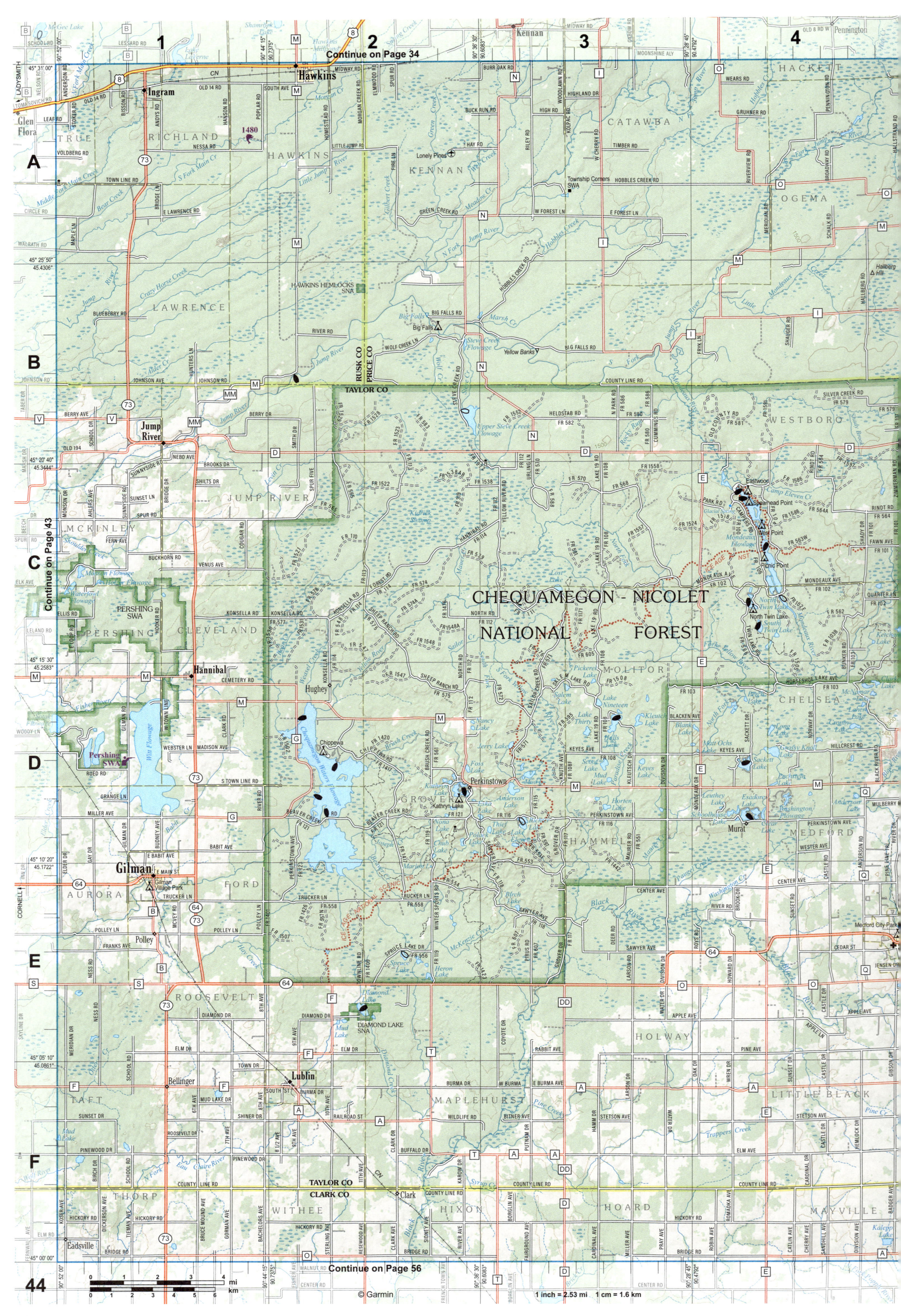

Continue on Page 34

Continue on Page 43

CHEQUAMEGON - NICOLET

NATIONAL   FOREST

Continue on Page 56

44

© Garmin

1 inch = 2.53 mi   1 cm = 1.6 km

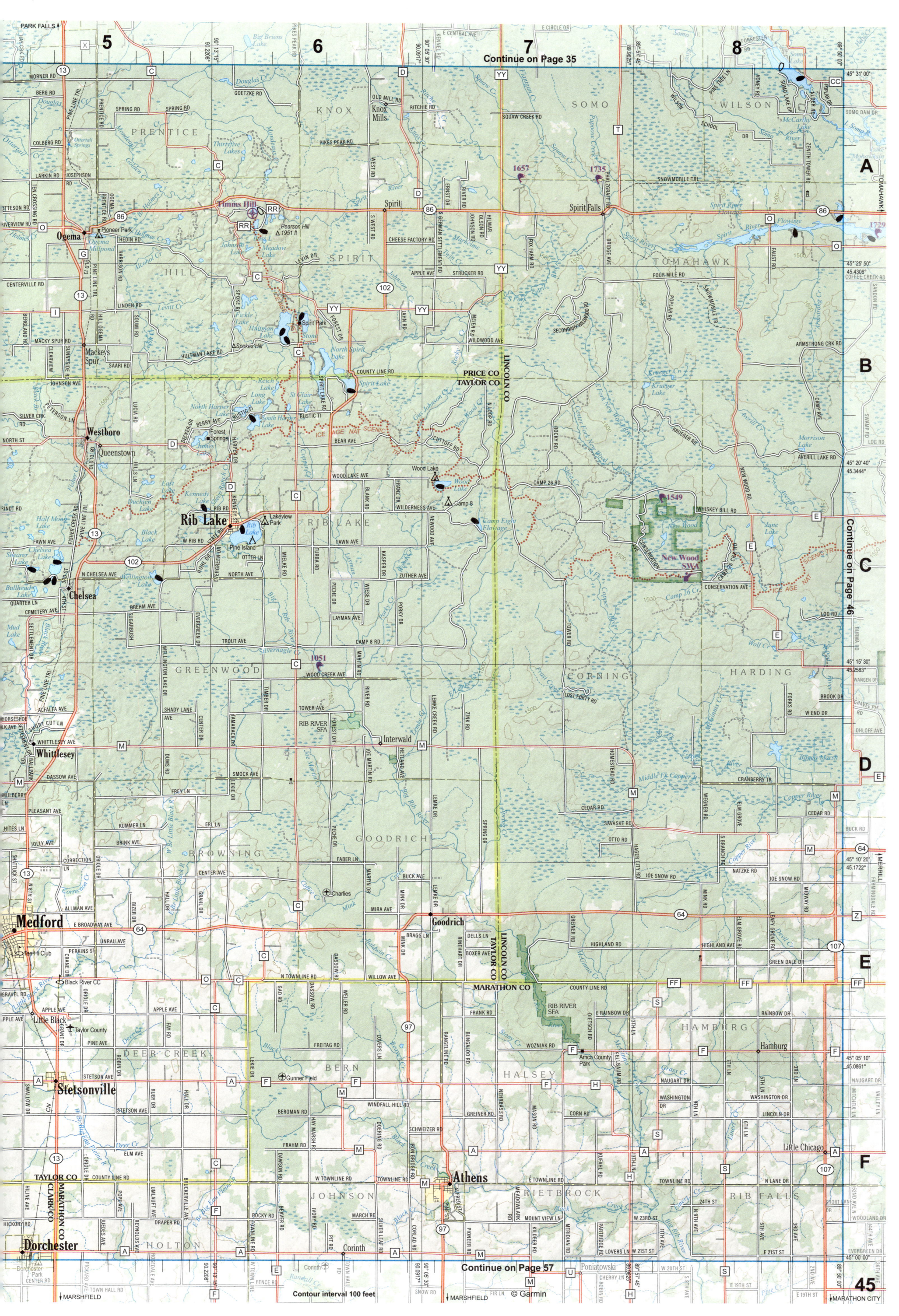

Continue on Page 46

Contour interval 100 feet

© Garmin

45

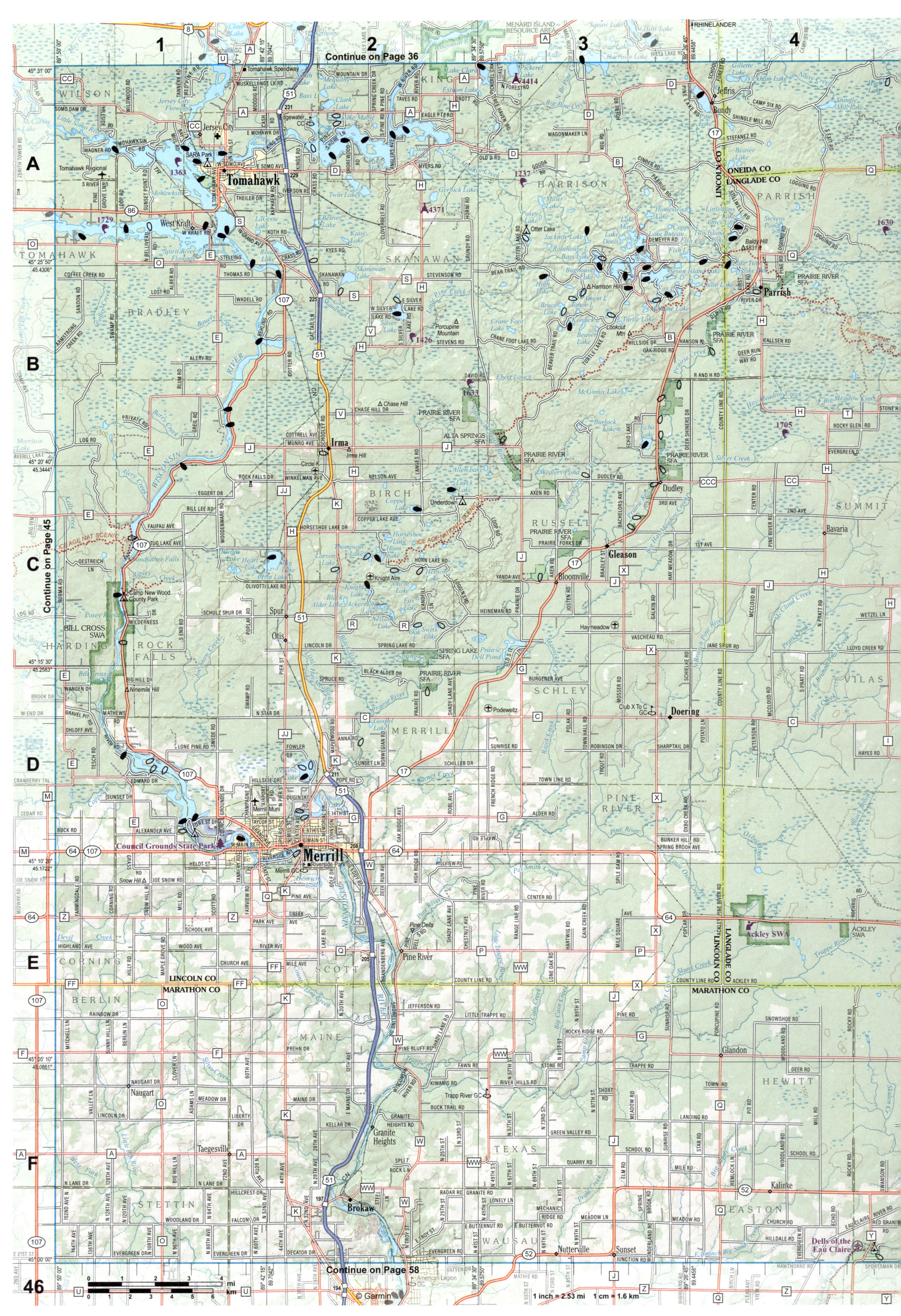

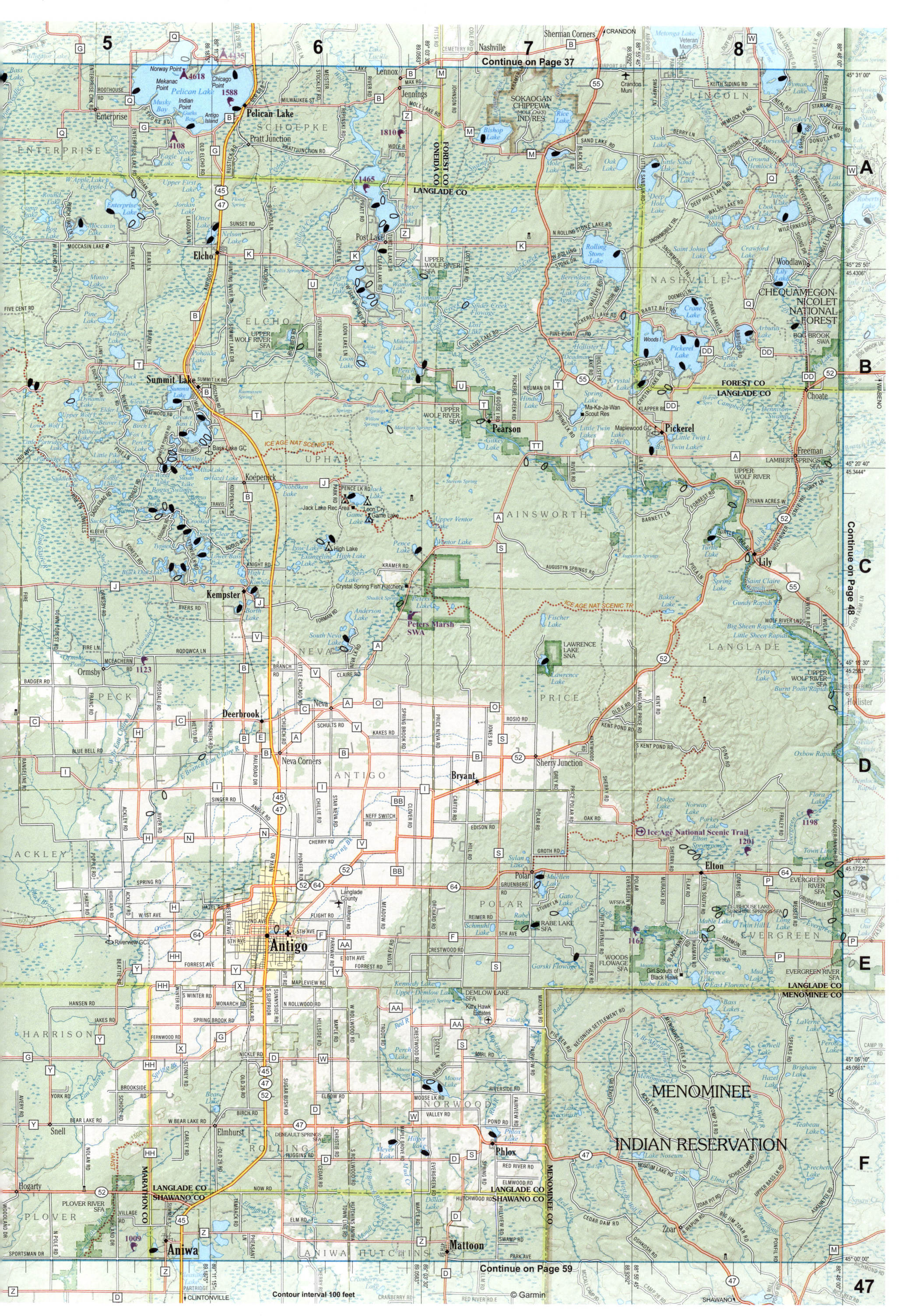

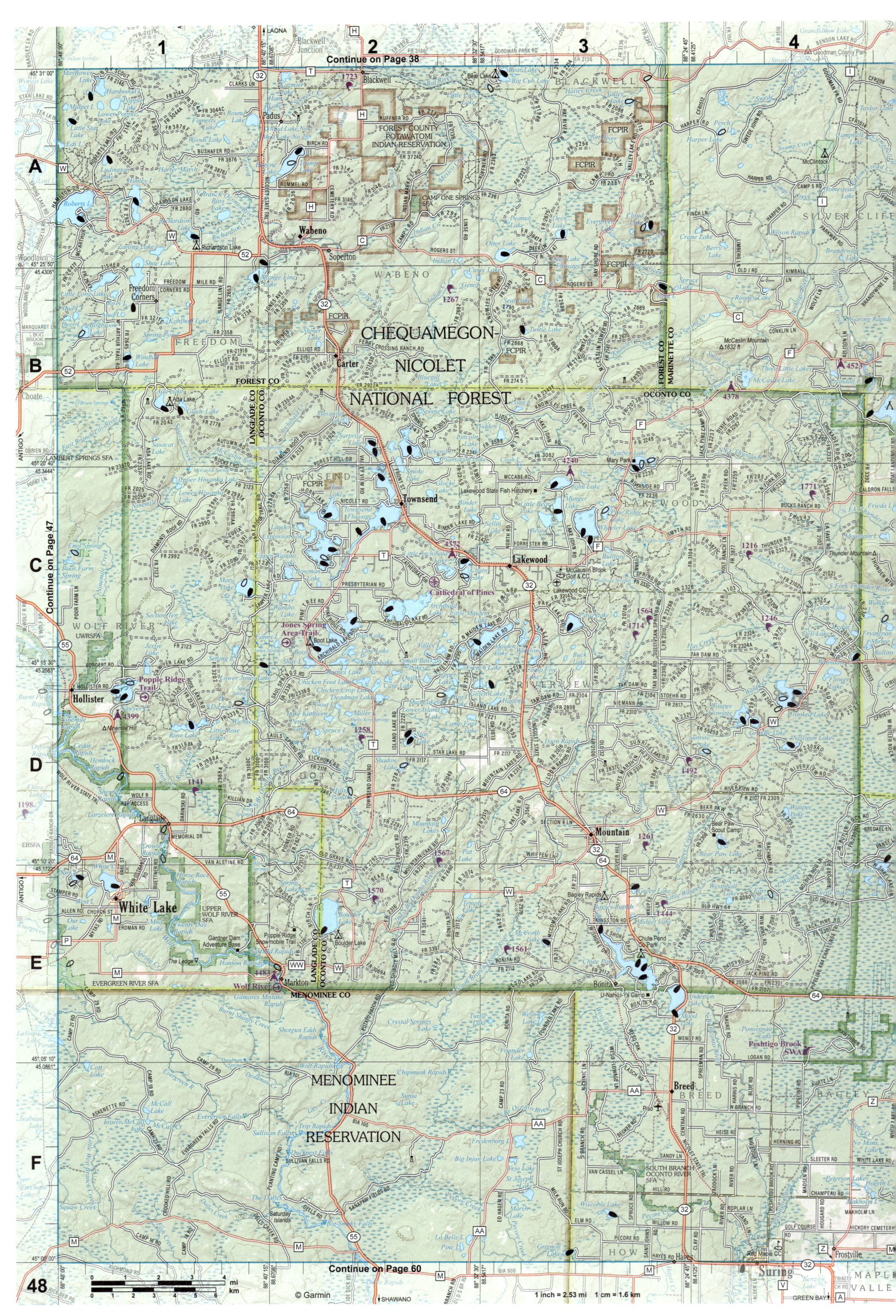

Continue on Page 38

Continue on Page 47

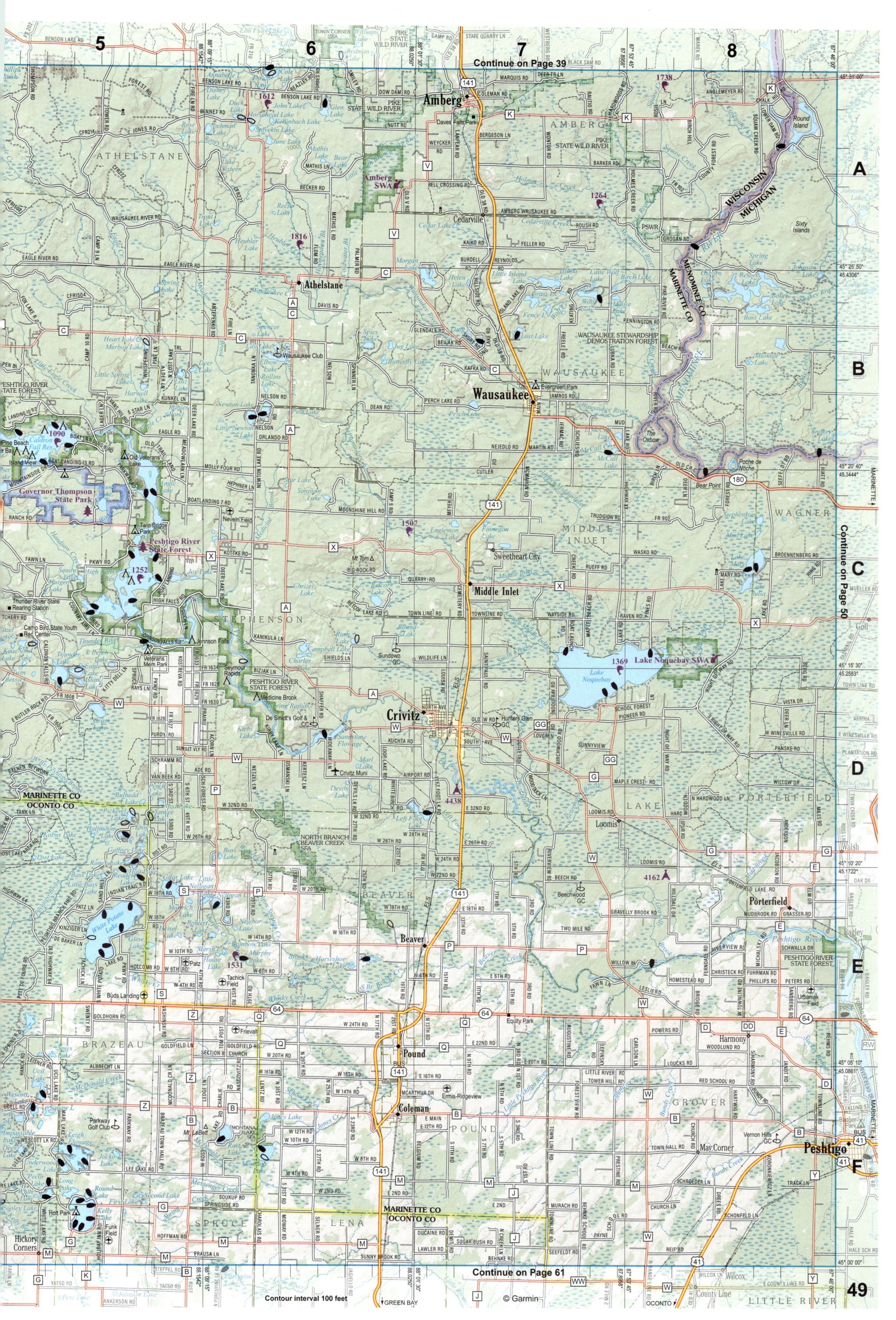

Continue on Page 39

Continue on Page 50

Continue on Page 61

Contour interval 100 feet   © Garmin

49

GREEN BAY NWR

St Martin Island

Gravelly Island Shoals

45° 31' 00"

A

MICHIGAN
WISCONSIN

MENOMINEE CO
DELTA CO
DOOR CO

45° 25' 50"
45.4306°

Saint Martin Island +Shoals

ROCK ISLAND PASSAGE

Boyer Bluff

Washington Harbor

Little Lake Rd

COFFEY SWAMP SNA

Jacobsen Museum

McDONALD RD

Washington

Rock Island State Park
Rock Island

JACKSON HARBOR RIDGES SNA
Jackson Harbor

SWENSON RD

JACKSON HARBOR RD

GUNNLAUGSSON RD

Fish Island

W

MAIN RD

W

Washington Island

W HARBOR RD

W HARBOR RD

AIRPORT RD

DEER LINE RD

RANGE LINE RD

WASHINGTON ISLAND

West Harbor

Deer Run

BIG & LITTLE MARSH SNA

+Fisherman Shoal

B

Figenscaus Harbor

MICHIGAN RD

LAKE VIEW RD

Detroit Harbor

▲4609

Detroit Harbor

W

Washington Island

Lobdells Point

W

AZNOE RD

SIDE RD

South Point

GRAND TRAVERSE ISLAND SP

BAY

Detroit Island Passage

Porte des Morts Passage (Death Door Passage)

GREEN BAY NWR
Plum Island

FERRY

Detroit Island

C

Deathdoor Bluff

Door Bluff Park

DOOR BLUFF RD

Table Bluff

Hedgehog Harbor

Wisconsin Bay

Garret Bay

Gills Rock

Northport

Waverly Shoal

+Nine Foot Shoal

Pilot Island

Ellison Bluff

Ellison Bluff Park

Ellison Bay

Ellison Bay

E WISCONSIN BAY RD

BLACKBERRY RD

ISLE VIEW RD

Europe Lake

42

EUROPE LAKE RD

EUROPE BAY RD

Europe Bay

Gravel Island
GRAVEL ISLAND NWR

PORCUPINE BAY RD

HIGH RD

BADGER RD

MINK RIVER RD

NP

FERDINAND HOTZ RD

Ferdinand Hotz Park

Europe Bay Hotz Loop

Newport State Park
Newport Bay

Newport Conifer Hardwoods

+Horseshoe Reefs

Sister Islands

SEAQUIST

GREEN RD

LAKEVIEW RD

HIGHVIEW RD

MINK RIVER RD

LIBERTY GROVE

1354

BEACH RD

42

HILL RD

ZZ

4606

Rowley Bay

Rowleys Bay

Sand Bay Park

Gravel Island
GRAVEL ISLAND NWR

Spider Island
GRAVEL ISLAND NWR

D

LAKE MICHIGAN

+Sister Shoals

Sister Bay

Sister Bluffs

Bay Ridge

WATERS END RD

OLD STATE RD

HILL RD

SCANDIA RD

APPLEPORT RD

N SHORE RD

S BAYSHORE RD

Sister Bay

PLATEAU RD

ZZ

ORCHARD RD

WOODCREST RD

KINSEY BAY LN

N BAY RD

45° 10' 20"
45.1722°

Welcker's Point
Eagle Bluff

Horseshoe Island

North Nicolet Bay
South Nicolet Bay

PENINSULA STATE PARK

Shanty Bay

57

Eagle Harbor

Ephraim

Peninsula PGC

SETTLEMENT RD

CHURCH RD

TOWNLINE RD

GERMAN RD

Q

4018

Q

+Four Foot Shoal

North Bay

MIDDLE RD

Peninsula State Park

Sunset Trail

Ephraim-Fish Creek

42

Tennison Bay

Eagle Tower
Nicolet Bay

GIBRALTAR RD

PIONEER RD

LIME KILN RD

GROVE RD

E MEADOW RD

N BAY RD

E

Fish Creek

F

MAPLE GROVE/EAST RD

W MEADOW RD

PINE RD

Mud Lake

E

GIBRALTAR

F

Baileys Harbor

BAILEYS HARBOR BOREAL FOREST SNA

Q

SPRING RD

CEDAR RD

Mud Lake SWA

PENINSULA PLAYERS RD

F

Moonlight Bay

Cana Island

JUDDVILLE RD

HIGHLAND RD

TRIANGLE RD

57

WANDERING LN

THORP POND SNA

QUARTERLINE RD

4039

Ridges Sanctuary

45° 05' 10"
45.0861°

BAILEYS HARBOR

EE

MARSH RD

PLATEAU RD

HIGH RD

OLD GRAMM RD

EE

Peninsula Center

Baileys Harbor

E

SCHOOL RD

MAPLE TREE RD

WOODED LN

BLUFF RD

SUMMIT RD

S MAPLE RD

Baileys Harbor

F

BEACH RD

FAIRVIEW RD

CHERRY RD

Maxwelton Braes Golf Club

HILLSIDE RD

HONOLD RD

ELM RD

FLINT RD

MEMORIAL DR

LOGERQUIST RD

Kangaroo Lake

IST-PL

T

JACKSONPORT

57

V

SHANTY SLOPE RD

Contour interval 100 feet

© Garmin

87° 20' 00"
87° 20' 48"

45° 00' 00"

87° 00' 00"

44° 51' 45"
86.8625°

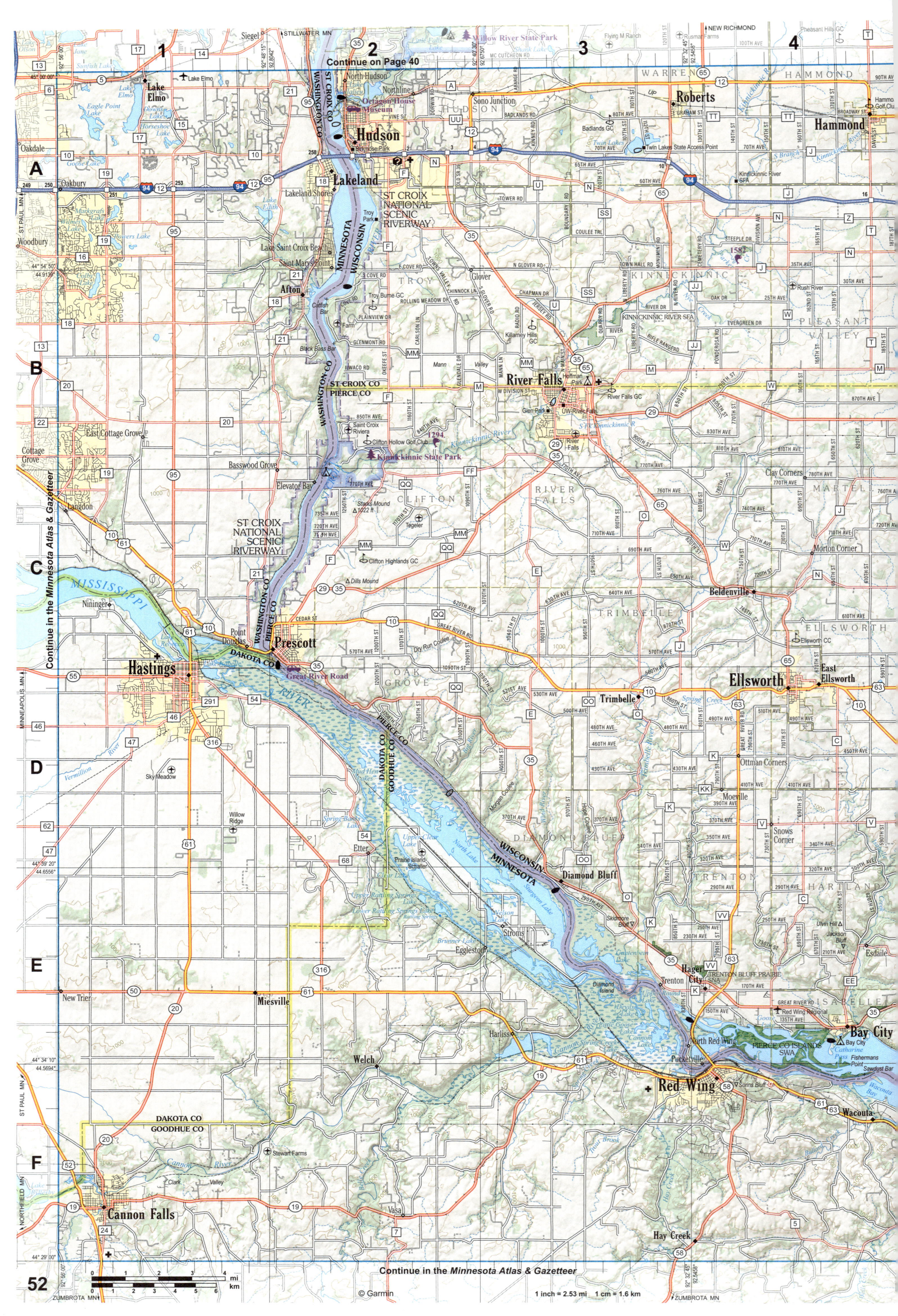

Continue on Page 54

Contour interval 100 feet

© Garmin

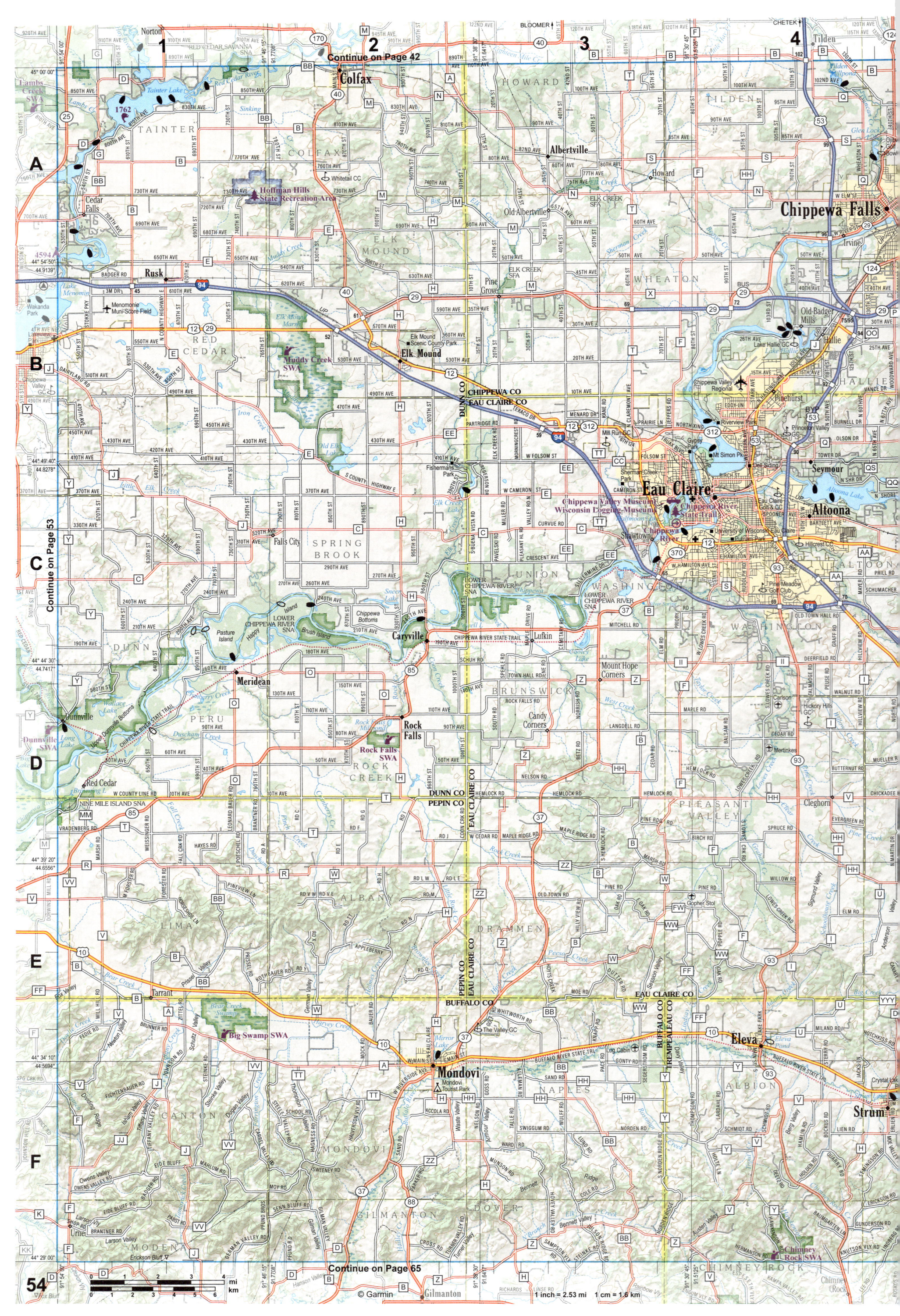

Continue on Page 42

Continue on Page 53

Chippewa Falls

Eau Claire

Altoona

Colfax

Albertville

Howard

Elk Mound

Mondovi

Eleva

Strum

Continue on Page 65

© Garmin

1 inch = 2.53 mi   1 cm = 1.6 km

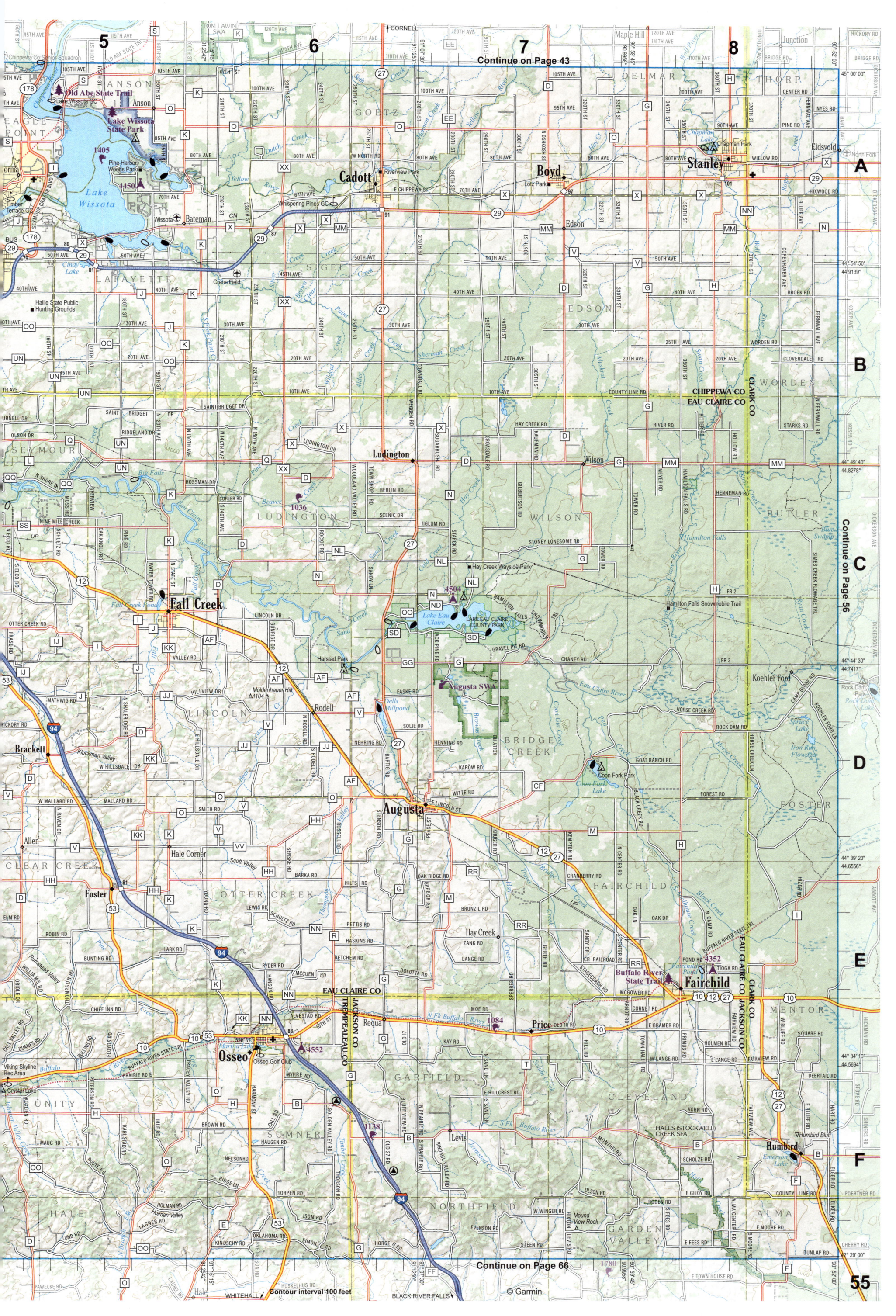

Continue on Page 56

Contour interval 100 feet

© Garmin

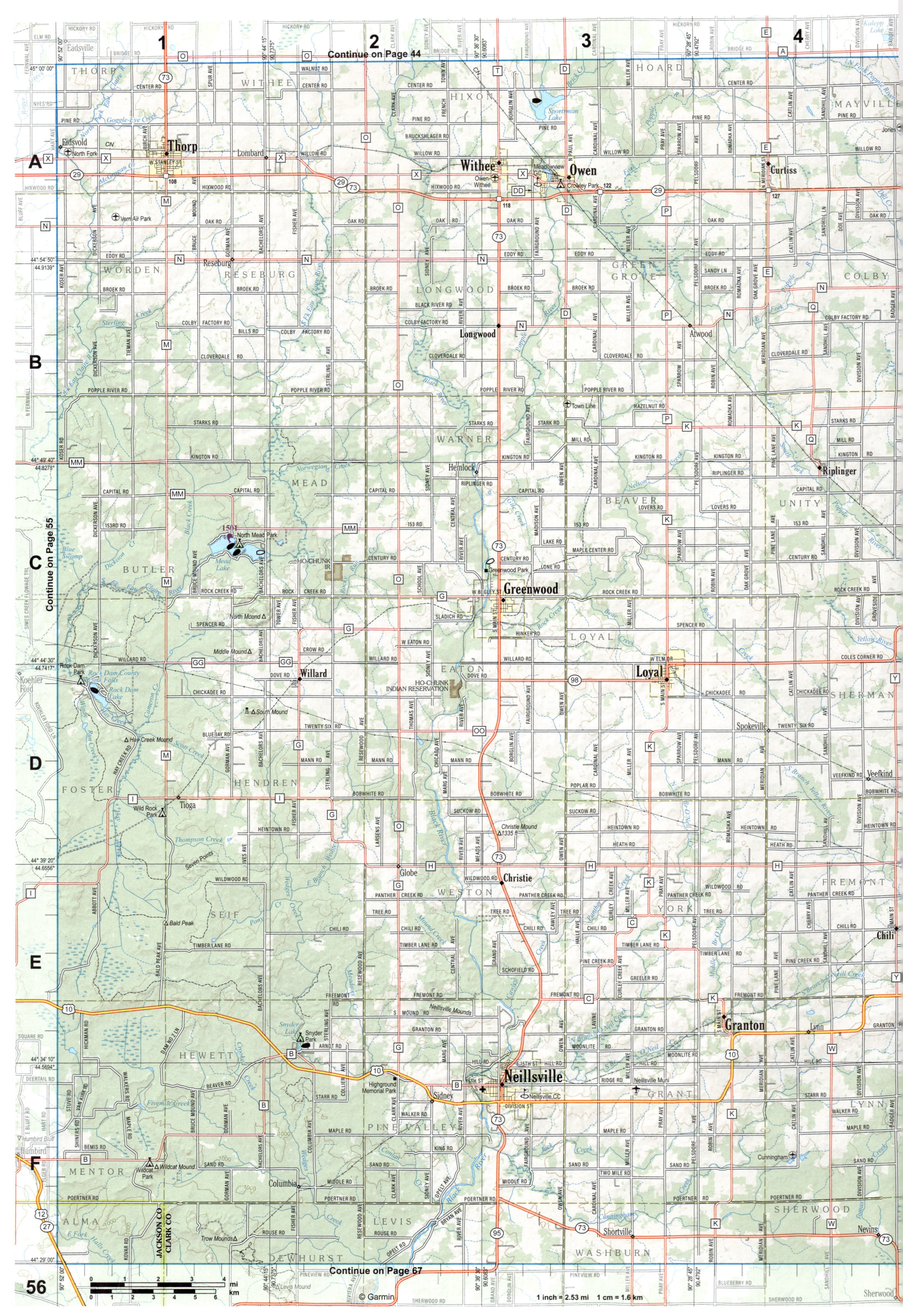

Continue on Page 44

Continue on Page 55

Continue on Page 67

1 inch = 2.53 mi   1 cm = 1.6 km

© Garmin

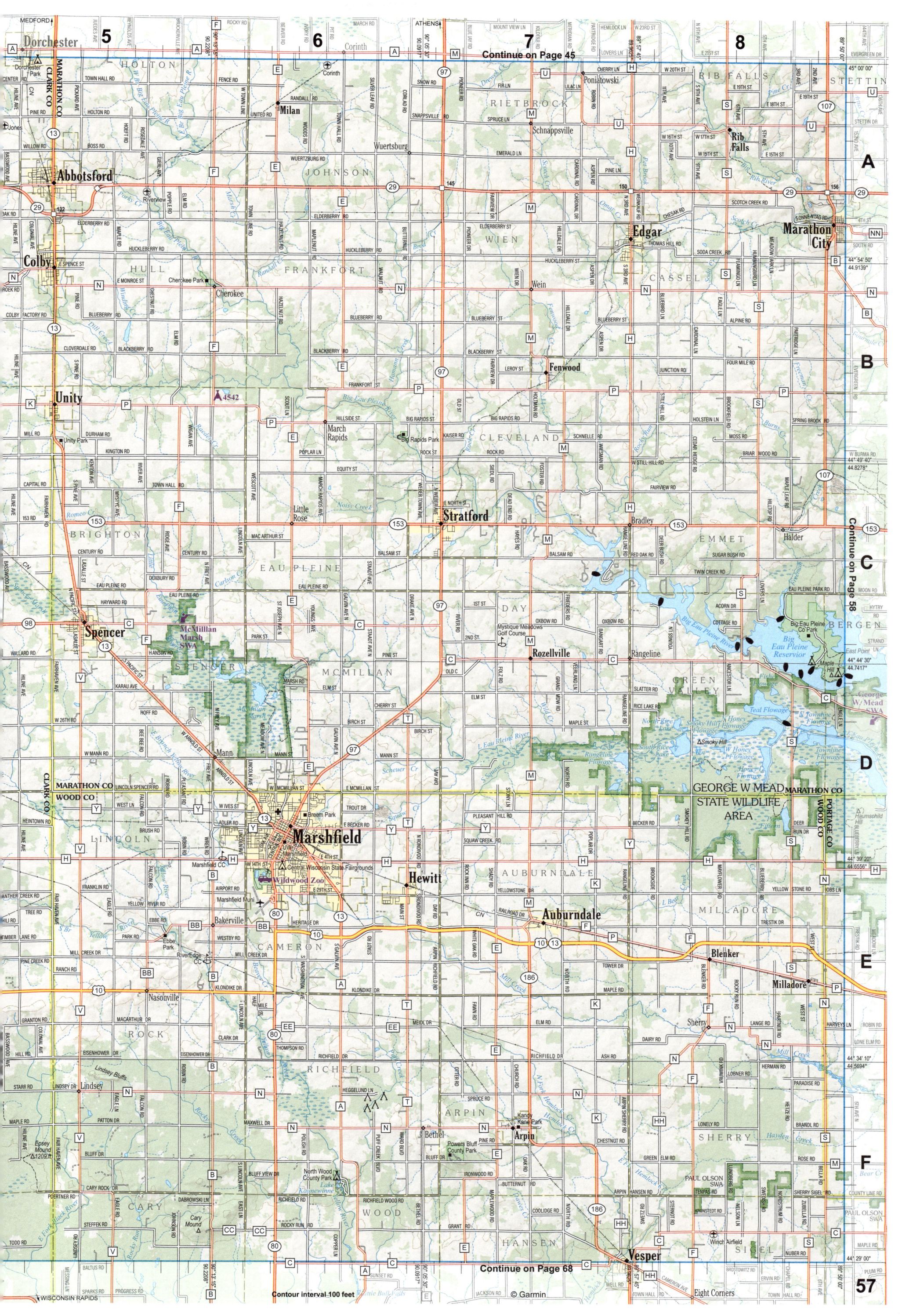

Continue on Page 45

Dorchester

Milan

Abbotsford

Colby

Cherokee

Unity

March Rapids

Stratford

Spencer

Rozellville

Marshfield

Hewitt

Auburndale

Bakerville

Nasonville

Lindsey

Bethel

Arpin

Vesper

Poniatowski

Schnappsville

Rib Falls

Edgar

Marathon City

Fenwood

Halder

GEORGE W MEAD STATE WILDLIFE AREA

Big Eau Pleine Reservoir

Blenker

Milladore

Sherry

Paul Olson SWA

Continue on Page 58

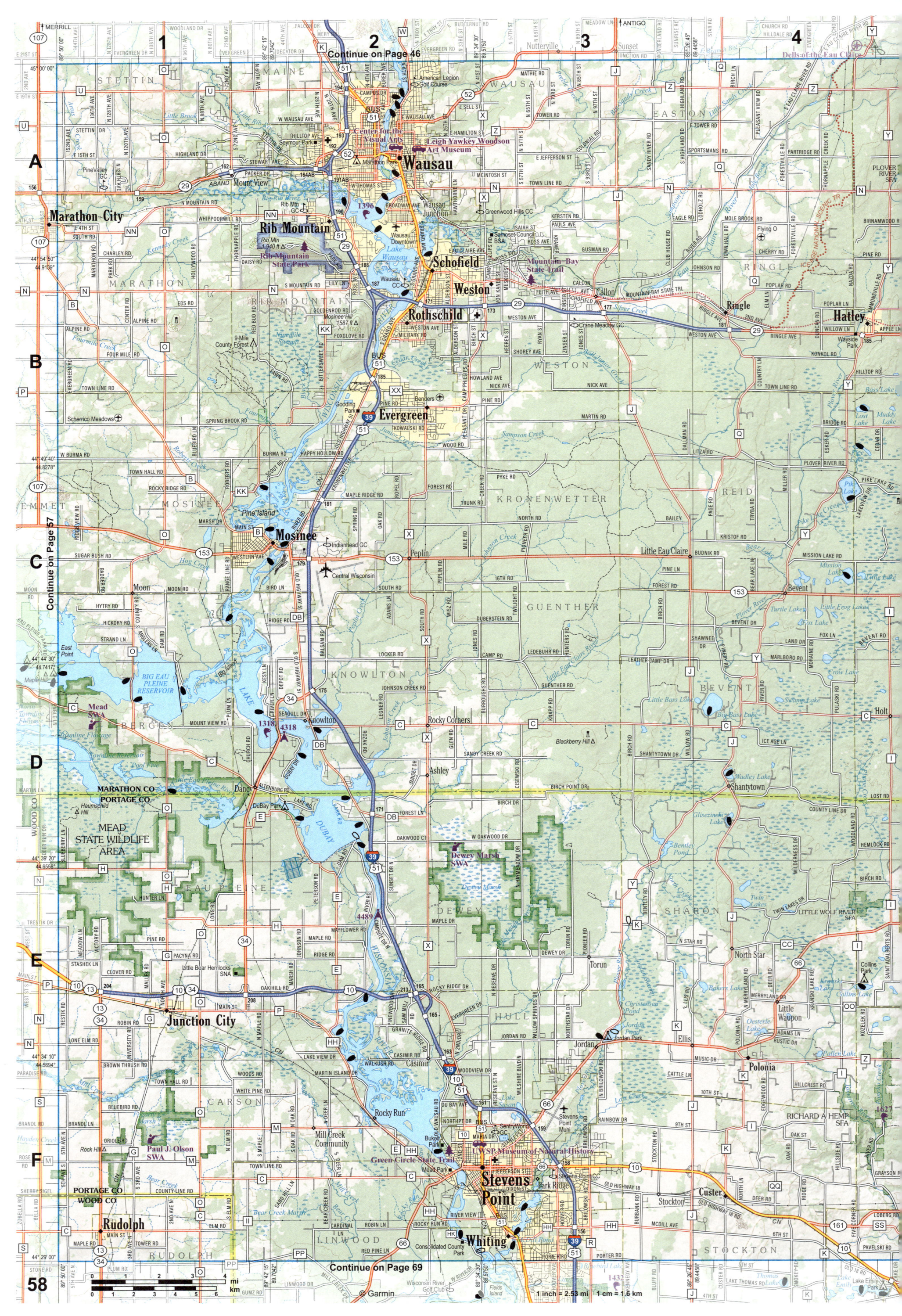

Continue on Page 46

Continue on Page 57

Continue on Page 69

58

1 inch = 2.53 mi   1 cm = 1.6 km

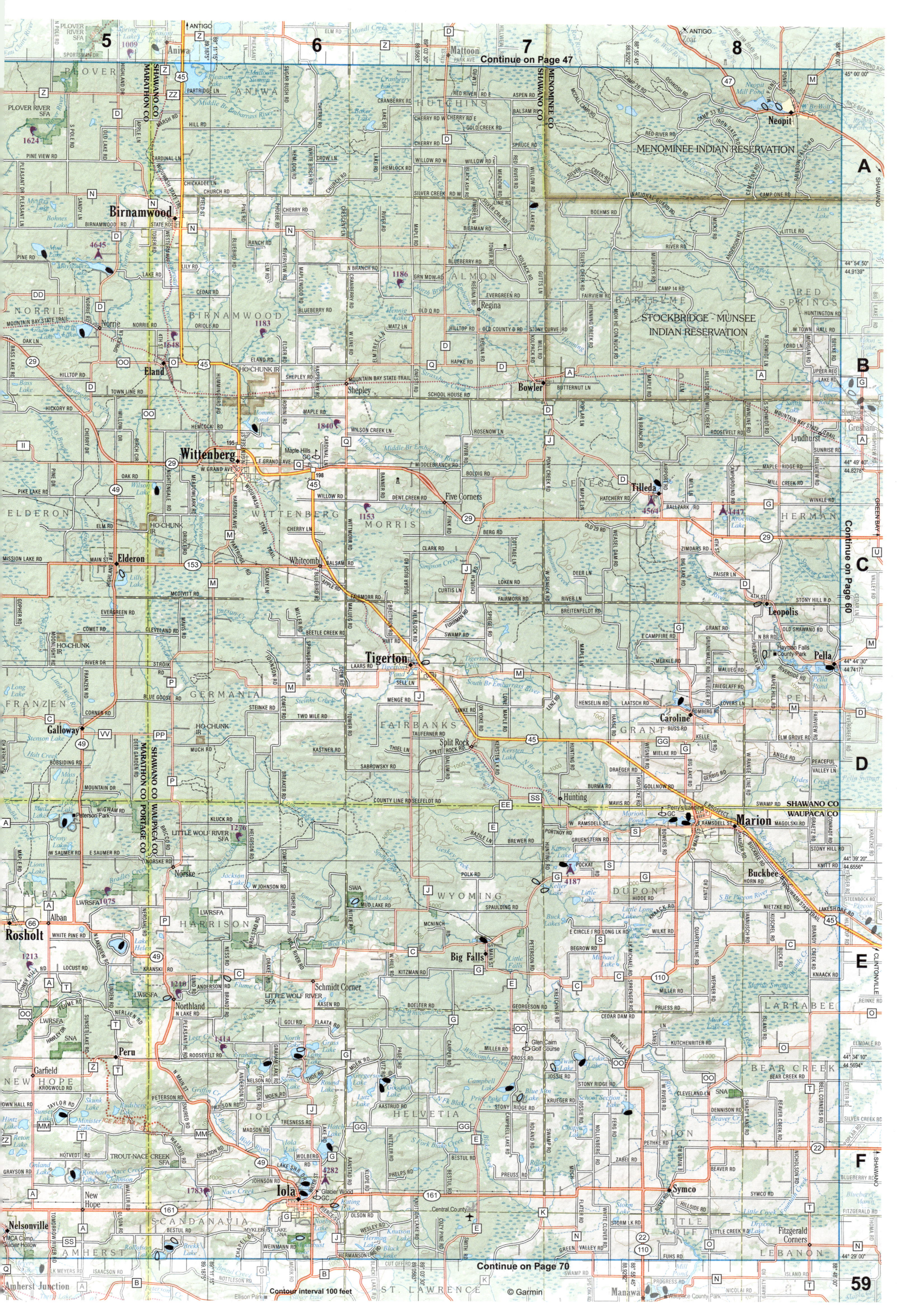

Continue on Page 47

Continue on Page 60

Continue on Page 70

MENOMINEE INDIAN RESERVATION

STOCKBRIDGE - MUNSEE
INDIAN RESERVATION

Contour interval 100 feet

© Garmin

59

Continue on Page 48

Continue on Page 59

Continue on Page 71

MENOMINEE INDIAN RESERVATION

Keshena

Gresham

Lyndhurst

Red River

Thornton

Shawano

Shawano Lake

Cecil

Bonduel

Zachow

Pella

Belle Plaine

Lunds

Angelica

Embarrass

Frazer Corners

NAVARINO STATE WILDLIFE AREA

Clintonville

Navarino

Briarton

Rose Lawn

Deer Creek SWA

Leeman

Nichols

Cicero

Bear Creek

Maine SWA

WOLF RIVER BOTTOMS SWA

Outagamie SWA

Black Creek

Seymour

Suring

Frostville

Gillett

Underhill

Mosling

Pulcifer

Hintz

60

0 1 2 3 4 mi
0 1 2 3 4 km

© Garmin

1 inch = 2.53 mi · 1 cm = 1.6 km

Continue on Page 49

Continue on Page 62

Continue on Page 72

GREEN BAY

ONEIDA INDIAN RESERVATION

Continue on Page 50

Continue on Page 61

Continue on Page 73

GREEN BAY

DOOR PENINSULA

Carlsville

Sevastopol

Valmy

Institute

Sturgeon Bay

Maplewood

Forestville

DOOR CO
KEWAUNEE CO

Algoma

Rio Creek

Casco

Luxemburg

1 inch = 2.53 mi   1 cm = 1.6 km

© Garmin

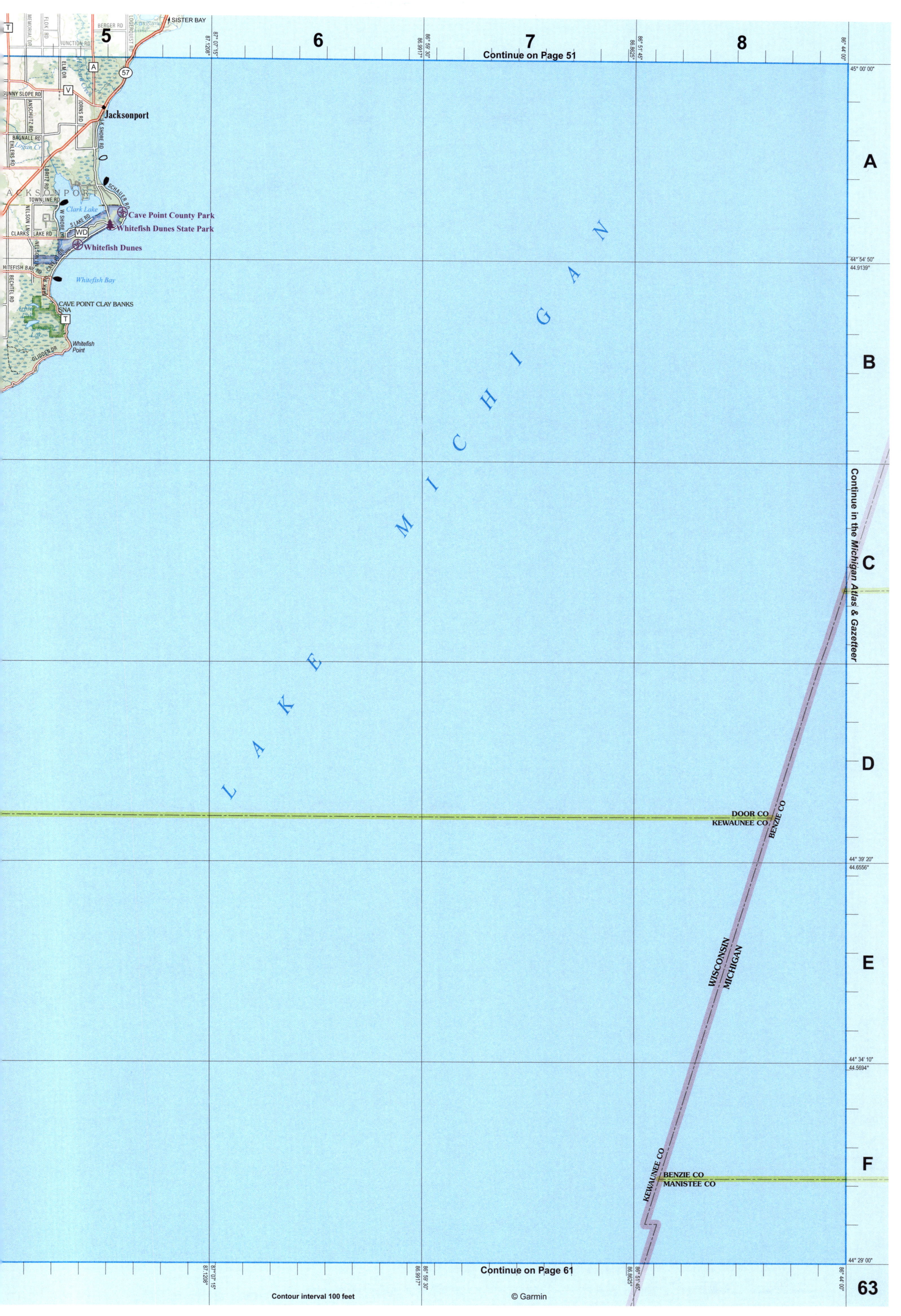

5

6

7

8

Continue on Page 51

SISTER BAY

Jacksonport

Cave Point County Park
Whitefish Dunes State Park
Whitefish Dunes

JACKSONPORT

Clark Lake

Whitefish Bay

CAVE POINT CLAY BANKS
SNA

Whitefish Point

A

B

C

D

E

F

L A K E   M I C H I G A N

Continue in the *Michigan Atlas & Gazetteer*

45° 00' 00"

44° 54' 50"
44.9139°

DOOR CO
KEWAUNEE CO

44° 39' 20"
44.6556°

WISCONSIN
MICHIGAN

BENZIE CO

44° 34' 10"
44.5694°

KEWAUNEE CO
BENZIE CO
MANISTEE CO

44° 29' 00"

87° 07' 15"
87.1208°

86° 59' 30"
86.9917°

86° 51' 45"
86.8625°

86° 44' 00"

Continue on Page 61

Contour interval 100 feet

© Garmin

63

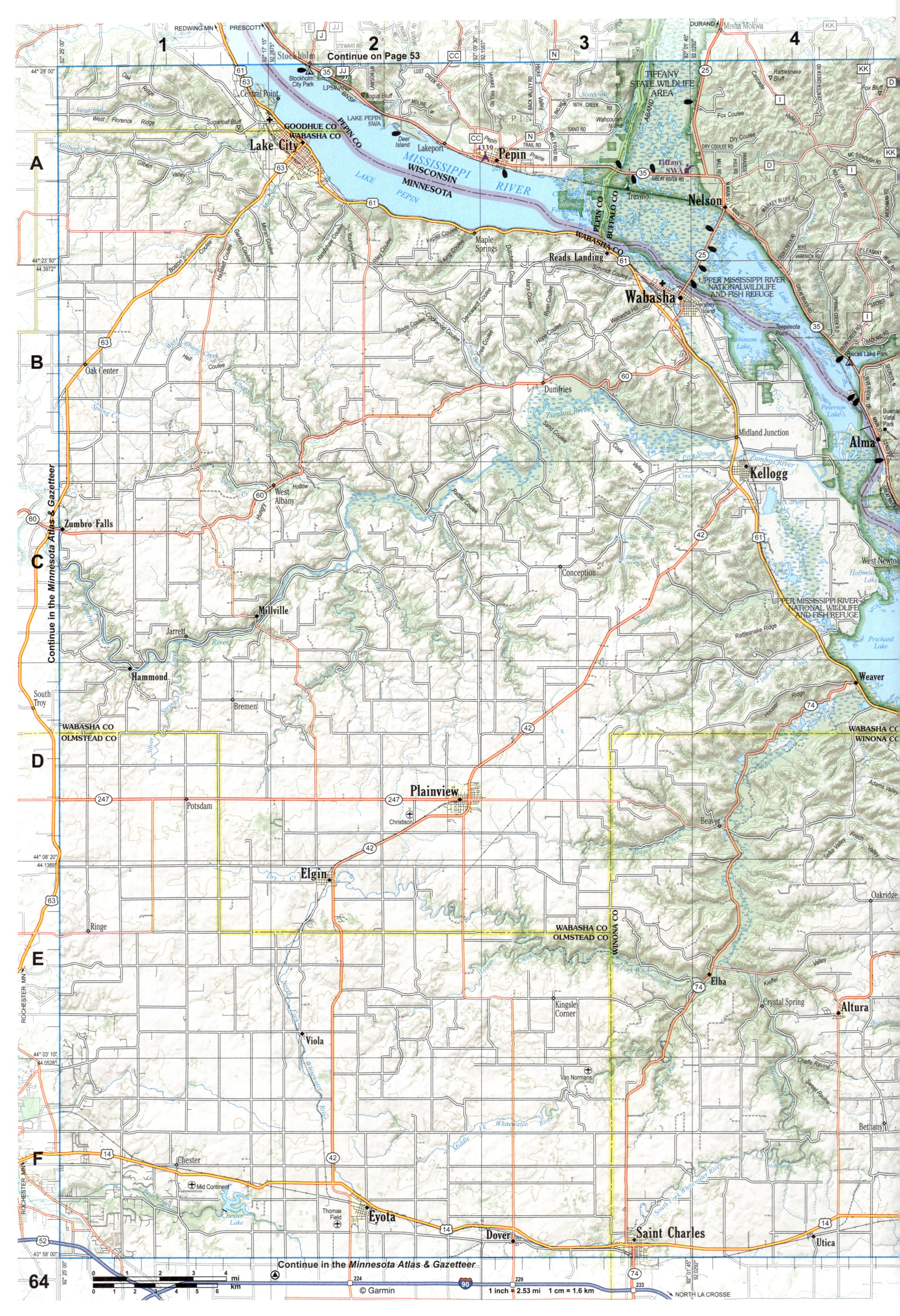

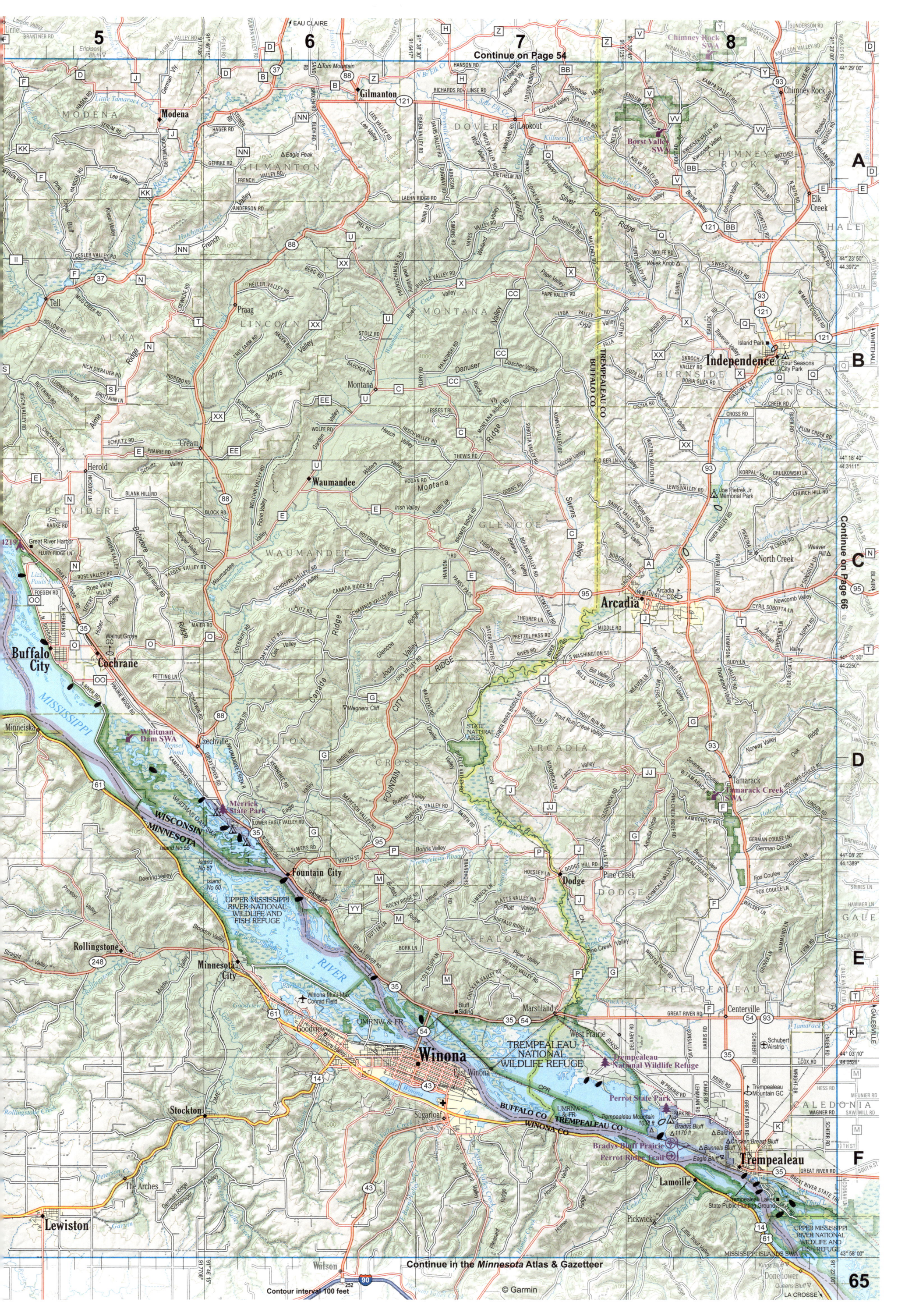

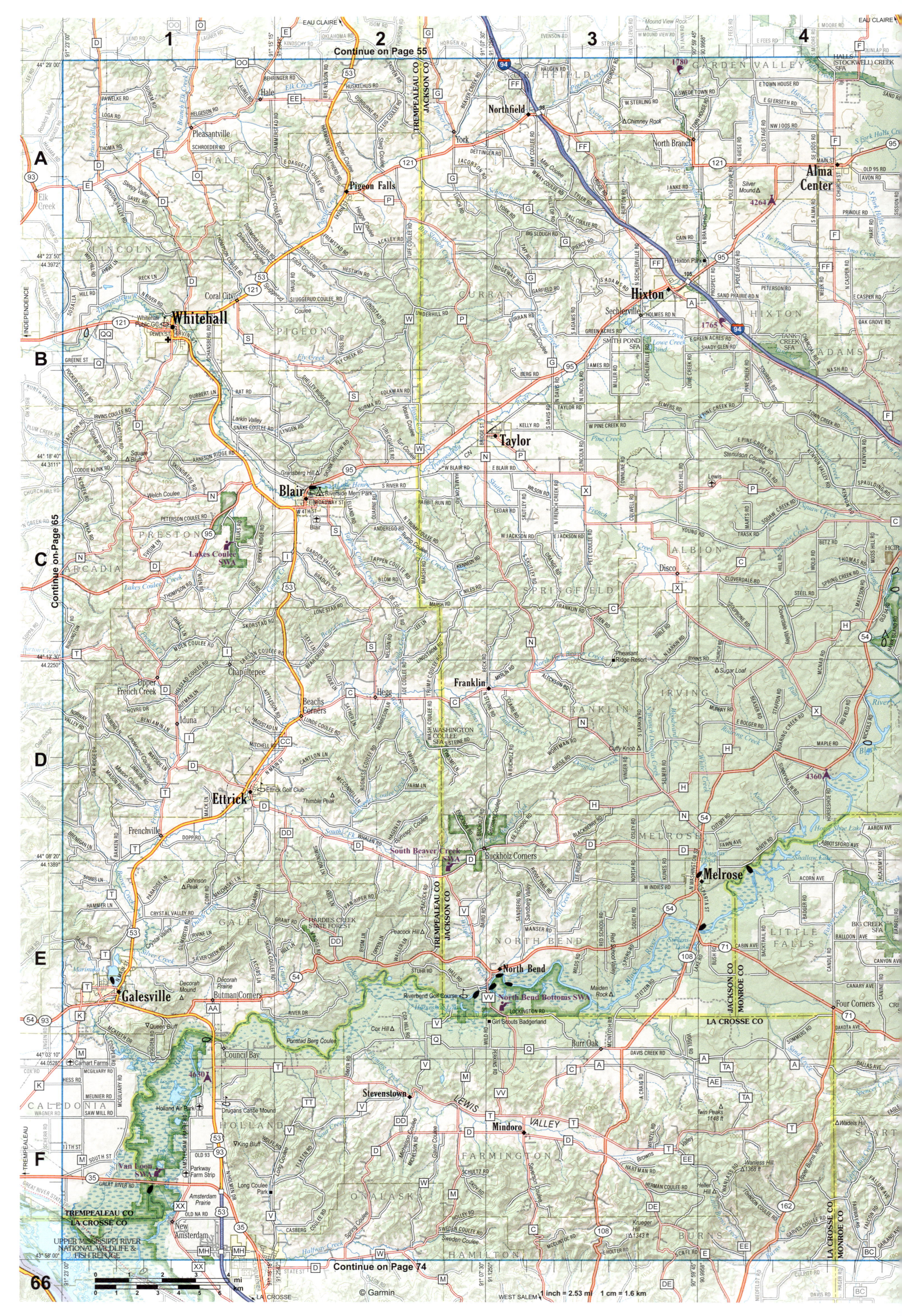

Continue on Page 74

Continue on Page 65

© Garmin

inch = 2.53 mi   1 cm = 1.6 km

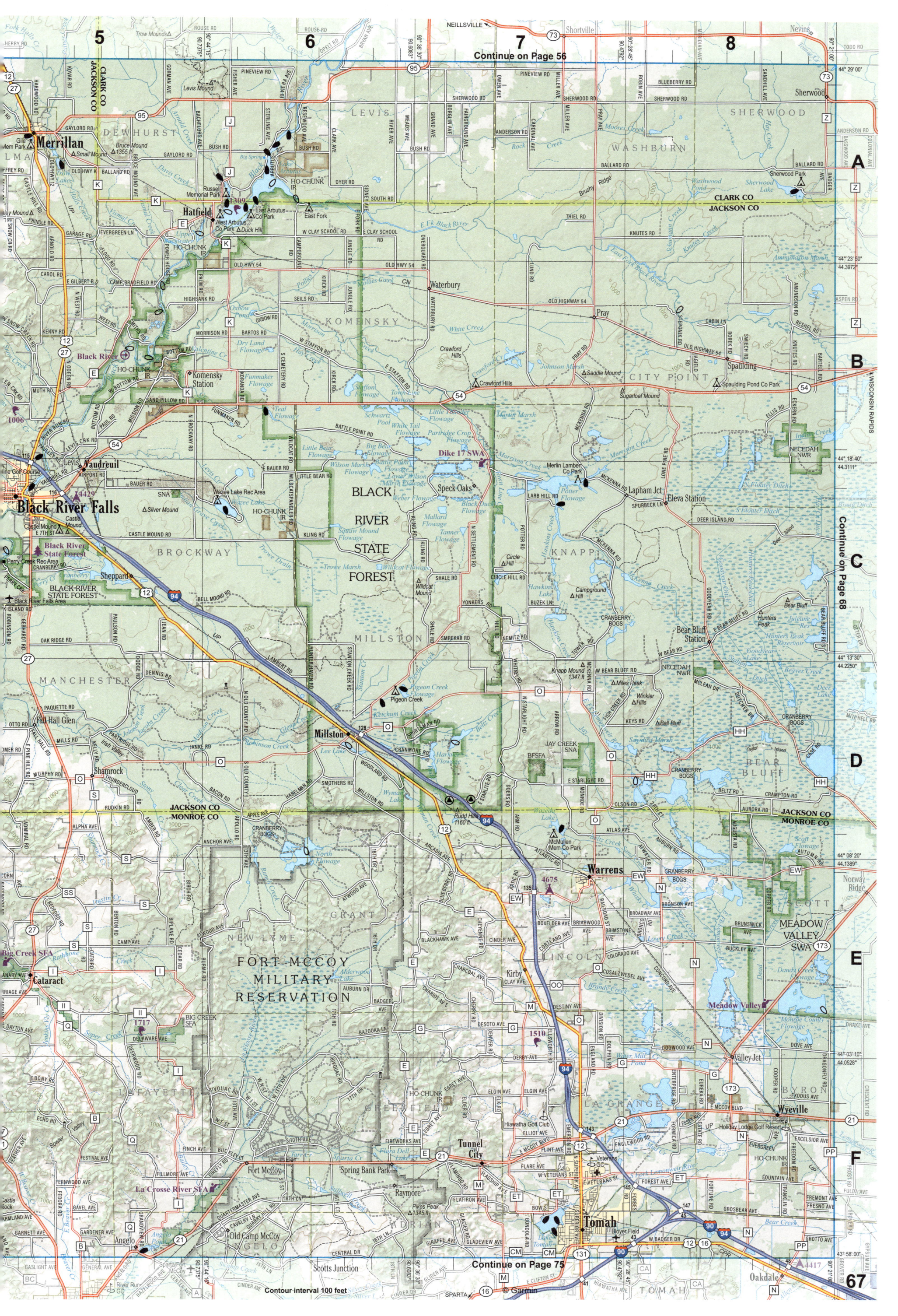

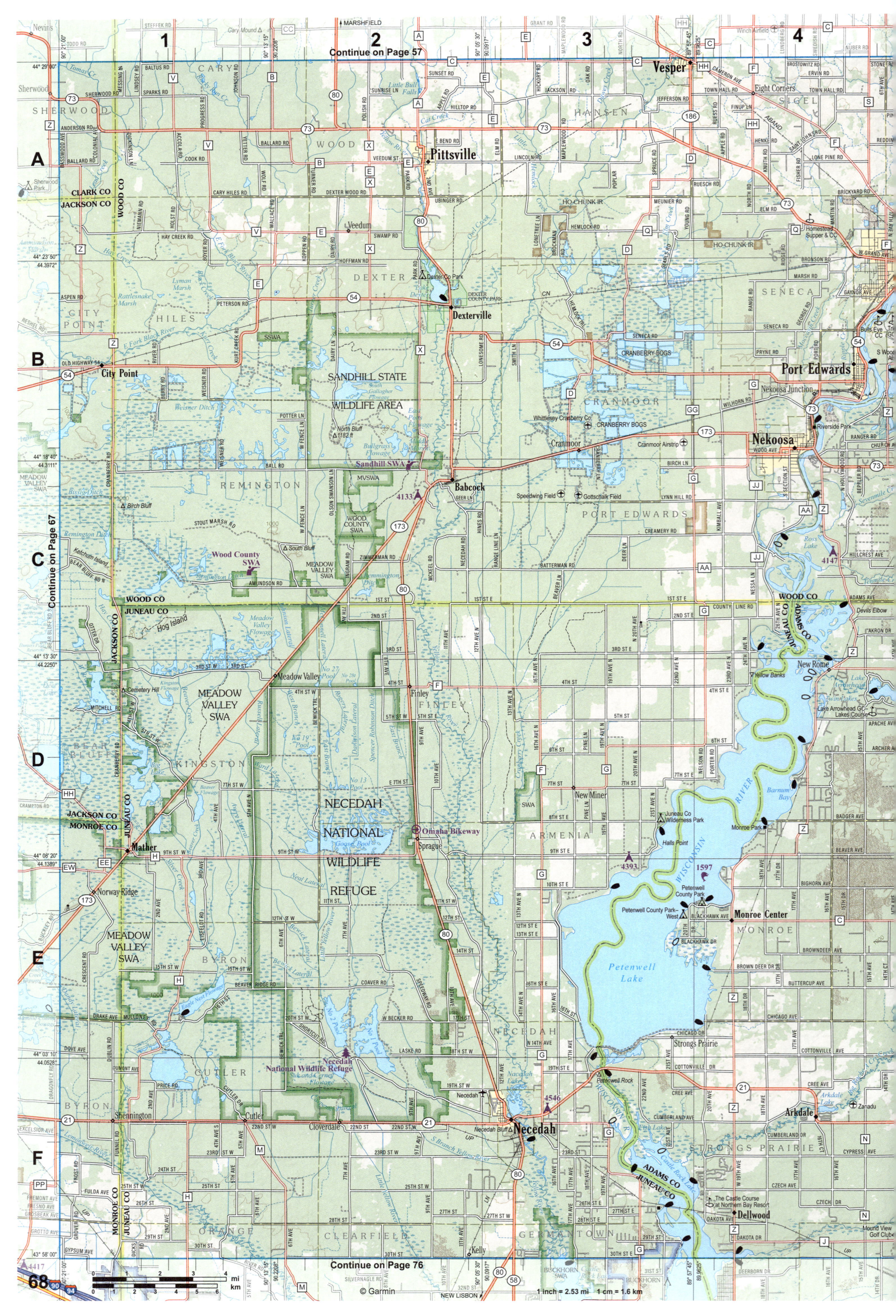

Continue on Page 67

1 inch = 2.53 mi   1 cm = 1.6 km

© Garmin

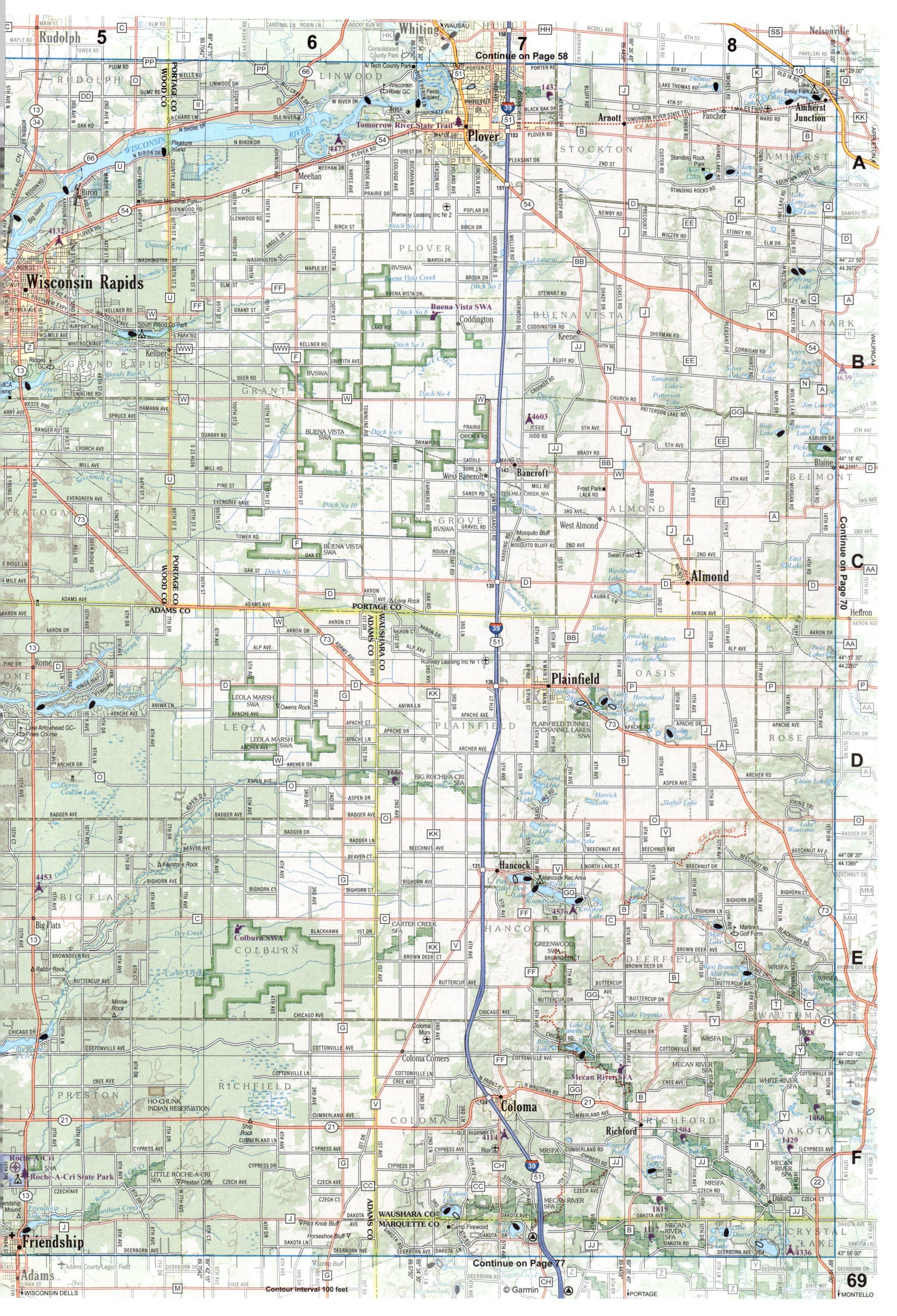

Continue on Page 58

Continue on Page 70

Continue on Page 77

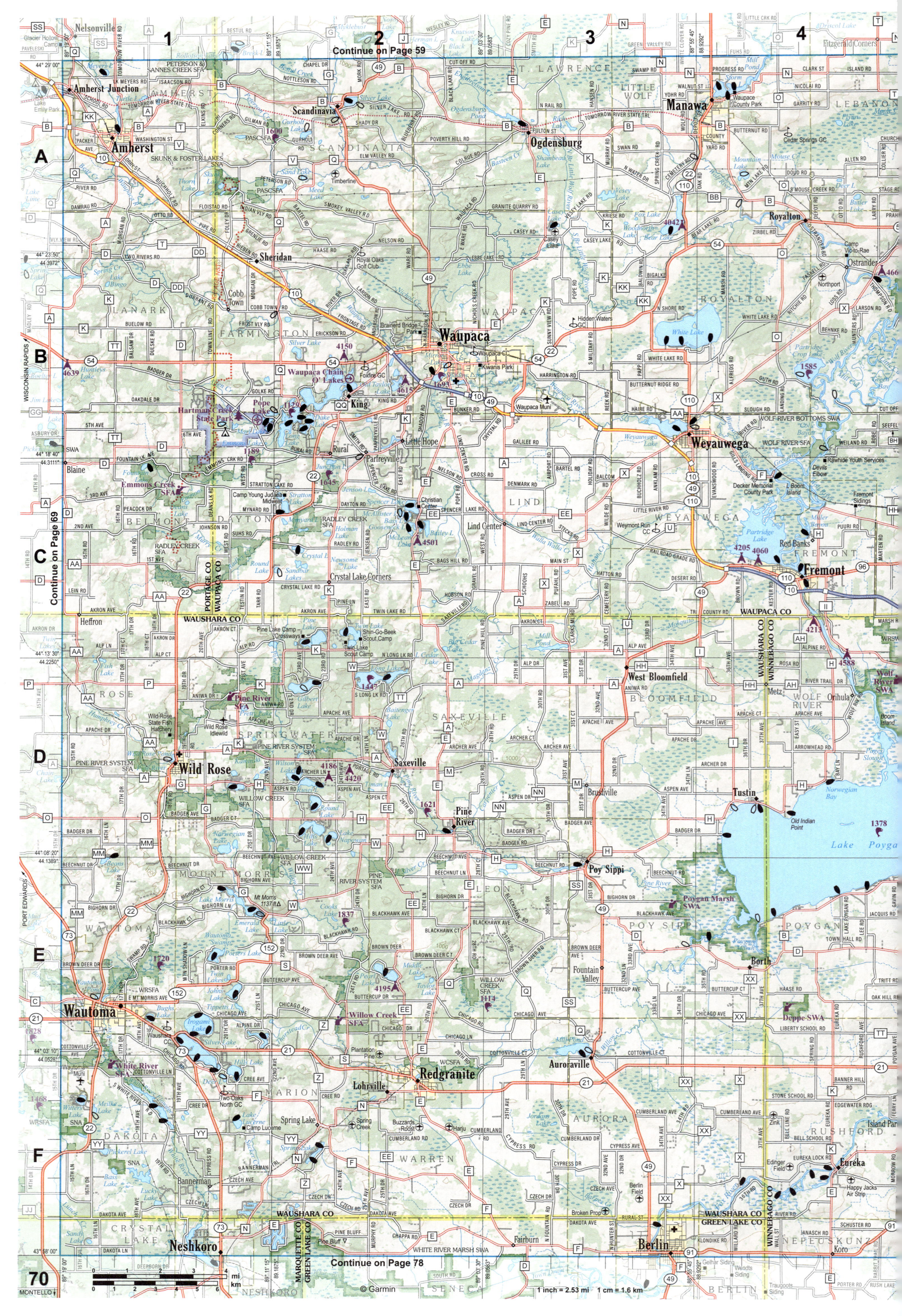

Continue on Page 69

Continue on Page 78

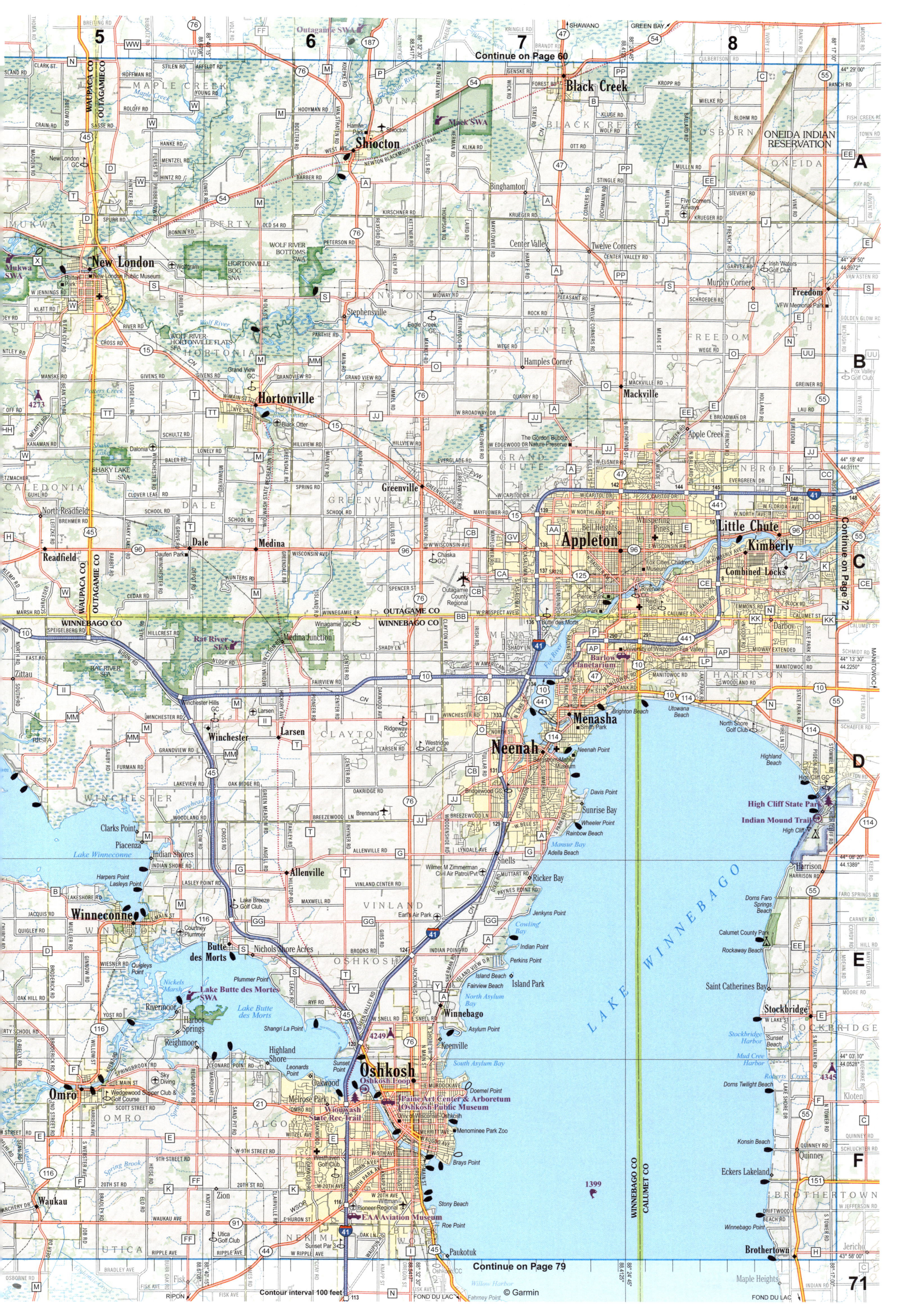

Continue on Page 60

Black Creek

ONEIDA INDIAN RESERVATION

Shiocton

New London

Freedom

Hortonville

Mackville

Appleton

Little Chute
Kimberly
Combined Locks

Readfield

Dale   Medina

Greenville

Grand Chute

Continue on Page 72

Winchester

Larsen

Menasha

Neenah

High Cliff State Park
Indian Mound Trail

Winneconne

Allenville

Butte des Morts

Lake Winnebago

Calumet County Park

Saint Catherines Bay

Stockbridge

Omro

Winnebago

Keenville

Highland Shore

Oshkosh

Quinney

Waukau   Zion

EAA Aviation Museum

Brotherton

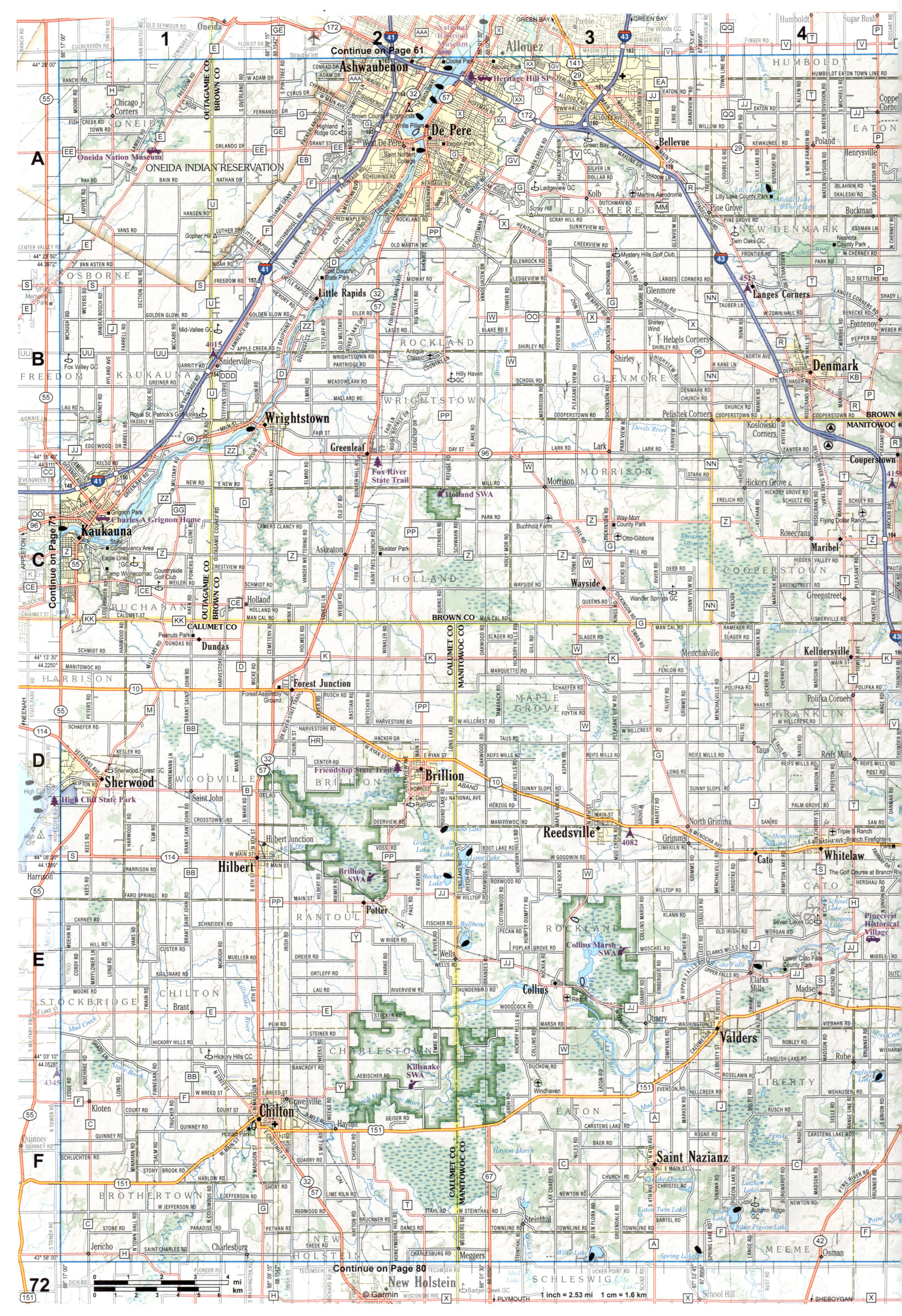

Continue on Page 61

Continue on Page 71

Continue on Page 80

1 inch = 2.53 mi   1 cm = 1.6 km

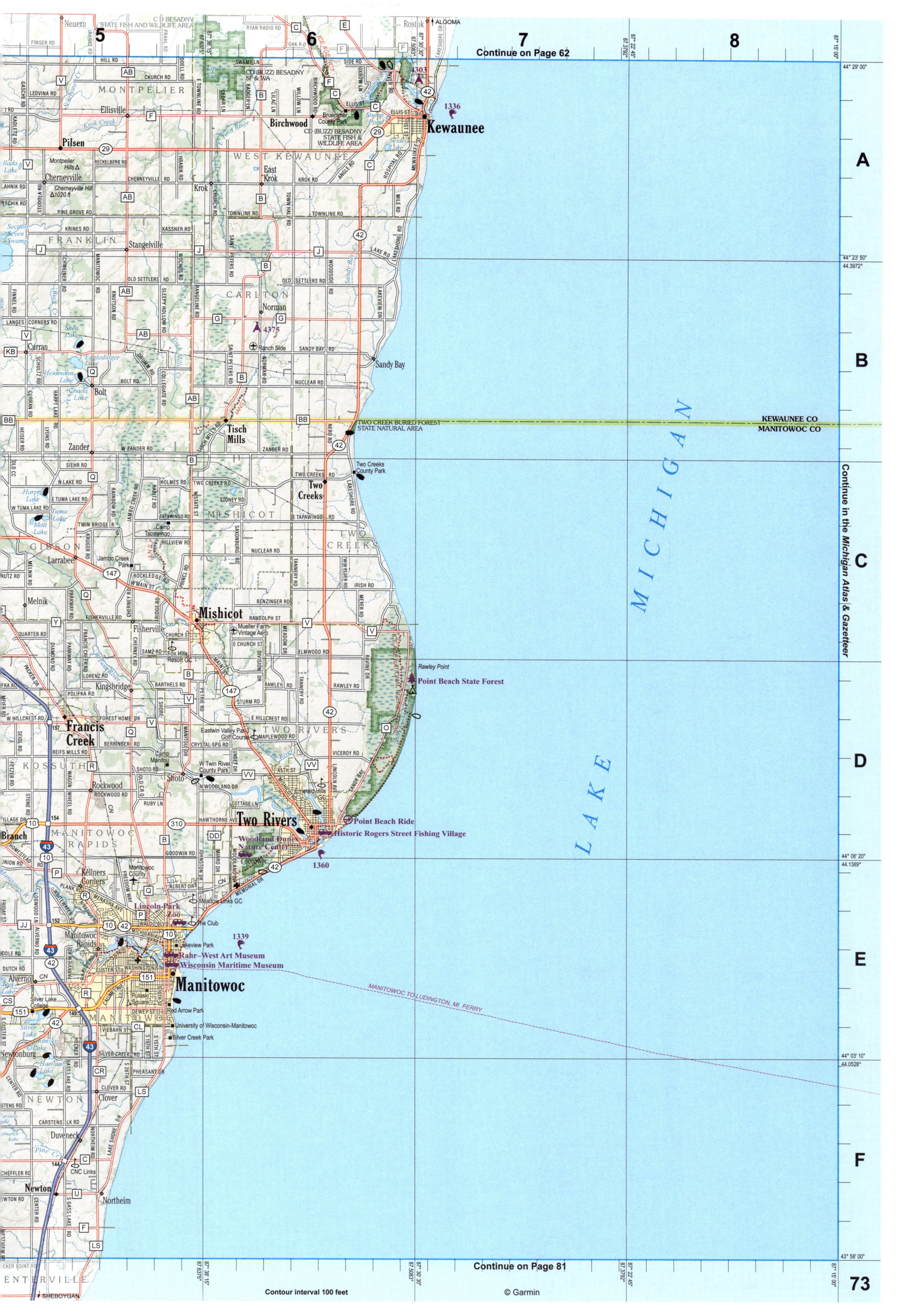

Continue on Page 62

Continue on Page 81

Contour interval 100 feet

© Garmin

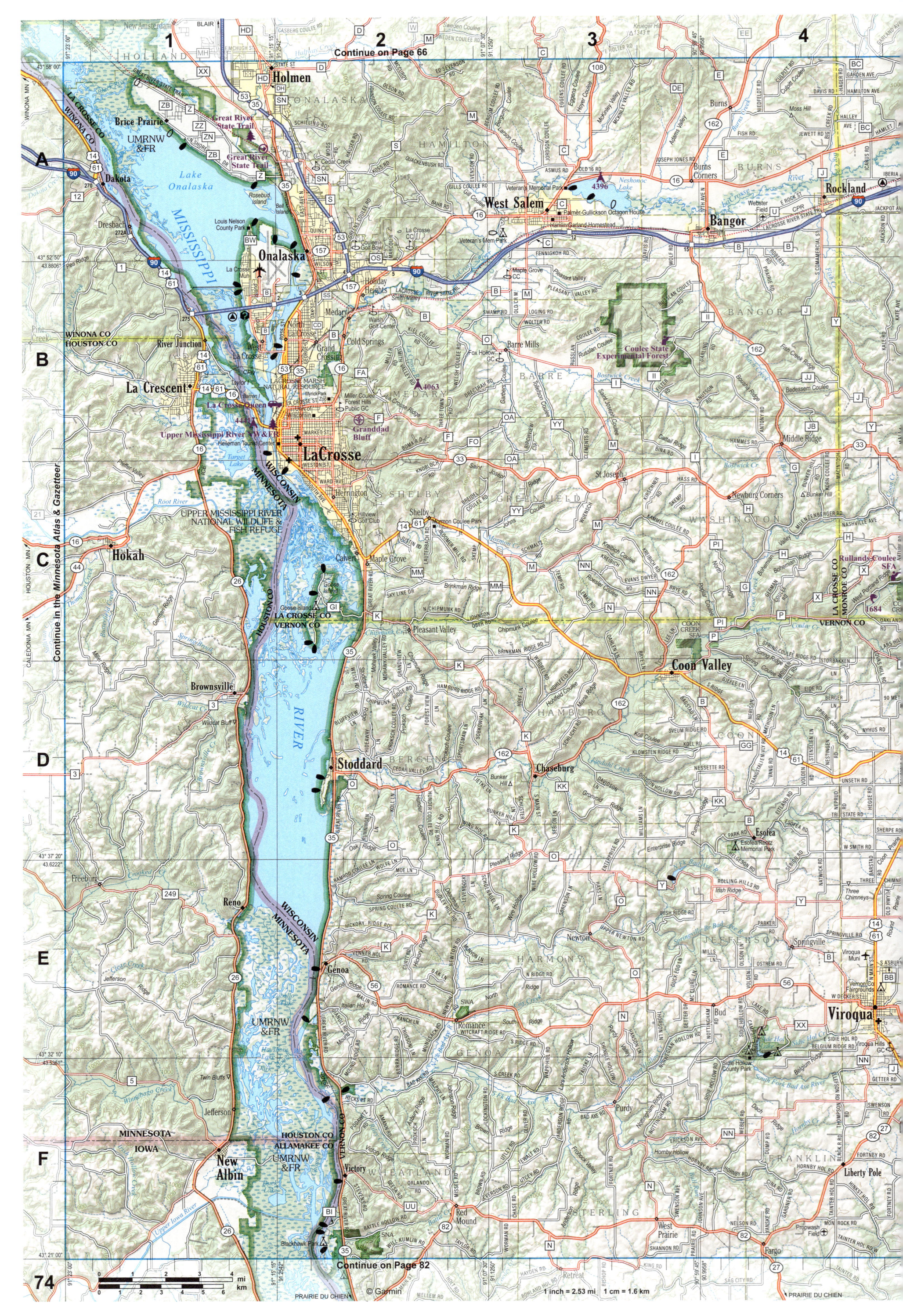

Continue on Page 66

Continue on Page 82

74

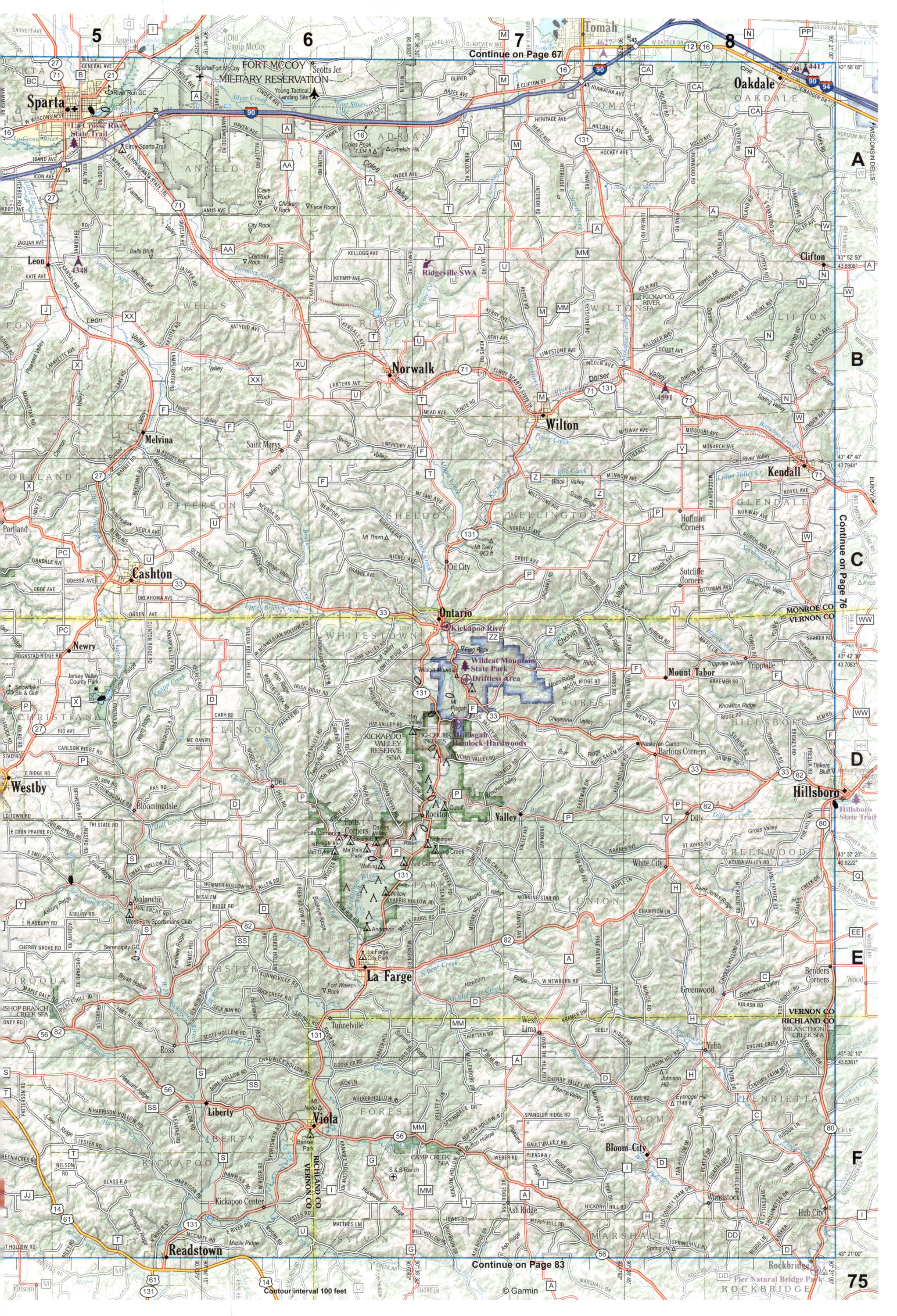

Continue on Page 76

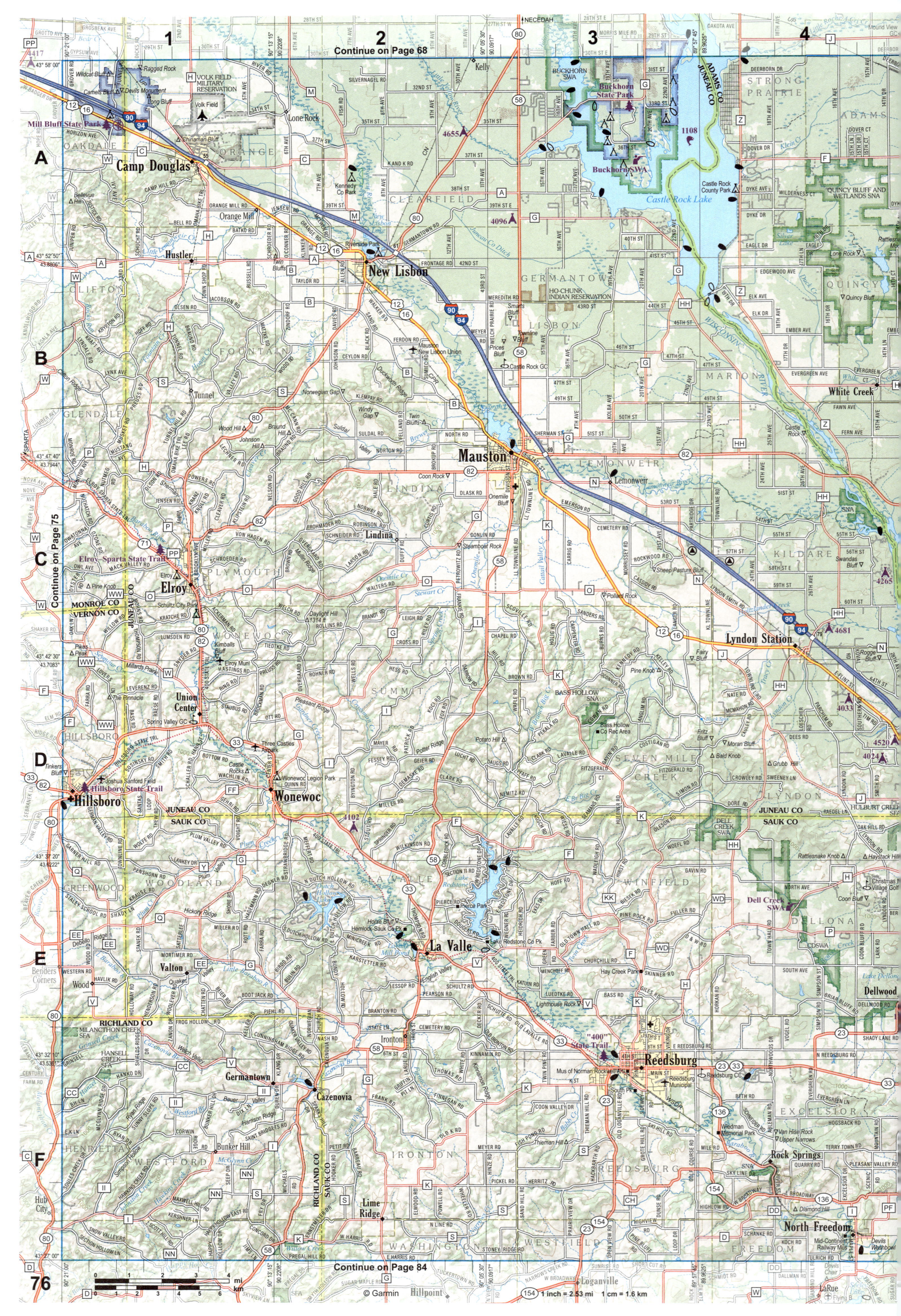

Continue on Page 75

© Garmin   Hillpoint

1 inch = 2.53 mi   1 cm = 1.6 km

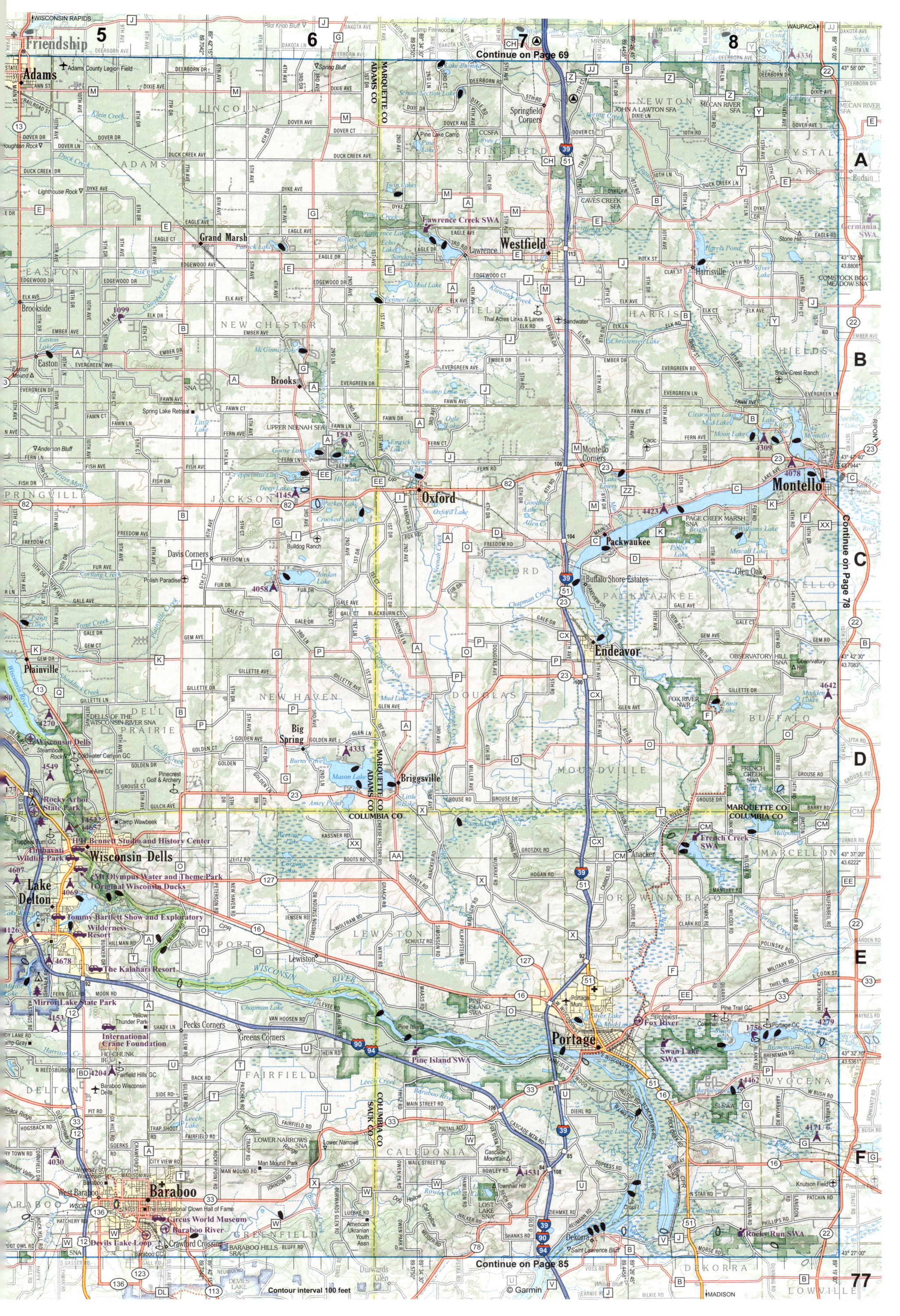

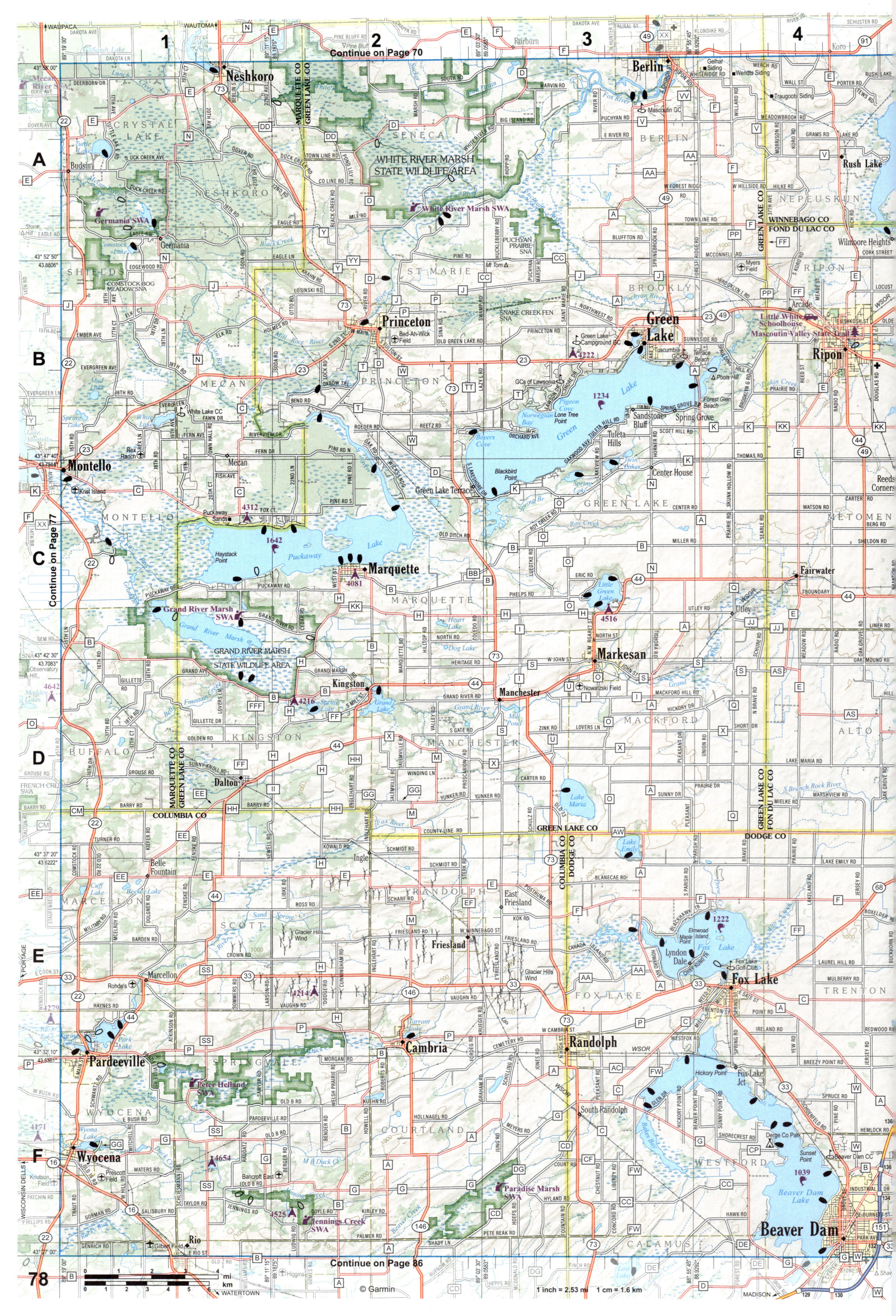

Continue on Page 70

Continue on Page 77

Continue on Page 86

78

1 inch = 2.53 mi   1 cm = 1.6 km

© Garmin

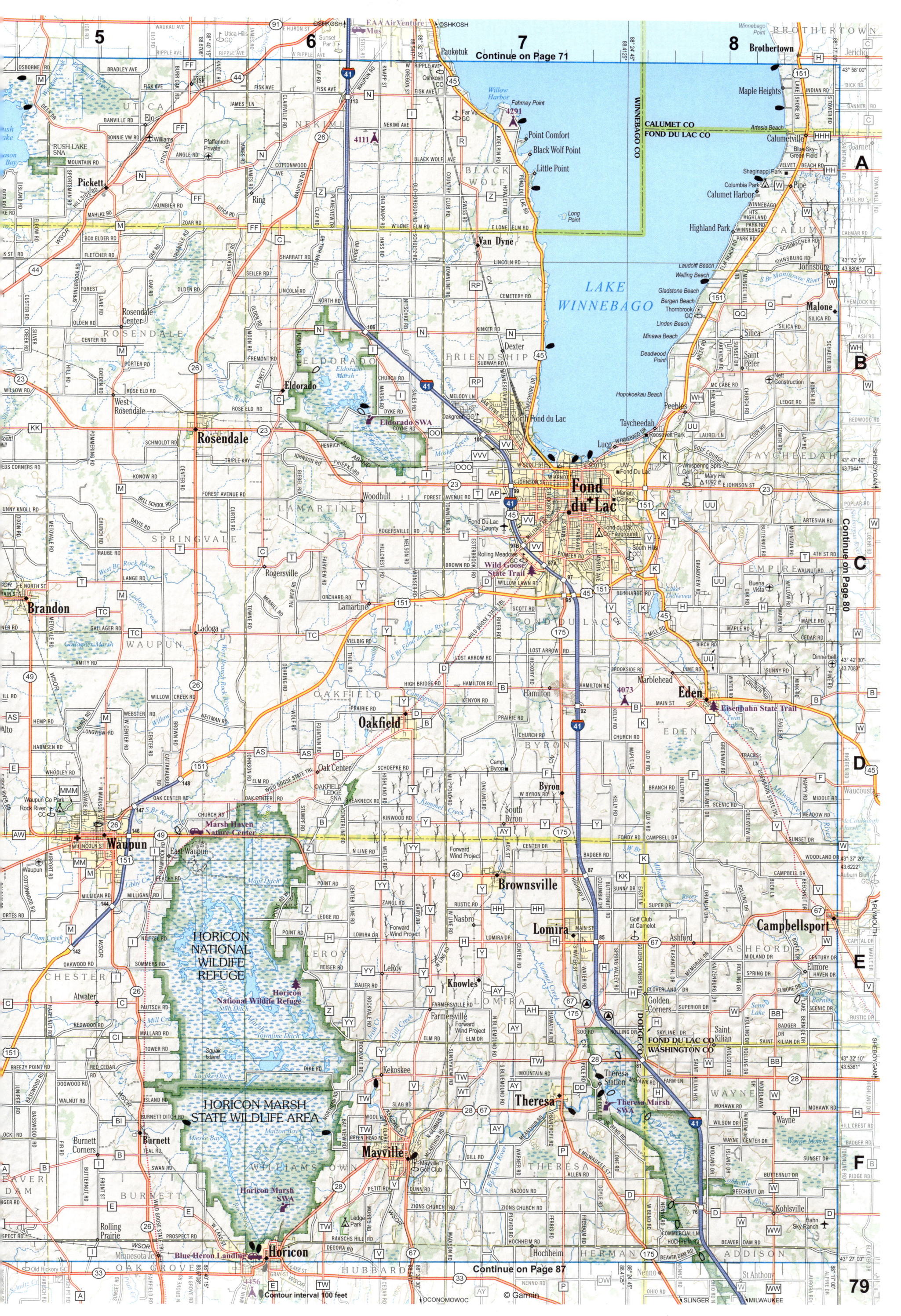

Continue on Page 80

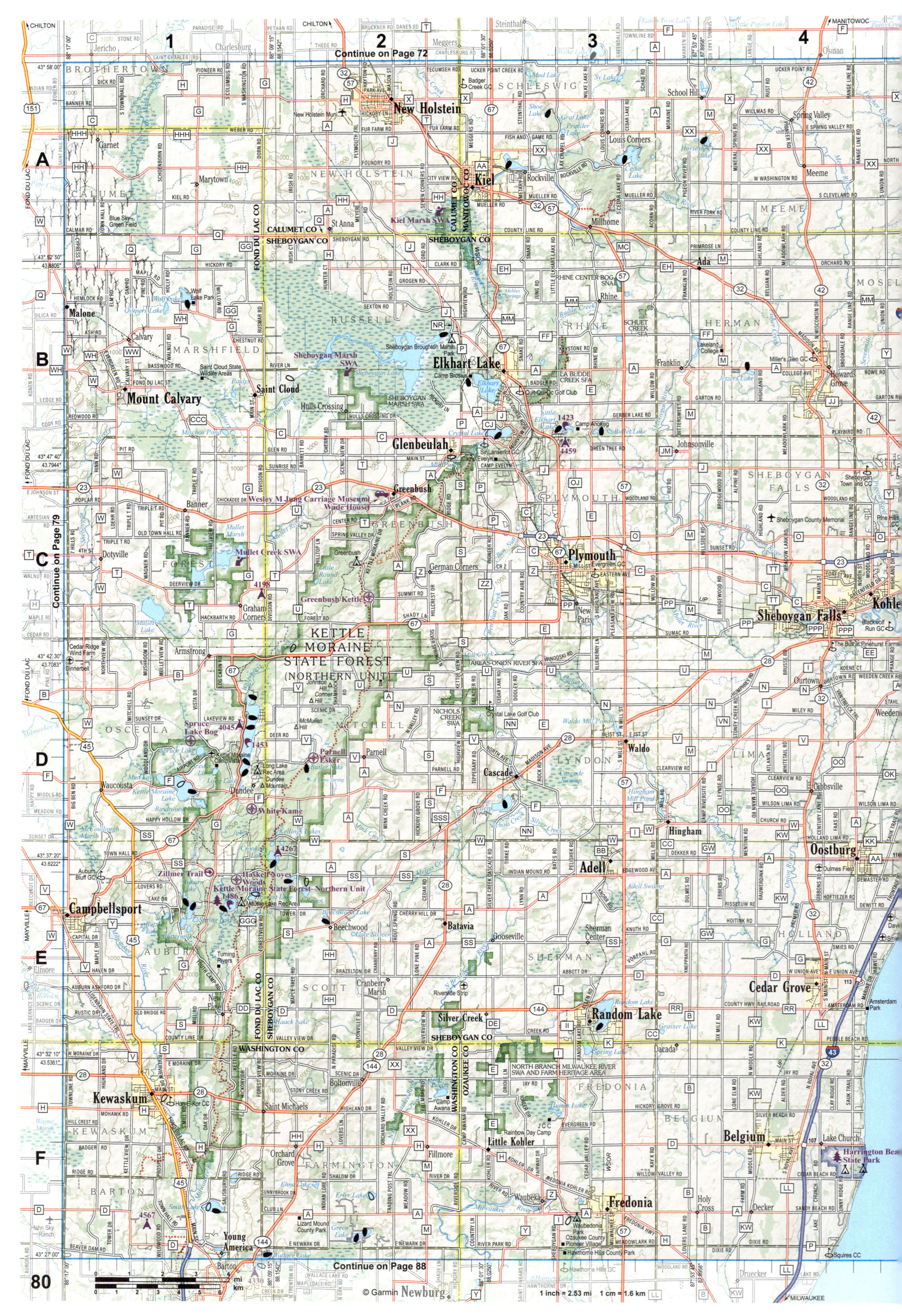

Continue on Page 72

Continue on Page 79

Continue on Page 88

80

1 inch = 2.53 mi 1 cm = 1.6 km

© Garmin

87° 45'
87° 38' 15"
87° 30' 30"
87° 22' 45"
87° 15' 00"

43° 58' 00"

A

MANITOWOC CO
SHEBOYGAN CO

43° 52' 50"
43.8806°

B

C

D

43° 37' 20"
43.6222°

E

SHEBOYGAN CO
OZAUKEE CO

43° 32' 10"
43.5361°

F

43° 27' 00"

MANITOWOC
CENTER RD
S GASS LAKE RD

F

CENTERVILLE

CEDARVIEW RD
FISCHER CREEK RD

43

XX
NORTH AVE

Cleveland
S CLEVELAND RD

X
LS

FISCHER CREEK
CONSERVATION AREA

Whistling Straits
Golf Club

MM
LUELLOFF RD

FF
aven

ROWE RD

LAKESHORE RD

GARTON RD

Bell's

PLAYBIRD RD
Mosel

Van Der Vaart

Erdman

42

AB

Sheboygan Point

John Michael Kohler
Arts Center

23

TA

Sheboygan

28

1351

Lake View Park

WASHINGTON AVE

EE

123

28

OK

WEEDEN CREEK
EE

Riverdale CC

KK

STAHL RD

Black River Point

OK
KK

Hilbe's

V

120

KK
Kohler Park Dunes

Kohler–Andrae State Park

WILSON
WILSON LIMA RD

Black River

K

OWN LINE RD

ER RD

ASTER

LAKE
MICHIGAN

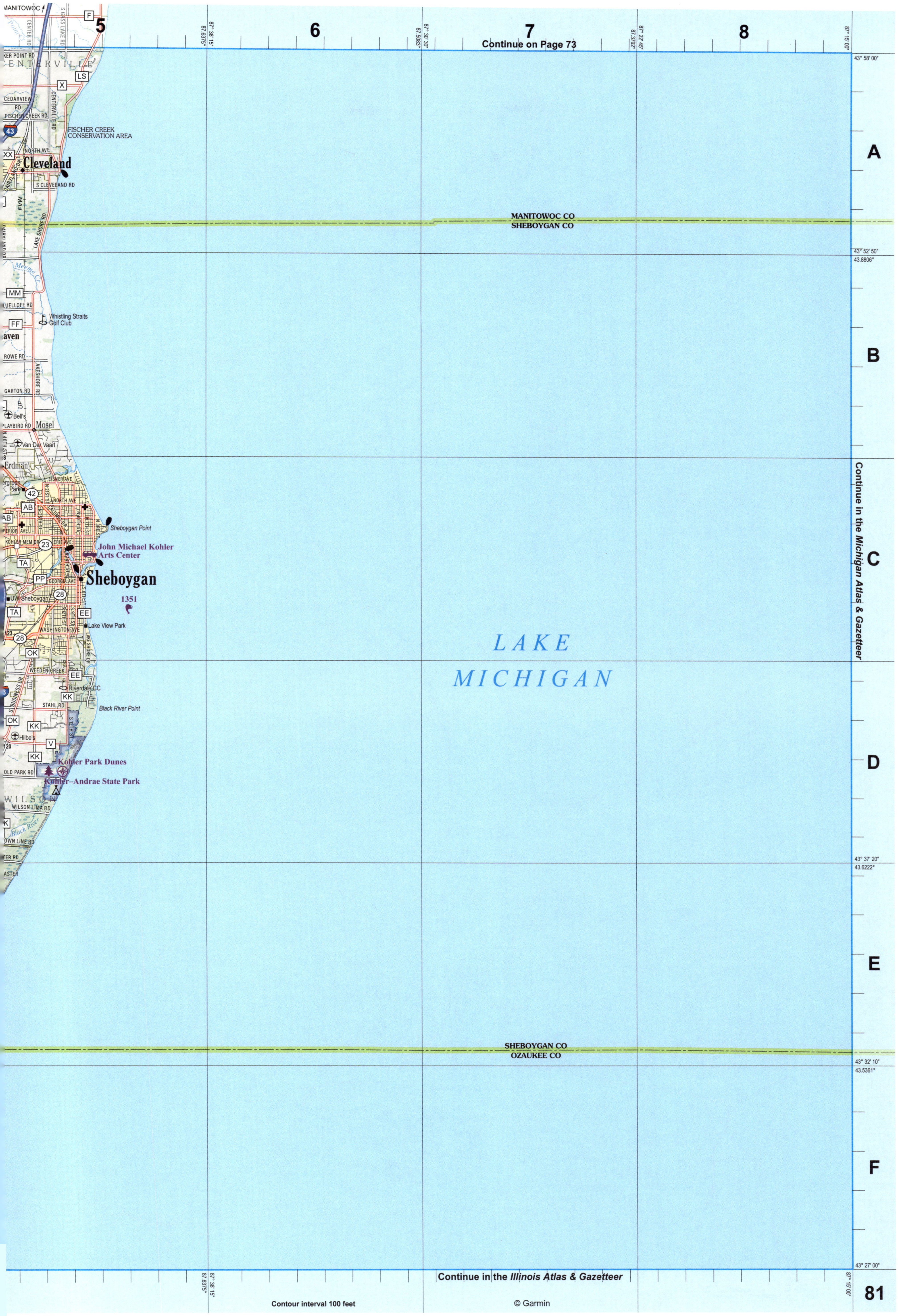

Continue in the *Michigan Atlas & Gazetteer*

Continue in the *Illinois Atlas & Gazetteer*

Contour interval 100 feet

© Garmin

81

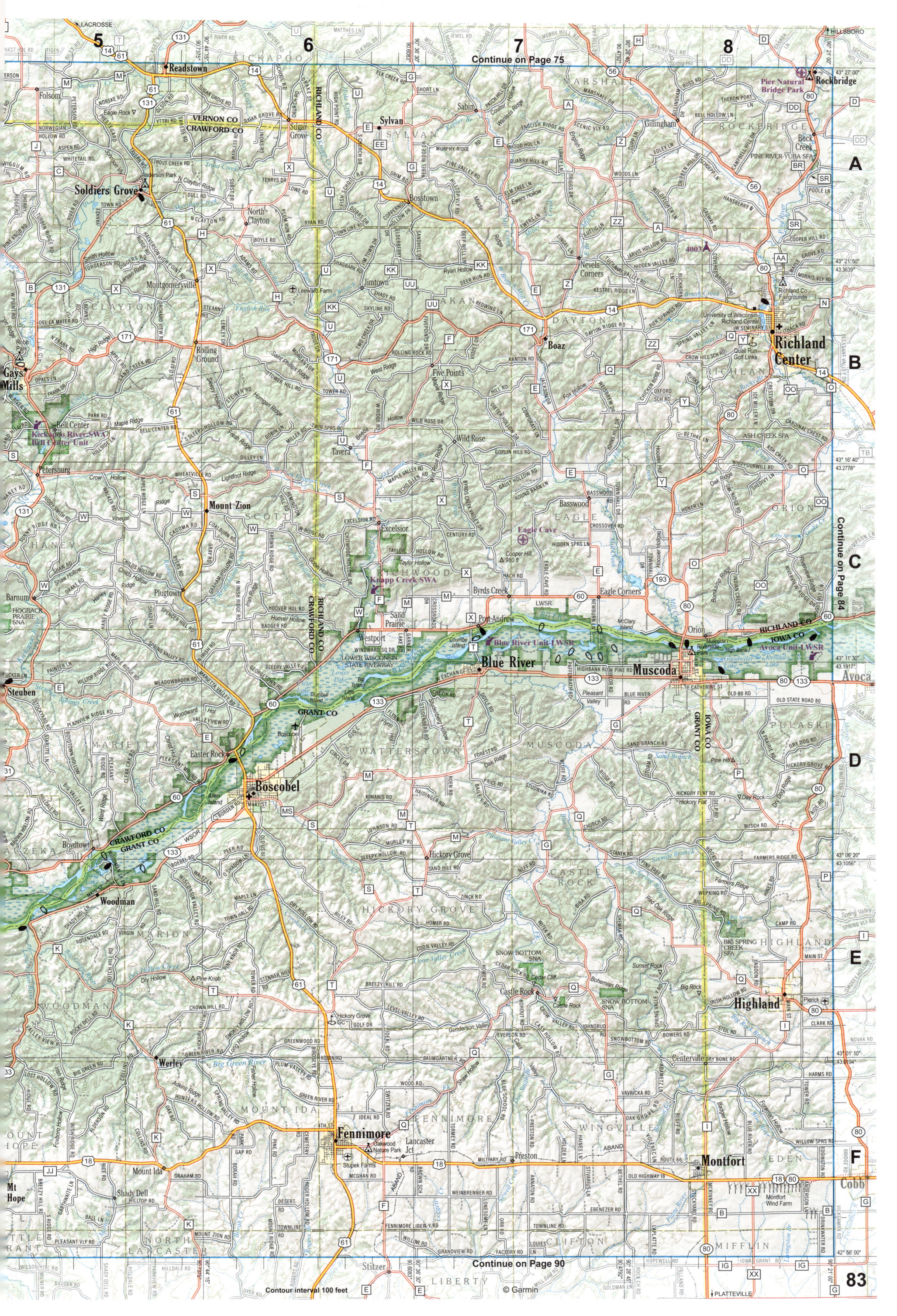

Continue on Page 84

Contour interval 100 feet

© Garmin

Continue on Page 76
Continue on Page 83
Continue on Page 91

North Freedom

Loganville
LaRue

Loyd
Hill Point
Wards Corners

Natural Bridge State Park
Leland

Neptune
Loreta

Ithaca
Keysville

Aubrey
Bear Valley
Plain
Black Hawk

Sextonville
Twin Bluffs
Richland

Gotham

Lone Rock
Spring Green
Helena
Arena

Avoca

Taliesin & Frank Lloyd Wright Visitor Center
Tower Hill State Park
Coon Rock

Clyde
Wyoming

The House on the Rock

Hyde

Blue Mound State Park

Governor Dodge State Park

Blackhawk Lake SRA

Ridgeway
Barneveld

Cobb
Edmund
Dodgeville
Military Ridge State Trail

1 inch = 2.53 mi
1 cm = 1.6 km

© Garmin

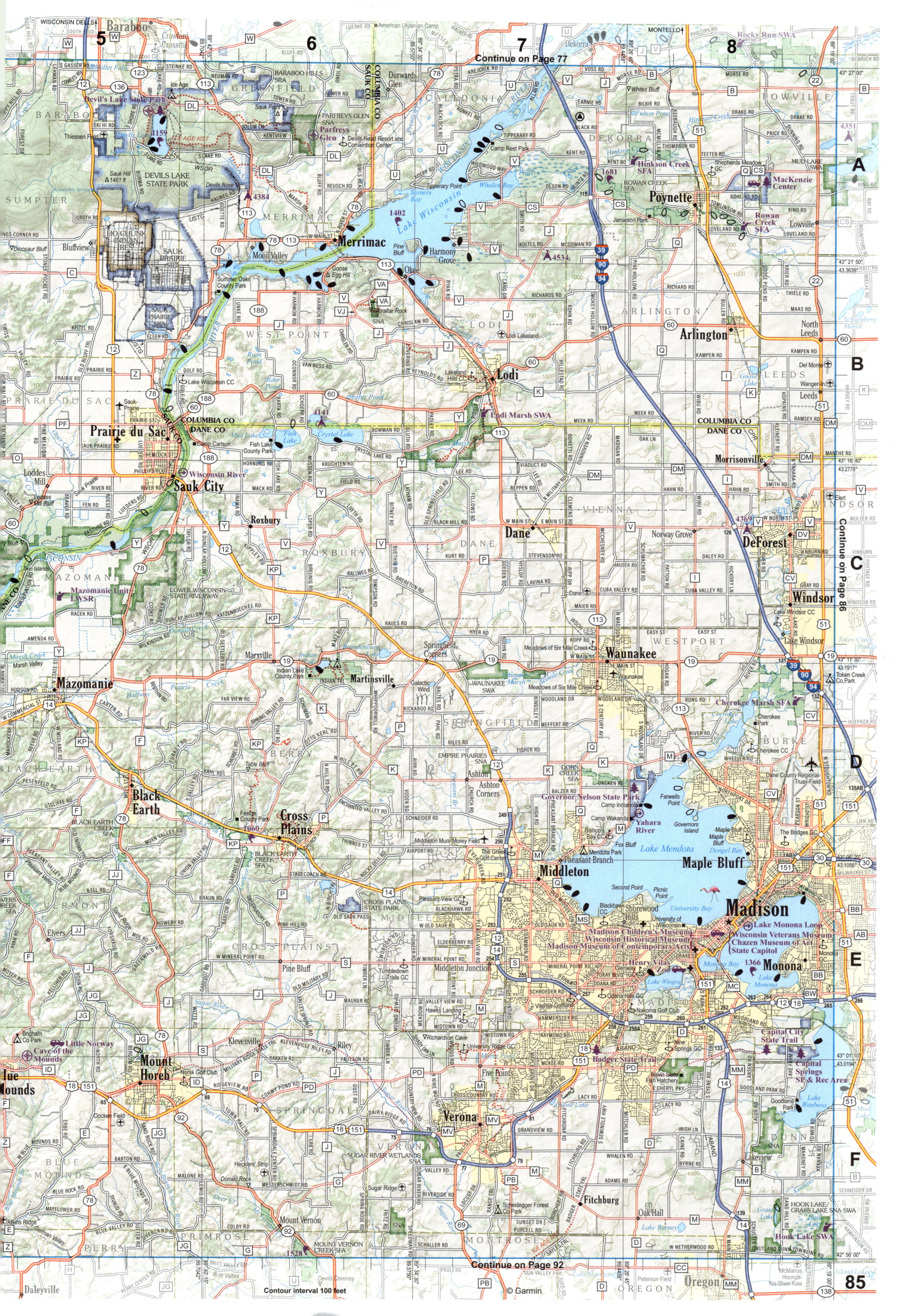

Continue on Page 77
Continue on Page 86
Continue on Page 92

Contour interval 100 feet

© Garmin

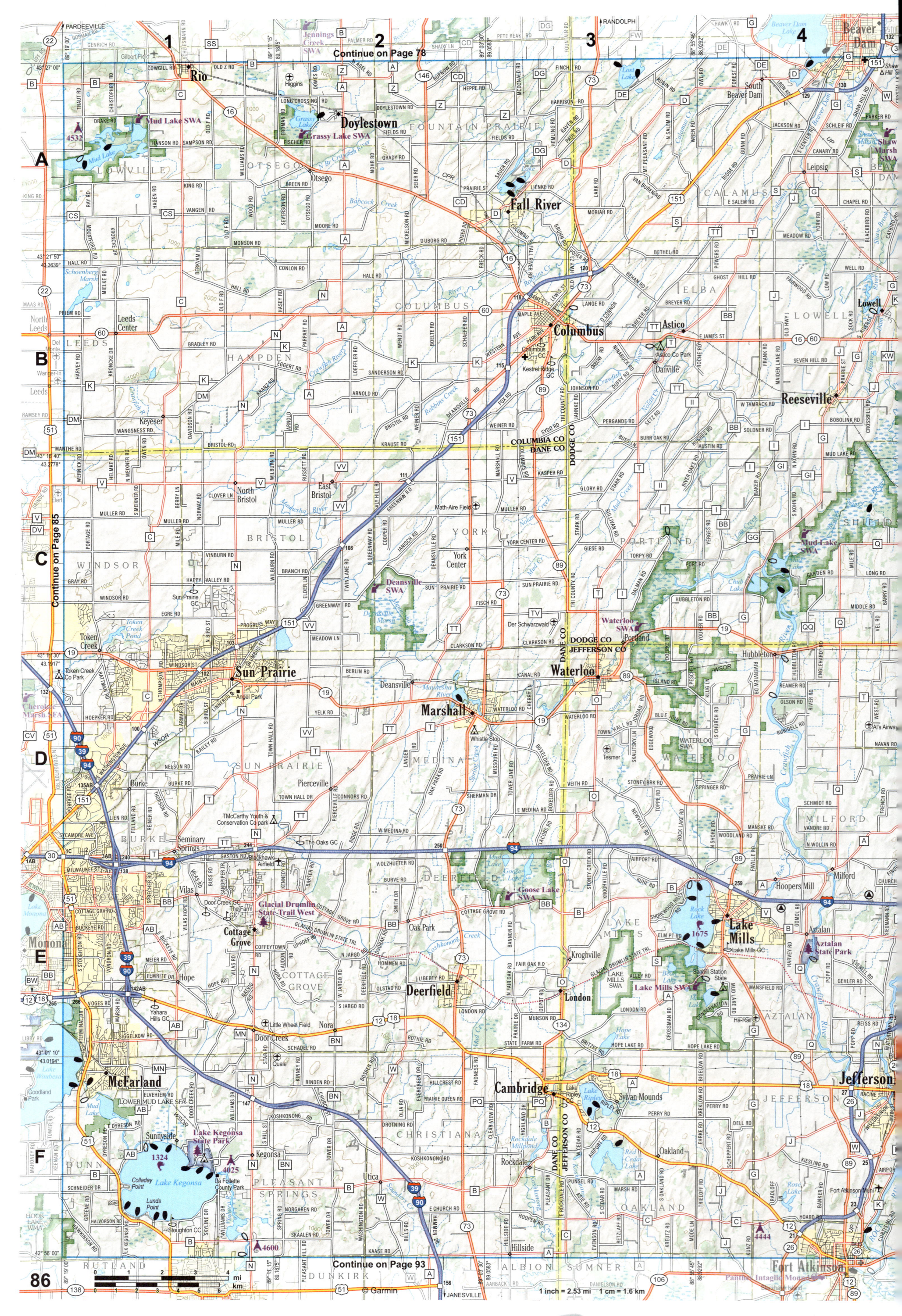

Continue on Page 78

Continue on Page 85

Continue on Page 93

1 inch = 2.53 mi   1 cm = 1.6 km

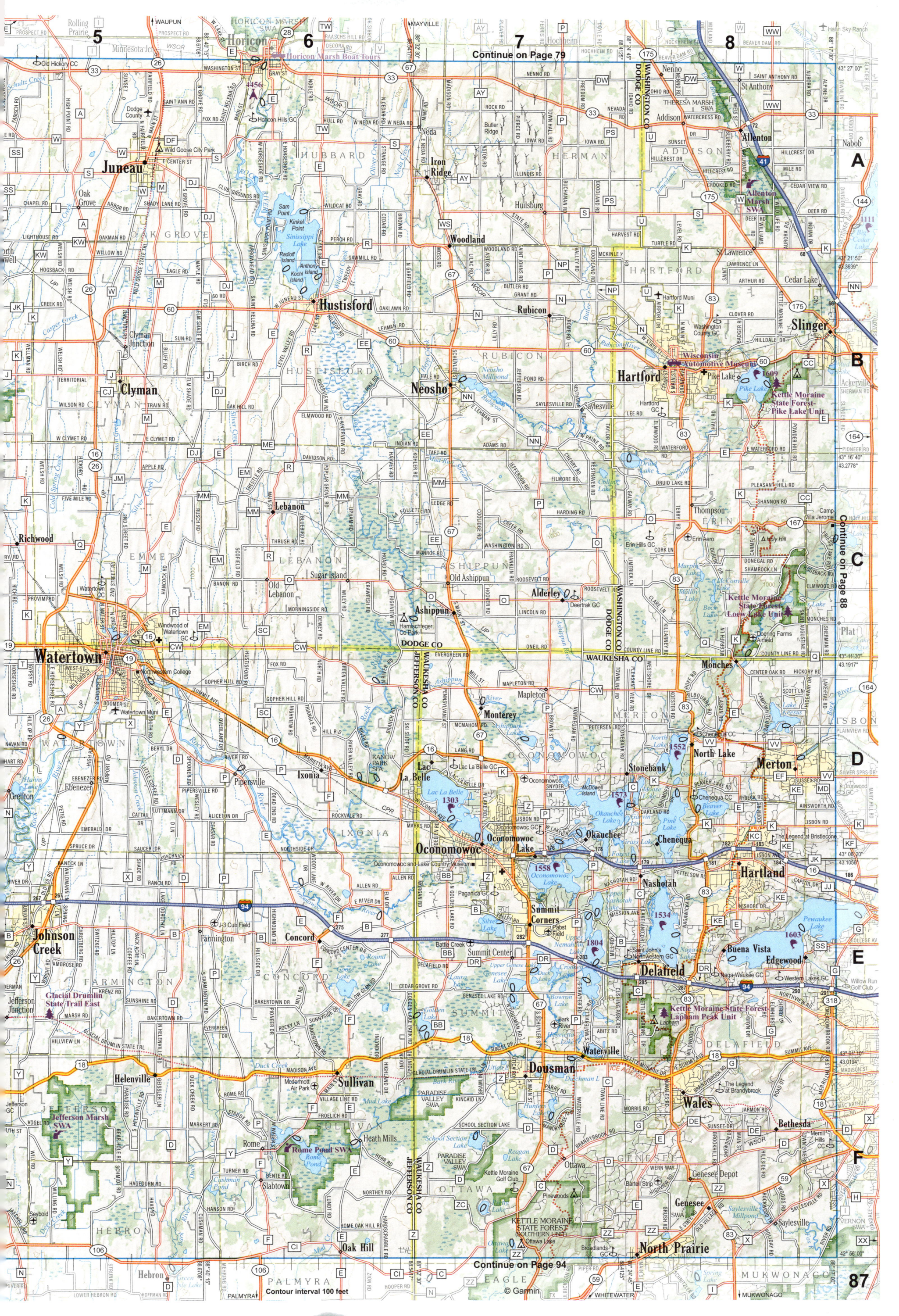

Continue on Page 88
Continue on Page 94

Continue on Page 87

LAKE MICHIGAN

Continue on Page 95

1 inch = 2.53 mi   1 cm = 1.6 km

© Garmin

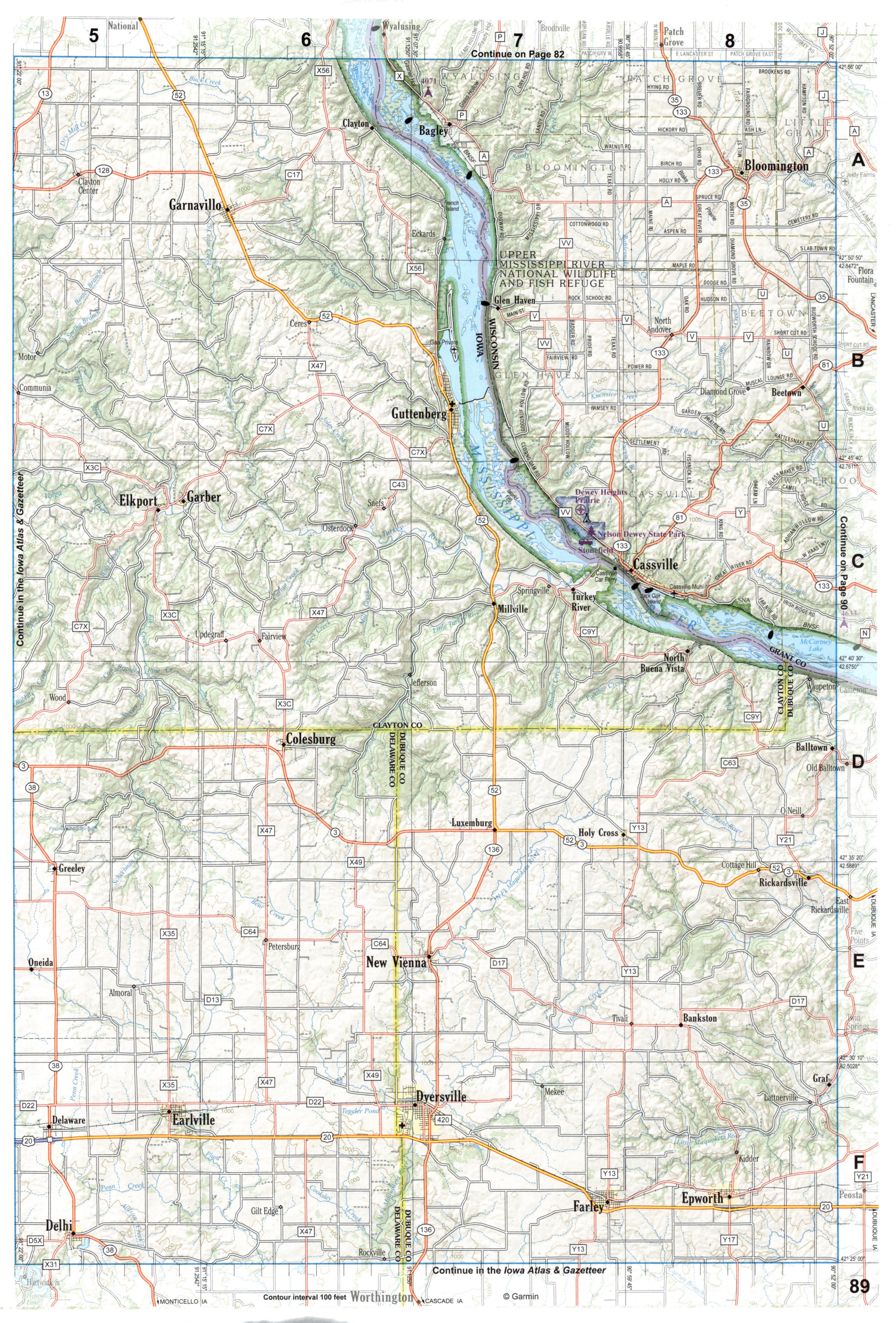

Continue on Page 82

National

Wyalusing   Brodtville

Patch Grove

Clayton   Bagley

Bloomington

Garnavillo

Eckards

UPPER MISSISSIPPI RIVER NATIONAL WILDLIFE AND FISH REFUGE

Glen Haven

North Andover

BEETOWN

Ceres

Motor

Communia

Guttenberg

Diamond Grove   Beetown

WATERLOO

Elkport   Garber

Snefs

Osterdock

Dewey Heights Prairie

CASSVILLE

Nelson Dewey State Park
Stonefield

Updegraff   Fairview

Springville

Millville

Turkey River

Cassville

Wood

Jefferson

North Buena Vista

Waupeton

Continue in the Iowa Atlas & Gazetteer

Continue on Page 90

CLAYTON CO

Colesburg

DUBUQUE CO
DELAWARE CO

Balltown
Old Balltown

O'Neill

Greeley

Luxemburg   Holy Cross

Cottage Hill

Rickardsville
East Rickardsville

Petersburg

Oneida

New Vienna

Tivoli   Bankston

Almoral

Five Points

Delaware

Earlville

Dyersville

Mekee

Graf

Cattnerville

Delhi

Farley

Epworth

Peosta

Kidder

Gilt Edge

Rockville

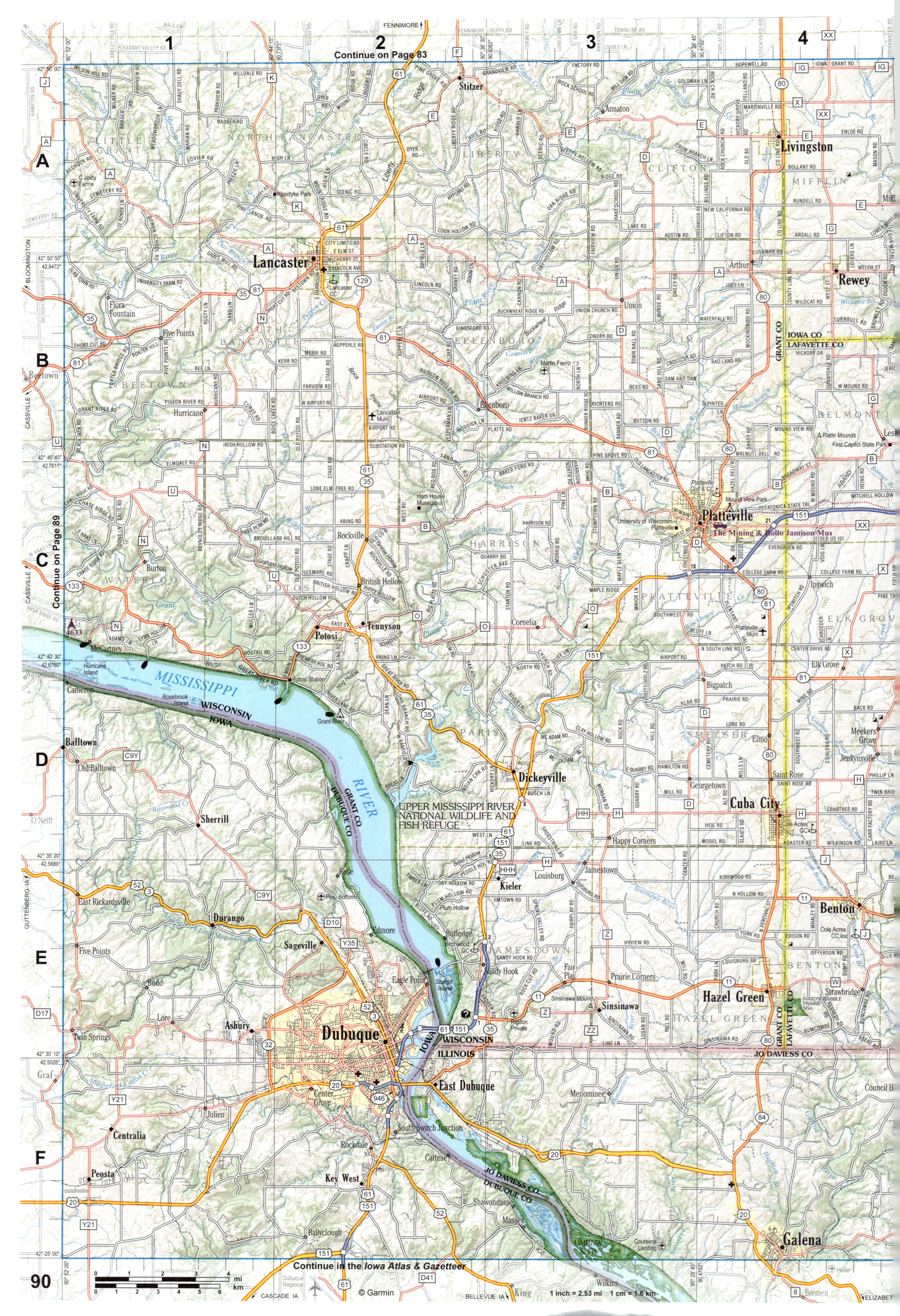

Continue on Page 89

© Garmin

1 inch = 2.53 mi   1 cm = 1.6 km

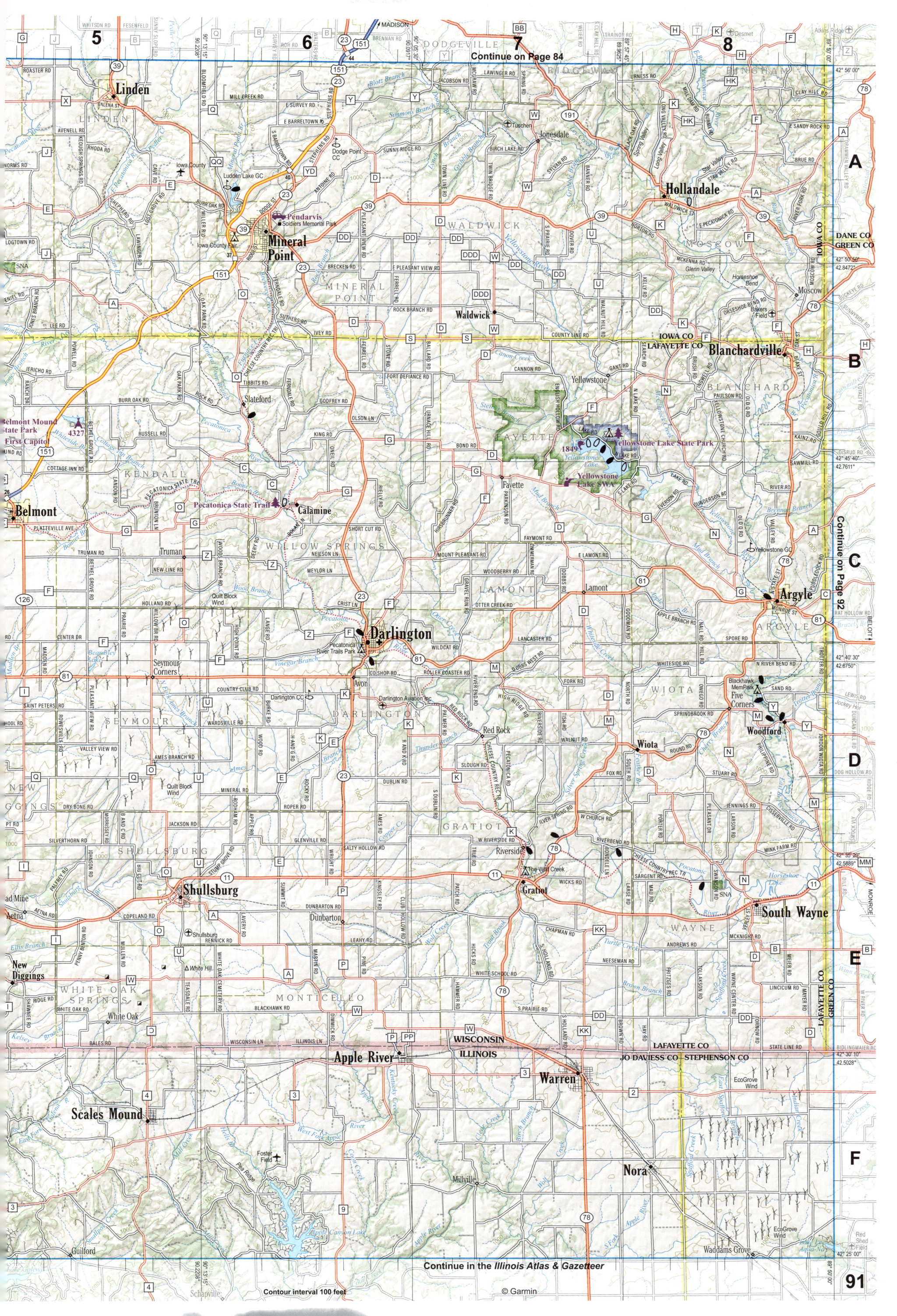

Continue on Page 92

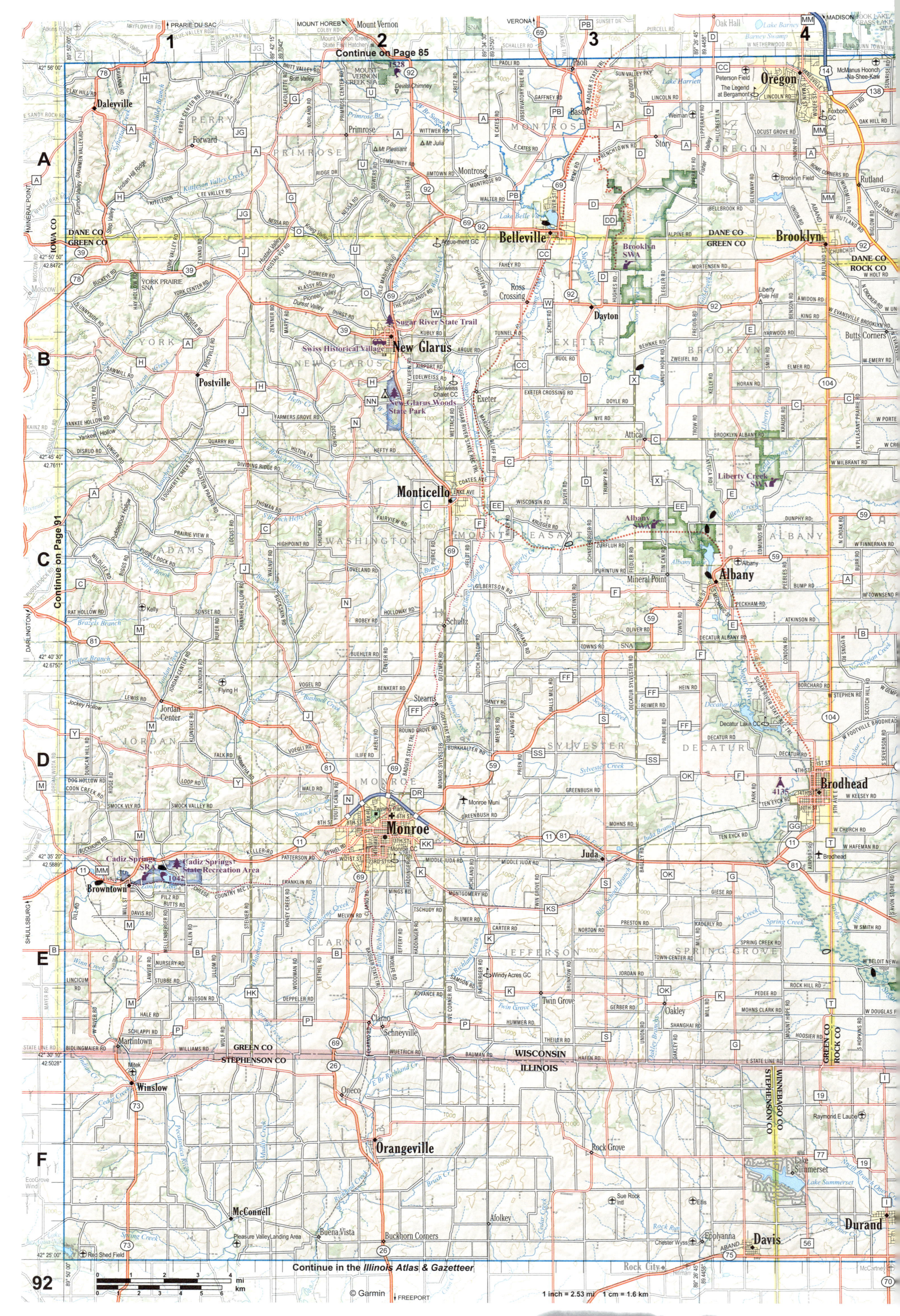

Continue on Page 85

Continue on Page 91

Continue in the *Illinois Atlas & Gazetteer*

© Garmin   FREEPORT

1 inch = 2.53 mi   1 cm = 1.6 km

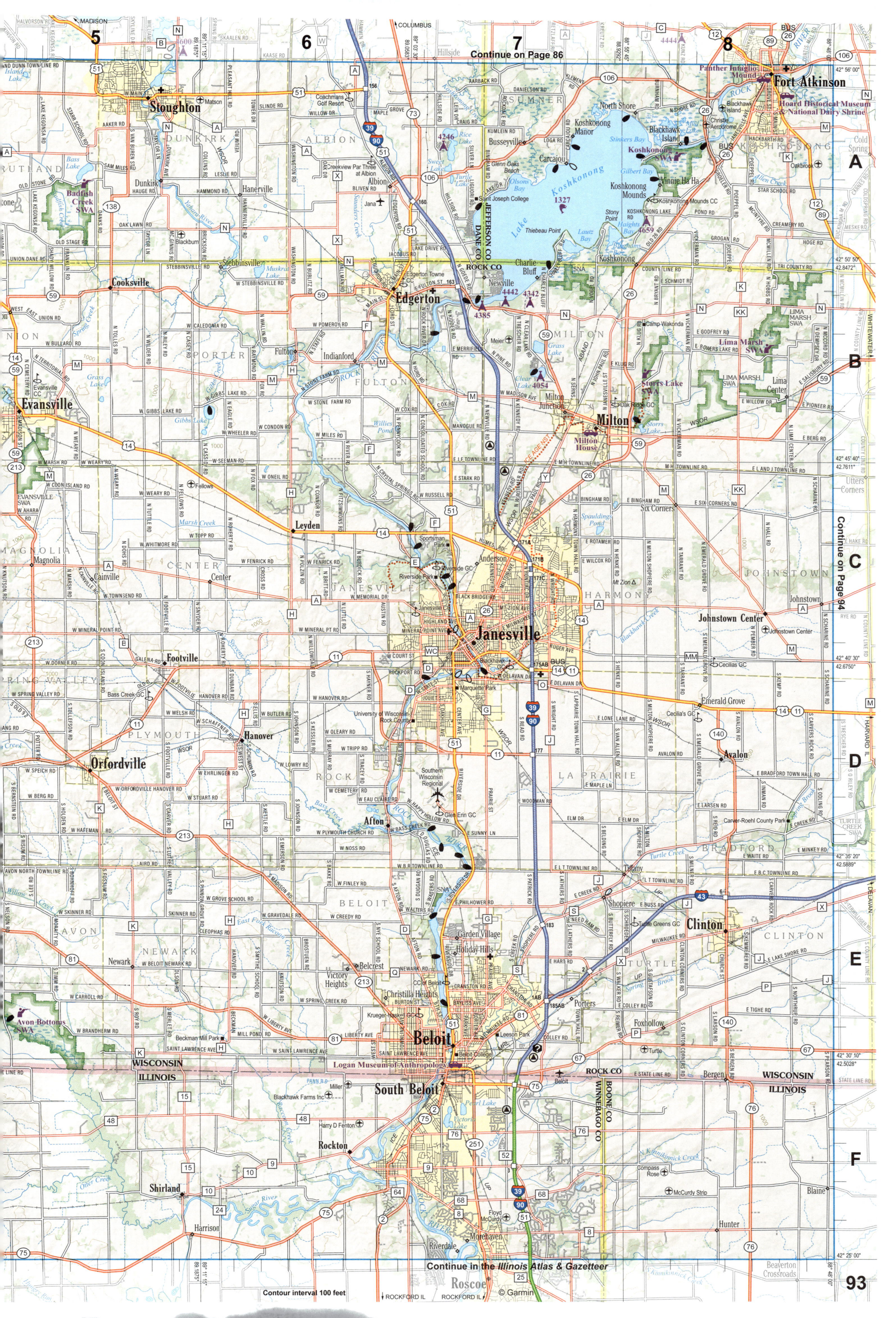

Continue on Page 86

Continue on Page 94

Stoughton

Fort Atkinson

Hoard Historical Museum & National Dairy Shrine

Koshkonong

DUNKIRK

ALBION

Badfish Creek SWA

JEFFERSON CO
DANE CO

Lake Koshkonong

Koshkonong Mounds

Cooksville

ROCK CO

Edgerton

Milton

PORTER

FULTON

Evansville

Indianford

Fulton

MILTON

Lima Center

Lima Marsh SWA

Storrs Lake

Leyden

Six Corners

Magnolia

CENTER

Center

JANESVILLE

HARMON

JOHNSTOWN

Johnstown

Footville

Janesville

Johnstown Center

Hanover

PLYMOUTH

ROCK

Emerald Grove

University of Wisconsin Rock County

Avalon

Orfordville

Afton

LA PRAIRIE

Tiffany

BRADFORD

NEWARK

AVON

Newark

BELOIT

Clinton

CLINTON

Garden Village

Holiday Hills

TURTLE

Belcrest

Victory Heights

Christilla Heights

Burton St

Porters

Foxhollow

Avon Bottoms SWA

Beloit

Beloit College

Logan Museum of Anthropology

WISCONSIN
ILLINOIS

WISCONSIN
ILLINOIS

ROCK CO
WINNEBAGO CO

BOONE CO

Bergen

South Beloit

Blackhawk Farms Inc

Rockton

Shirland

Harrison

Compass Rose

McCurdy Strip

Blaine

Hunter

Riverdale

Morehaven

Contour interval 100 feet

Roscoe

ROCKFORD IL

© Garmin

Continue on Page 87

Continue on Page 93

North Prairie

Hebron

Palmyra

Eagle

Mukwonago

Cold Spring

Whitewater

La Grange

East Troy

Honey Creek

Heart Prairie

Lauderdale

Richmond

Elkhorn

Spring Prairie

Lyons

Springfield

Delavan

Lake Geneva

Darien

Williams Bay

Fontana

Walworth

Pell Lake

Sharon

Zenda

Genoa City

Continue in the Illinois Atlas and Gazetteer

WISCONSIN
ILLINOIS

Hebron

Richmond

Alden

Harvard

1 inch = 2.53 mi   1 cm = 1.6 km

© Garmin

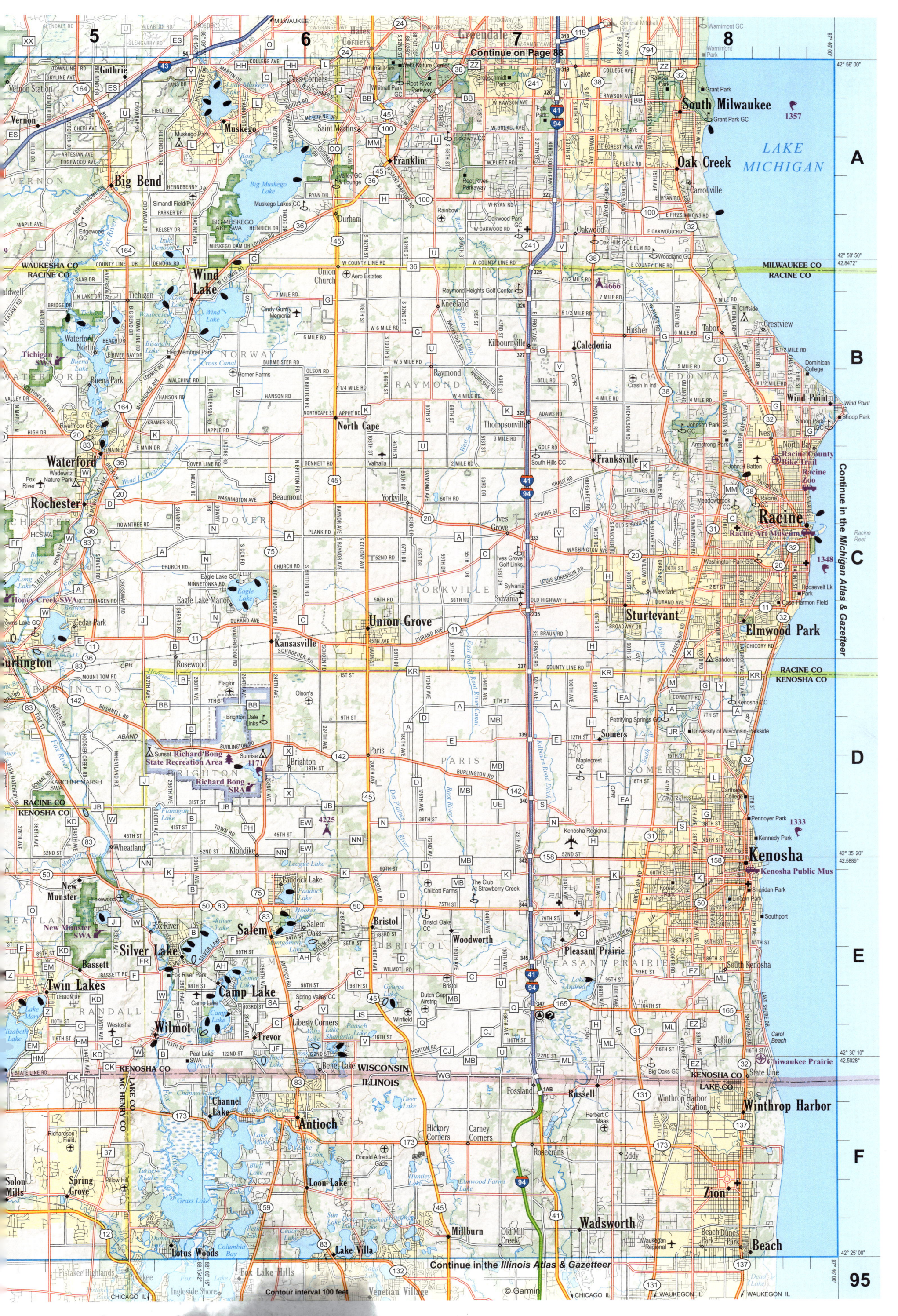

Continue in the *Michigan Atlas & Gazetteer*

Continue in the *Illinois Atlas & Gazetteer*

NAME, TOWN	PAGE & GRID	ACRES	DEER	BEAR	SQUIRREL	RABBIT	FURBEARERS	TURKEY	GROUSE	PHEASANT	QUAIL	WOODCOCK	WATERFOWL	HABITAT
St Croix Islands SWA, Somerset	40 E2	1,046	•	•	•	•	•	•					•	River, islands
Storrs Lake SWA, Milton	93 B8	750	•							•			•	Marsh, potholes, timber, lake, farmland
Straight River SWA, Luck	30 E4	1,325	•	•	•	•	•	•	•			•	•	Hardwood forest, grassland
Swan Lake SWA, Portage	77 E8	2,335	•		•	•	•	•					•	Marsh, timber, cropland
Tamarack Creek SWA, 65 miles north of Centerville	65 D8	542	•		•	•			•	•	•			Marsh, bog, timber
Theresa Marsh SWA, Theresa	79 F7	5,300	•		•	•	•	•					•	Marsh, flowage, stream, lowland timber, lowland brush
Thunder Lake SWA, Three Lakes	37 C5	3,000	•					•					•	Marsh, lake
Tichigan SWA, Waterford	95 B5	1,521	•		•	•				•			•	River, marsh, farmland, timber
Tiffany SWA, Nelson	64 A3	13,000	•			•	•		•				•	River slough, timber, lake, marsh
Totagatic Lake SWA, 6 miles southwest of Cable	25 E8	14,000	•	•					•				•	Lake, timbered upland
Totagatic River SWA, 7 miles northwest of Hayward	25 F7	272	•	•		•	•		•		•	•	•	River, marsh, timbered upland, flowage
Turtle Creek SWA, 2 miles northwest of Delavan	94 D1	1,035	•		•	•				•			•	Stream, marsh, timber, lowland brush
Underwood SWA, 17 miles north of Mercer	28 C3	1,602	•	•	•	•	•	•	•				•	Timbered upland, cedar swamp
Van Loon SWA, Holmen	66 F1	3,918	•		•	•			•				•	River, sloughs, marsh, timber
Vernon SWA, Mukwonago	94 A4	4,655	•			•	•			•			•	Marsh, flowages, river, lowland timber
Washington Creek SWA, 9 miles south of Bruce	43 C6	515	•					•				•	•	Flowage
Waterloo SWA, Waterloo	86 C3	4,000			•	•	•			•			•	Marsh, potholes, timber, farmland, river
Weirgor Springs SWA, Weirgor	33 D5	2,243	•	•	•	•		•						Springs, stream, marsh, timbered upland
White River Marsh SWA, Princeton	78 A2	12,000	•		•	•				•			•	Farmland, marsh, wood lots, river
White River SFA, 5 miles south of Ashland	27 A5	2,406	•					•					•	Stream, timber
White River SFA, Wautoma	70 F1	616	•		•				•	•				Stream, brush, timber
White River SWA, Ashland	27 A5	1,120	•				•	•			•			River bottom, timbered upland
Whitman Dam SWA, Cochrane	65 D5	2,253	•		•	•	•	•	•				•	River slough, lowland timber, marsh
Willow Creek SFA, Redgranite	70 E2	2,172	•						•	•				Stream, brush, timber
Wolf River SWA, Zittau	70 D4	1,800	•				•			•			•	River, marsh
Wood County SWA, 5 miles northwest of Babcock	68 B1	959	•		•	•			•		•	•	•	Marsh, timber
Woodman Unit–LWSR, Woodman	82 E4	3,643	•		•	•			•		•	•	•	River, sloughs, marsh, timber
Yellow River SFA, 5 miles east of Cumberland	31 F8	708	•			•		•						Stream, marsh, timbered upland
Yellowstone Lake SWA, 8 miles northwest of Argyle	91 C7	4,000	•		•	•	•			•			•	Lake, marsh, potholes, timber, cropland

DEPARTMENT OF NATURAL RESOURCES SERVICE CENTERS

Northern Region Co-Headquarters
Rhinelander DNR
107 Sutliff Ave
Rhinelander, WI 54501
(715) 365-8900

Northern Region Co-Headquarters
Spooner DNR
810 W Maple St
Spooner, WI 54801
(715) 635-2101

Northeast Region Headquarters
1125 N Military Ave
PO Box 10448
Green Bay, WI 54307
(920) 492-5800

West Central Region Headquarters
1300 West Clairemont
Box 4001
Eau Claire, WI 54702
(715) 839-3771

Southeast Region Headquarters
2300 N Dr Martin Luther King, Jr Dr
Milwaukee, WI 53212
(414) 263-8500

South Central Region Headquarters
3911 Fish Hatchery Rd
Fitchburg, WI 53711
(608) 275-3266

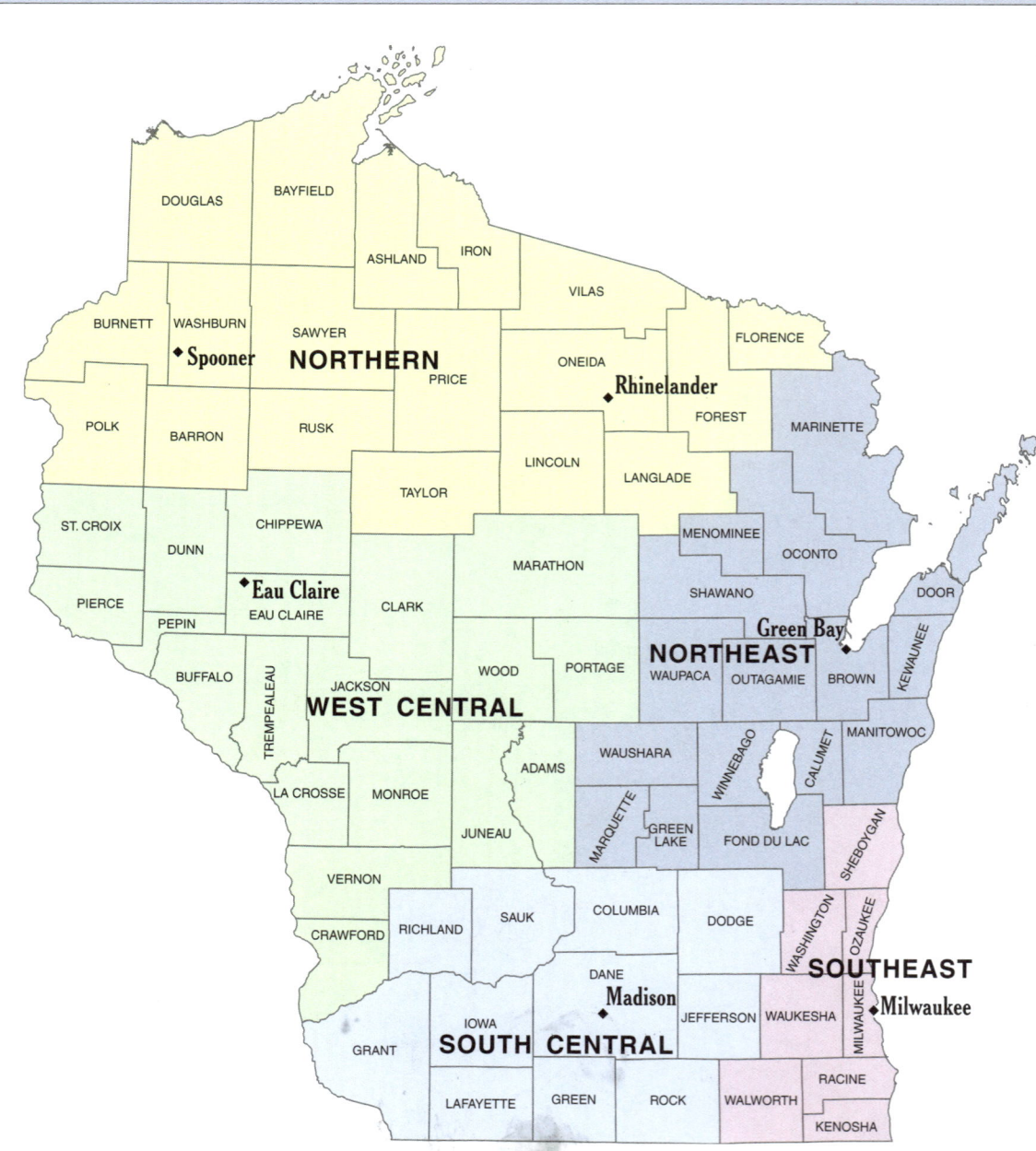